"This is a fascinating story about the many steps and missteps involved in the design and construction of this magnificent airplane. But the book is far more than that. It is a valuable case study on engineering management as well as airplane design.

I don't know which I have more admiration for, the 747 or Joe Sutter. This book is an excellent read for the engineer, the manager and the layman alike."

—Donald S. Lopez, Deputy Director,
National Air and Space Museum

"Sutter tells his story . . . from his boyhood on Beacon Hill watching planes take off from the Boeing factories down below to the design, building and launch of the 747 and beyond. [I]ts simplicity is a blessing."

—*The Seattle Times*

"Joe Sutter took on an inchoate idea, a brilliant but fractious team of engineers, and a merciless deadline and produced a machine that transformed world travel. This book reveals how much the project tested his nerve and his character. It also describes a quality that no amount of science can provide: uncanny intuition. Each time Sutter made a decision crucial not only to the 747's success but to the very survival of The Boeing Company, he got it right."

—Clive Irving,
author of *Wide-Body:
The Triumph of the 747*

"[Sutter] takes readers from the highs of the first 747 takeoff on Feb. 9, 1969, to the lows when the project nearly bankrupted the company."

—*Chicago Tribune*

"A candid retrospective of the why, the who, and the how of the creation of an airliner that forever changed long distance travel, by the leader of its design team."

—Neil Armstrong

"Sutter places this narrative in the context of his life; he shares interesting details about coming of age in the first half of the 20th century."

—*Library Journal*

"Joe Sutter literally changed the world with the 747. His example of leadership, integrity, vision, courage, and technical excellence continue to shape Boeing today."

—Alan Mulally, President and CEO,
Boeing Commercial Airplanes

"[An] engaging look at the technical, political and corporate forces that clashed over the 747."

—*Publishers Weekly*

747

747

CREATING THE WORLD'S FIRST
JUMBO JET AND OTHER ADVENTURES
FROM A LIFE IN AVIATION

JOE SUTTER
with JAY SPENSER

Smithsonian Books

Collins
An Imprint of HarperCollinsPublishers

HarperCollins books may be purchased for educational, business, or sales promotional use. For information, please write: Special Markets Department, HarperCollins Publishers, 10 East 53rd Street, New York, NY 10022.

Published 2006 in the United States of America by Smithsonian Books
In association with HarperCollins Publishers.

FIRST EDITION

Designed by Stephanie Huntwork

All photographs throughout the text are courtesy of the Boeing Corporation except where noted.

ISBN: 978-0-06-088242-6

The Library of Congress has catalogued the hardcover edition as follows:

Sutter, Joseph F.
    747: creating the world's first jumbo jet and other adventures from a life in
    aviation/by Joe Sutter with Jay Spenser.
        p. cm.
    ISBN: 978-0-06-088241-9
        1. Sutter, Joseph F. 2. Aeronautical engineers—United States—Biography.
    3. Boeing 747 (Jet transports)—Design and construction. I. Spenser, Jay P.
    II. Title.

TL540.S8865A3 2006
629.13'0092—dc22
    [B]   2005057965

    07 08 09 10 WBC/RRD 10 9 8 7 6 5 4 3 2

In memory of my beloved wife, Nancy, my pillar of strength

CONTENTS

ACKNOWLEDGMENTS

I am grateful first and foremost to my friend Larry Dickenson, senior vice president of sales at Boeing Commercial Airplanes. Larry feels that this story should be told, and agrees with me that it may inspire young men and women to pursue careers in aerospace. Thank you, Larry, for single-handedly doing so much to see this book come into being.

My gratitude also goes to Pierre Vellay, a senior vice president of Air France. A friend of many decades, Pierre was the first to propose that I write my story. Without his continued enthusiasm and encouragement over the years, this book might not exist today.

Since much of what I describe happened decades ago, I called on many friends and former colleagues to refresh my memory. Ardell Anderson, Row Brown, Matt Chen, Jim Chorlton, Ruth Howland, Ron King, Bob Larson, Dix Loesch, George Nible, Jim Norman, Lynn Olason, Bob Potter, Clancy Wilde, and Brien Wygle are among the Boeing retirees who helped me get the details right by providing information and insights. I also benefited from the help and guidance of Alan Mulally, Allen Rohner, and many other current Boeing people.

Additional appreciation goes to my good friend John Borger, a legend at Pan American World Airways, and to Barbara Townsend, his daughter. I am likewise grateful to Judy Mahoney and Nancy Anderson at the University of Washington, and to Mary Widseth at Boeing, for their unflagging support of this project.

On the historical front, I am beholden to Michael Lombardi and Thomas Lubbesmeyer of the Boeing Historical Archives, as well as to current Boeing executive Dave Knowlen, the driving force behind Boeing's restoration of the Dash 80 and the last surviving Stratoliner. Together with aviation writer and historian Jay Spenser, my talented coauthor, they checked countless facts to ensure accuracy.

My heartfelt thanks also go to Barbara Murphy of Clipper Communications for helping me find the best agent, to Farley Chase of the Waxman Literary Agency for bringing me to the best of publishers, and to Elisabeth Dyssegaard of Smithsonian Books for an outstanding job in the physical realization of this book. I am grateful for the passionate interest of these individuals, which shaped my telling of commercial aviation's earlier days and the birth of the 747.

Finally, I thank my sister, Fran, now in her nineties, and my children, Gabrielle, Jonathan, and Adrienne, for consenting to be interviewed and otherwise enthusiastically supporting my humble efforts.

I was born in Seattle in 1921 and grew up thrilled by aviation. My friends all wanted to fly airplanes but I set my heart on designing them. The futuristic flying machines I sketched as a boy would carry passengers in safety and comfort to the far continents, conquering oceans in a single flight.

Little did I know I would grow up to realize these dreams. Starting at Boeing right after World War II, I participated in the design of this great U.S. company's pioneering 707 and other early jets. After two decades of work, the opportunity came my way to lead the team designing the new Boeing 747. It was the most challenging and thrilling job in the world.

Until recently, I have resisted telling my story because by its nature it is not a one-person tale. In fact, every single one of the 4,500 talented Boeing people who reported to me contributed to this legendary airplane, which is theirs as much as mine. We did it together in a collaboration unlike any other.

Others have already written about the development of the 747, which is the world's first twin-aisle or widebody airplane. While

I assisted the authors of those worthy efforts, people have long told me it wasn't enough. If I didn't write about the 747 from my own perspective, they claimed, much of the real story might be lost.

My hesitation crumbled when they pointed out that telling my story might inspire youngsters who dream of getting into the airplane design business just as I did so many decades ago. I'm happy to say that these arguments, and the prospect of another opportunity to extend well-deserved credit to others, at last tilted the scales in favor of my embarking on this project.

The 747 has a unique majesty. Passengers love it and so do pilots, but it's what this airplane has done for humanity that's significant. Since the first 747 entered service in 1970, the world 747 fleet has transported more than 3.5 billion passengers—the equivalent of more than half the world's population—a distance of more than 35 billion statute miles (56 billion kilometers), which is the equivalent of 75,000 trips to the Moon and back.

Travel to far lands probably springs to mind when you think of the 747. So might short-haul shuttle flights if you live in Japan. But the 747 is also the workhorse of global air freight. In fact, almost half the world's goods that are shipped by air fly aboard 747 freighters. These cargo-hauling 747s bring us consumer electronics, perishable foodstuffs, fresh-cut flowers, and a host of other high-value cargoes.

But more than passengers and cargo take flight aboard 747s. These hardworking jets also carry ideas, human energy, and cultural perspectives that broaden our horizons and enrich us all. In this sense, they are aerial ambassadors that draw the world together and promote understanding.

As of this writing, the 747 has been in production for well over three decades. The 747-400—an improved version introduced in 1989—gave rise to today's 747 family, and tomorrow's is now on the horizon. After two abortive starts preempted by shifting market conditions, Boeing is now developing the 747-8, a second major 747 derivative that could see production of this famous airliner continue for several more decades. If so, newer and more efficient versions of the world's most recognizable jetliner will continue to serve humanity for at least another half century.

The main focus of this book is the latter half of the 1960s, when I led the engineering team that created the 747. I served as part of this amazing industrial effort from the beginning, guiding the 747 through its definition, design, testing, certification, and debut in service.

Of course, telling the tale of the 747 requires that I also tell you about myself. I ask you to bear with me while I delve into my childhood, education, and service in World War II. I assure you that I do so sparingly and with the specific intent of showing how these earlier chapters in my life were formative, and what lessons I drew from them that stood me in good stead in my career.

I hasten to add that this is the story of the 747 as I *remember* it. Human memory is fallible, as I'm reminded when friends say, "Hey Joe, the way you tell it isn't quite the way I recall it." I have checked my facts as best I can; I also imposed on many others to perform rigorous reviews of my manuscript.

The latter 1960s were heady days. It was an audacious time in U.S. history, and the same "can do" attitude that put men on the Moon also infused and inspired each person on my 747 team.

The 747 was launched when Boeing was overcommitted on too many fronts. Boeing's leaders literally bet the company on this airplane and we came perilously close to losing the gamble. If the 747 jetliner's success seems inevitable in retrospect, it certainly didn't at the time.

It is a source of continuing pleasure for me that for many decades now 747 jumbo jets have safely and reliably connected the farthest-flung regions of the world. I'm proud of what Boeing accomplished with this airplane. I'm also proud to see that the traditions of product excellence, technical innovation, and market leadership continue to define Boeing today.

Above all, I'm grateful for having led "The Incredibles," an unforgettable bunch of men and women who pulled a rhinoceros-sized rabbit out of Boeing's hat at a time when failure would have spelled disaster. It was an honor and a privilege.

May this book bring fond memories to those who were there and insight and enjoyment to everyone else.

Joe Sutter
Seattle, Washington
October 2005

747

1

GROWING UP WITH AVIATION

The 747 flew for the first time on February 9, 1969. It was a cold winter's day and a highly emotional one for me. We'd had to create this huge new jet so rapidly that its design phase was shorter than that of just about any jetliner before or since. Every challenge had seemed as outsize as the 747 itself. So it was only when I saw the world's first jumbo jet in the air that I knew my team had done it—we'd created a *real* airplane.

I couldn't have done it without my late wife, Nancy. When I'd come home beaten down with problems for which there seemed no solution, Nancy was always there to help lift me out of the dumps. Intelligent, beautiful, full of humor and life, she shared the burden of the 747's development.

She felt the pressure of our community's hopes and fears. "Does your husband know what he's doing?" her doubting friends would ask. "Do you think that big thing he's designing will actually *fly?*" Of course, they were only giving voice to the question on everybody's mind in Seattle in the late 1960s, but it still left Nancy feeling none too great.

On the morning before that first flight, I sensed Nancy needed me to reassure her that our big airliner would fly. I promised her it would. "What's more," I added confidently, "I'll show you just where it'll leave the ground."

I bundled her into a Boeing station wagon and drove us out to the calculated "unstick" point along the snow-fringed runway. "Kid, you stand right here," I said, letting her out on dry grass a hundred yards off, "and as that airplane goes by, you'll see its wheels lift off the ground right in front of you."

With a muted whine entirely different from the flaring hiss that jetliners made back then, the prototype 747 taxied to the distant threshold. The pilots completed their last checks, the engines spooled up, and that huge airplane accelerated down the runway.

Before Nancy's eyes, a jetliner two and a half times bigger than anything then in service broke ground and surged skyward, effortlessly carrying away with it the weight of the world.

When I picked Nancy up, she was crying. "Oh Joe," she exclaimed, tears of relief running down her cheeks, "it took off just where you said it would!"

I saw then that she'd gone through just about as much hell as had I or, for that matter, any of the 4,500 people on my engineering team. On that unforgettable day, Nancy and I knew we'd weathered a great and thrilling storm.

———————

I was born in Seattle, Washington, on March 21, 1921. The world was very wide back then, and our part of it—the Great Northwest—was a remote region in one far-flung corner of the United States. The transcontinental rail line came up through Tacoma and pretty well ended in Seattle, so unless your destination was British Columbia or the Yukon, you had to board a ship to go much farther.

Young and raw, Seattle was itself a bit of a frontier. It was a seaport village, not a city, and it had no skyscrapers except for Smith Tower, which for decades was the tallest U.S. building west of the Mississippi River. Located in Pioneer Square, the old part of downtown Seattle,

Smith Tower is today the smallest spire in a bustling skyline. It has glass-doored offices and brass open-frame elevators with human operators and is a universally loved symbol of a vanished era.

My home state is equally colorful. Washington gained statehood only in 1889, and its wild and wooly days as a western territory were within the living memory of people I knew as a boy. Washington's abundant natural resources made Seattle the jewel of the Northwest, a cosmopolitan universe of big timber, fishing fleets, large ships braving the Pacific to Asia, smaller ones working the Inside Passage to Alaska, and ferryboats plying Puget Sound.

The spectacular backdrop to all this human activity was nature on a grand scale. My childhood world was a universe of vast wilderness, the sparkling blues of Puget Sound with its orcas and salmon, and towering snow-capped mountains so perfect they look like operatic backdrops. With all the rain that sweeps in off the Pacific, though, there are a lot of days in Seattle when you can't see the mountains.

We Sutters lived in Beacon Hill, a lower-middle-class neighborhood to the south of downtown Seattle. Ours was a working neighborhood of emigrants from Europe and Asia. There were many nationalities all living together with a real sense of community. Houses had verandahs and—in those days before air-conditioning or television—people sat outside enjoying summer evenings, so you got to know your neighbors pretty well.

My father, Frank Sutter, arrived in the United States from Slovenia at the age of 17. His last name was actually Suhadolc, but like so many immigrants he received an easier last name when passing through Ellis Island. I adored and respected my dad, although I didn't get to spend much time with him. He worked pretty much all the time.

As a young bachelor, my dad traveled to Alaska in hopes of making his fortune in the Klondike gold rush. He spent a long and very difficult decade toiling in the far north. Family legend has it he helped build a bridge across the Yukon River. He also survived being mauled by a hungry bear that broke into his cabin one night in search of food.

Dad did ultimately find a small gold deposit. After staking out his claim, he sold it to a Swede for $15,000—a very large sum in those days. Giving up the frontier life, he moved to Seattle, where he and a partner started a meat-cutting shop called the Union Packing Company. Soon thereafter, Dad met and fell in love with my mother, Rosa, a recent widow. They were married in 1912.

My mother was born Rosa Plesik in what was then the Austro-Hungarian Empire. Her family left Europe when she was two years old and settled in Leadville, Colorado, so she grew up in the Rocky Mountains. Rosa's first husband was a miner who labored in the silver and lead mines. Together they had three children—my half siblings Fred, John, and Rose—before her husband succumbed at an early age to diseases associated with lead mining. Rosa packed up the children and moved to an area near Ravensdale, Washington, where she had relatives in the coal mining trade.

My father's business was successful, but it required him to work 10 hours a day, 6 days a week. I hardly saw him except in the evenings and for a little while each weekend. I don't recall him and my mother ever taking so much as a one-week vacation. Not ever.

Frank and Rosa—or Rose, as she was nicknamed—had five children. Aside from Frances, the eldest, we were all boys: Vincent, Louis, me, and Robert. Fran was always busy around the house helping my mother raise four boys. She remains an inspiration to me to this day.

Vin was serious and didn't play sports. Later on, he could often be found down at Dad's plant helping out. Lou, in contrast, was carefree and happy-go-lucky. During his teens, he got hold of a beat-up old Plymouth—about a '33 or '34 and dark blue—that greatly improved his mobility and social life. Between dates, he found time to teach me to drive when I was 15.

I was the bookish member of the family. Although I lived outside and played plenty of sports, I always seemed to have my nose in a book when I wasn't doing chores at home. As the baby of the family, Bob got away with murder as far as doing chores and whatnot. Lou was two years older than me, and we tended to play together. Sometimes

Bob joined in, but for the most part he just banged around with friends his own age.

In short, we all got along and learned to share, pitch in, and rely on each other. There was always enough good-natured teasing between us that nobody was ever allowed to get a swelled head. Anyone showing symptoms of that was promptly taken down a notch or two by the others. All in all, I remember it as a happy and busy childhood with lots of give-and-take. I wasn't quite as close to my half-siblings because they didn't live in the immediate area and were older.

When I was three, Fran, Lou, and I all contracted scarlet fever, which was a very serious childhood illness back then. I've heard we had diphtheria too, so we were in great danger. My father summoned the doctor while my mother cradled me in blankets she'd heated in her kitchen woodstove. I'd turned blue and was reportedly on the verge of death, and those hot blankets probably saved me.

When the doctor arrived, he took one look and said I might be beyond help. But Rose Sutter wasn't about to write her son off. She held a mirror to my face and showed the doctor the condensation from my breath. "You see, Doctor," she said, "Joey is still alive."

They transferred us to a sanitarium called Firlands where we were quarantined for many long weeks. It was very hard on my mother. Vin, my eldest brother, also worried about us. He was seven years old and, being the responsible one, decided that he'd better join us so that he could watch out for us. With that noble thought in mind, he intentionally ate the rest of an orange we sick Sutters had been sharing at our table. Fortunately he didn't come down with scarlet fever.

The first thing I can recall in my life is in fact that dingy room that Fran, Lou, and I shared at Firlands. I even remember the hole in the plaster wall by my bed. Needless to say, the quality of my memories improved enormously the moment the staff there pronounced us fit again and set us free.

We Sutters lived a simple European-style life. My mother did the cooking and baked our bread, which in the early days was by woodstove. In the 1930s, though, my father replaced it with an electric stove. That innovation was supposed to make Mom's life easier, but it initially had little effect because she kept right on baking her breads, pies, and cakes in a little woodstove off to one side of our kitchen.

I had lobbied hard for the electric stove because it would mean less firewood, and firewood was the bane of my existence. From the time I was little, in fact, I dreaded the month of August each year, because that was when our family had a year's worth of firewood delivered to our home.

My task each August was to haul those bark-covered slabs of fir and hemlock to my older brothers for them to chop up. I'd take that wood away and stack it into neat rows, one on top of the other, until I'd built another woodpile. When each pile got too high for me to put more logs on, Vin or Lou would take breaks from the chopping and stack them higher still.

It was hot, sticky, dirty work for all of us except Bob, who was too small to be of much use. Hard as my older brothers swung their axes, though, I felt I had the worst of it because hauling all that wood inevitably left me with countless slivers, or splinters as they're called in other parts of the country. I'd have slivers all over my hands and up and down the insides of my arms. They were extremely painful and made me thoroughly miserable, particularly the ones I couldn't pluck out with tweezers.

My mother was a wonderful cook who hardly ever bought anything from our neighborhood grocery store. Instead each weekend we'd climb into our four-door Chrysler and head for Ravensdale, where we'd visit friends. We'd return from the country loaded down with wooden boxes of the freshest peas, corn, beans, cucumbers, pears, apples, cherries, strawberries, raspberries, and every kind of delicious produce you could imagine.

That Chrysler was originally green but faded over time to a light olive. I remember it well because it was our first family car. My father had never owned a vehicle before, so the dealer had to show him how to operate it. Dad got the hang of driving it all right, but he had trouble remembering to open the garage door before backing out.

He worked such long hours that it was often totally dark when he set off for work. He'd enter the garage from the rear, start up the car, shift into reverse, hit the gas, and *bang*—out through the garage door he'd burst with a clatter that woke half the neighborhood.

This happened a number of times and it struck me as funny each time. Today I realize how hard my father was working for us. I guess he was preoccupied with cares and maybe sleep deprived as well. That garage door looked pretty awful after Dad's third or fourth accident. Vin did the repair work and I helped, but we weren't carpenters, so it was a real lash-up job.

Thanks to Dad's business, we Sutters had excellent cuts of meat in addition to all the fresh fruits and vegetables we brought back from Ravensdale. And thanks to Dad's sideline business, we also had eggs and butter. As the colloquial saying went, "We ate good." That wasn't always true for everyone in the neighborhood, particularly after the Depression hit, so we considered ourselves very fortunate.

Sometimes I'd stay over by myself in Ravensdale, spending long days exploring the Cedar River Watershed and otherwise enjoying being out in the country. There were no city streetlights to contend with, so on moonless nights the sky was like black velvet strewn with stars and the diamond dust of the Milky Way. Washington State being so far north, I also saw magical displays of northern lights.

I slept on a bed of hay and straw in a barn when I stayed over in Ravensdale. I'd drift off hearing the sigh of wind in the trees. Sometimes the distant echoing hoots of owls or the rattling of rain on the barn's shingles would awaken me at night. Those visits instilled a deep and abiding love of nature.

Back in Seattle, I spent lazy summer days playing baseball, touch football, soccer, and even basketball when we could improvise hoops. Lou and I played with other kids in our blue-collar neighborhood, many of them the children of Boeing factory workers. There were no parks nearby; we played in empty lots or in the street.

One day I kicked a brand-new soccer ball as high as I could into the air. It came almost straight down and impaled itself on a spike atop our neighbor's ornamental wrought-iron fence. The ball instantly exploded, shredded beyond repair. It belonged to George Zipp and his five scrappy brothers next door, and they were pretty mad about it. None of us had the money for a replacement ball, so this accident effectively ended our soccer games.

Sometimes we'd take public transportation to Lake Washington and go swimming. Seattle had no city buses back then, just a system of beat-up streetcars. We were on Line 6, which started in Georgetown below Beacon Hill and passed through a flat area. The streetcars swayed so badly you'd swear they were going to jump the tracks. Turns were particularly harrowing because the land had been graded to make it flat and the mud used as fill was still settling. It was a wild ride!

In those days, we often built our own toys and invented our own games. One such improvised amusement brought me my first and only brush with the law. I was 9 or 10 at the time. Somehow my friends and I got hold of a huge old truck tire. Lugging it up to the top of a sloping street, we took turns climbing inside and rolling ourselves downhill.

All went well until, feeling brazen, I got that damn tire rolling much too fast. I bailed out just in time and saw it hit a bump, jump the barricade at the end of the street, and sail out of sight. In horror I recalled that the Olympic Foundry, a local business, was directly beneath. A moment later I cringed to the echoes of smashing wood and shattering windows.

The police promptly showed up to investigate, and we confessed what had happened. When my dad came home that evening, I had to tell him about it as well. While he certainly wasn't thrilled to hear what I'd done, he was very proud of me for telling the truth.

Three or four days later, Dad drove me down to the municipal court. There we saw a judge whose courtroom trappings and air of authority scared my friends and me to such a degree that we couldn't understand his odd behavior. Today I realize that the judge was simply trying very hard to keep from laughing over our story. I decided one encounter with the law was enough and resolved to be more careful.

The only other time I got in trouble was at St. George, the small

Catholic grade school we attended. Our teachers were nuns. Our principal was Sister Mary Alice. We were terrified of her in particular. She and her staff members used to rap our knuckles.

A student whose last name was Sperdutti sat behind me in the sixth grade. One day he must have been bored because he started poking me in the back with the eraser end of his pencil. I tried to ignore it but he just kept on poking, so I turned around and ordered him to quit it. The sister teaching the class scolded us both for the disruption.

I thought the matter settled but a few minutes later Sperdutti did the unbelievable. Reacting to another hard dig in my ribs, I balled my fist and spun around. I meant only to confront him but I happened to catch him just as he was leaning forward to jab me again. My fist connected solidly with his face and I damn near knocked him out.

They marched us down to the principal's office, a fate worse than death for us both. Somehow we survived, although I found it far worse than seeing that judge. In the days that followed, Sperdutti's black eye—a real shiner that ran its course—reminded me of my transgression.

Punky, our family dog, didn't seem to think any less of me for my lawlessness. A black-and-white mutt, he actually belonged to my mother and would always follow her to the store. Hundreds of times he just missed getting run over because he never learned to look before crossing the street. Dogs ran free in those days; nobody used leashes in our neighborhood.

Vin, Lou, Bob, and I loved playing with Punky, who was unflaggingly cheerful and always ready for anything. A favorite game for us kids was racing Punky around the block. Of course, he was so fast that we had to give ourselves a head start.

This was accomplished by one of us holding Punky while another ran to the end of the block. The dog would chafe against this restraint, his every limb straining in urgent desire to follow. Once the runner had rounded the corner, we'd release Punky and he'd shoot off in pursuit.

Try as we might, myself included, none of us ever made it all the way around the block before Punky caught up with us. That finally changed one cold and damp winter day when Mom dressed Punky in a little sweater she'd knitted for him. It was white with black trim, and he looked pretty sharp. Lou started the game by running around the corner and Punky shot after him, but when Lou reappeared from the other direction, there was no sign of the dog.

We backtracked in concern and found him looking as though he'd just been through the wringer. He was tired and no longer wore that sweater. Perplexed, we explored farther and finally found its shredded remains in an empty lot at a far corner of the block.

Now we knew the truth! Punky had been beating us by slipping under a fence and cutting through the corner lot. This time, though, his sweater had caught on the fence. Trapped, he'd extricated himself by pulling hard and using his teeth, as evidenced by tattered clumps of wool thrown all around.

———————

Our hilltop neighborhood provided dramatic views of Mount Rainier and the Cascades to the east, and Puget Sound and the Olympic Peninsula to the west. It also looked down on the industrial flatlands short of Elliott Bay, the part of Puget Sound fronting Seattle. By far the most interesting thing on those flatlands was a tiny airplane company called Boeing.

Founded in 1916, Boeing was just five years older than me. I've always kind of felt that we grew up together, and that its activities were a defining element of my childhood. I have been fascinated by anything that flies since I was tiny, and I continue to watch birds to this day. Seattle has bald eagles, ospreys, and red-tailed hawks. Thrilling as they were to me as a kid, though, I must admit that Boeing gave them some stiff competition.

About the time I came along, the company accepted a contract from the U.S. Army Air Service to rebuild several hundred war-surplus de Havilland DH-4 bombers. The DH-4 was a big British two-seat military biplane that the United States had built under license during World War I. Although Seattle was in the heart of some of the best timber country in the world, Boeing chose to replace the wooden fuselages of those DHs with welded steel-tube fuselages. That forward-looking decision is an early example of the vision that has long characterized Boeing.

On summer days, my brothers and I would walk down to the flying field beside old Plant 1, Boeing's first real factory after its humble beginnings in a converted boatyard. There we'd watch technicians working on the airplanes dotting the flight line. Occasionally a leather-clad test pilot would climb into a Boeing military biplane like a knight mounting his steed.

Aviators were more than mere mortals to us. They were a different breed, intrepid demigods in silk scarves, puttees, and leather flying helmets with goggles. Further burnishing our admiration were the dime novels we read that romanticized the exploits of World War I fliers in their Sopwiths, SPADs, Nieuports, and Fokkers. However subjective our perceptions, though, it was no exaggeration to say that flying back then was dangerous.

Watching those Boeing pursuit ships in the air was a real thrill. The angry snarl of their propellers filled the sky as they zoomed overhead. For a small boy, the throaty modulation of a radial aero engine is a song that's hard to ignore. It would bring me tearing down the stairs and out into the street at a flat run, sowing pandemonium in our household. If I was already outside when the airplane flew overhead, I was at severe risk of forgetting the ball just thrown my way.

I will always remember one spring day when I was 6. It was explained to me that a 25-year-old airmail pilot named Charles Lindbergh had taken off from New York for Paris. Of course, the former city seemed as distant and exotic to me as the latter, so wide was the world in those days.

On May 20, 1927, Lindbergh took off in a frail silver airplane named the *Spirit of St. Louis*. It was an early morning departure from a flying field on Long Island. His monoplane was overloaded with gasoline and he'd barely been able to coax it into the air. I pored over the newspaper accounts, studied pictures of the man and his machine, and willed them both to make it.

Breathless excitement gradually gave way to fading hopes in the long hours that followed. By the next day, they had dwindled almost to nothing when the electrifying news arrived that "Lucky Lindy" had just been spotted approaching Paris. Shortly afterward came confirmation that he'd landed safely at Le Bourget Aerodrome.

The world went absolutely wild. Others had already conquered the Atlantic Ocean by air, but nobody had ever flown all the way from New York to Paris without stopping. Even more astounding, Lindbergh had done it alone and on a single engine. His faithful Wright J5 Whirlwind ran for 33 1/2 hours straight.

The elemental poetry of this audacious achievement—a handsome young man in a beautiful silver airplane—explains much of the profound impact of Lindbergh's achievement, but I believe there is more to it than that. By directly linking New York with Paris, the flight fueled dreams of commercial air travel between the great cities of the world. It was this tantalizing possibility that resonated in the tickertape parades and thunderous acclaim to which the shy young American returned.

Before Lindbergh's flight, the idea that people might someday board "aerial liners" and fly from one continent to another was dismissed as sheer lunacy. People took ships and trains to go any distance; the airplane was little more than a novelty. Intercontinental air travel was strictly the stuff of science fiction writers like Jules Verne or H. G. Wells, not something that might actually come to pass.

Lindbergh changed all that. He showed the world that heavier-than-air flying machines devised by human minds and fashioned by human hands could indeed fly thousands of miles to link major population centers on different continents. This sensational realization profoundly altered the United States in particular. Almost overnight, my country became "air minded."

If so, it was just catching up with me. I'd been that way all along. As the 1920s drew to an end, in fact, I lived and breathed aviation. I studied the airplanes of the day, which were generally open-cockpit crates covered by doped fabric drawn so taut that it reverberated like a drum when you thumped it with your finger. I eyed their structures, examined their landing gears, and critically assessed the bracing struts and flying wires that held them together.

The same day Lindbergh took off for Paris, Boeing's first commercial model, the model 40A, took to the sky. Boeing was then a manufacturer of military biplanes with only about 450 employees on the payroll. The 40A was designed for airmail but it could also carry two passengers. They were strictly an afterthought, though, and ran the risk of being left behind if too many bags of mail waited at the next stop.

By 1927, Boeing had outgrown its small flying field next to Plant 1 and had taken to testing its larger designs at Seattle's Sand Point, a grassy field on the shore of Lake Washington. It was at Sand Point in 1924 that the first successful round-the-world flight began and then ended six months later. Douglas (which today is part of Boeing) had built the lumbering single-engine World Cruiser biplanes in which army pilots claimed this honor for the United States.

Just a year after Lindbergh's flight, Boeing introduced its first true passenger airliner, the model 80 trimotor. This big biplane had a fully enclosed cabin with seating for 14 passengers. An improved version called the 80A introduced the world's first stewardesses, or female flight attendants, to air travel. There was one stewardess per 80A and—perhaps to reassure the passengers in those early days—she was required to be a registered nurse.

Unfortunately for Boeing, the U.S. navy took exclusive possession of Sand Point and turned it into Seattle's naval air station. To prevent Boeing from having to relocate elsewhere for want of a flying field, county officials pulled together and created Boeing Field, which opened in July 1928. Boeing Field (officially King County International Airport) remains a center of Boeing jetliner testing and deliveries to this day.

The stock market crashed in October 1929, bringing on the Great Depression. That same month, famous flier Jimmy Doolittle successfully performed the world's first entirely blind flight using instruments and radionavigational aids that he helped develop. Heading up a scientific team at New York's Mitchel Field, Doolittle took off under a hood and landed again solely by reference to these new instruments. With this success, the last piece of the puzzle fell into place for commercial aviation. Regularly scheduled flights could be performed even in darkness and cloudy weather.

The far end of my Beacon Hill neighborhood looked down over the southern half of Boeing Field. I kept an interested eye on happenings there and was on hand in 1931 when two army pilots dropped into the field in a Douglas O-31 military observation plane. I was 10 years old and intrigued by the all-metal monoplane with its unusual high wings. Boeing clearly wasn't the only company building interesting airplanes.

I staked those two pilots out and was there watching when they returned from lunch at the airport restaurant. One flier climbed into the O-31's front cockpit to work the switches. After they got it running, the other man kicked out the wheel chocks and clambered aboard. I watched them taxi off across the grass and take off. I recall thinking that aviation was the best job in the world. But what exactly did I want to do in this exciting field? I just didn't know.

That same year, Clyde Pangborn and Hugh Herndon piloted a Bellanca monoplane from Japan to my home state of Washington in a 42-hour flight that was the first-ever nonstop crossing of the North Pacific by air. Also in 1931, Wiley Post and Harold Gatty circled the globe in 8 days and 16 hours, an astonishing feat back then.

Magellan's expedition took three years to circumnavigate the globe in the early sixteenth century. Jules Verne speculated about a faster trip in *Around the World in Eighty Days*, which seemed wildly improbable when the book came out in 1873. Now here was such a trip in eight days. And showing how breathless the pace of aviation was back then, before the 1930s ended, billionaire society aviator Howard Hughes would do it in less than four days.

I read all I could about these and other aerial exploits, including expeditions to the poles and the exploration of far continents. Each autumn the papers were filled with news of the National Air Races in

Cleveland, but racing didn't hold my attention. I was far more interested in technological developments and the doings of a new airline called Pan American Airways, with its audacious plans for air travel across the oceans.

Pan Am would in fact conquer the Pacific in the latter 1930s with island-hopping seaplane services to Asia via Hawaii, Midway, Wake, Guam, and the Philippines. Passengers boarded in San Francisco and arrived in Hong Kong just six days later. Glamorous as they were, those pioneering transpacific air services certainly weren't for the masses; they catered exclusively to the wealthy and to senior executives whose corporations placed a premium on speed.

Across the Atlantic, Germany would beat Pan Am to the punch with leisurely lighter-than-air passenger services linking Europe with the Americas. At the time, I felt intuitively that dirigibles weren't the right way to go from a technological standpoint. The fiery crash of the *Hindenburg* at Lakehurst, New Jersey, in May 1937 confirmed this belief and ended once and for all the use of dirigibles as airliners.

But I'm getting ahead of myself. As mentioned, the 1930s dawned as a decade of austerity. The Depression was hard on most families, ours included. I helped out by earning money delivering papers. I was 11 when I started and held that paper route until the summer before I went to college.

My newspaper, the *Shopping News*, was very popular because it listed all the bargains around Seattle. Housewives up and down my route would be waiting for me to pedal by on my bike and sling it up on their porches. If I missed and the paper landed elsewhere, they sometimes wouldn't want to pay for it because it was dirty. Money was scarce enough that I couldn't afford many such losses, so I learned to focus on the job at hand and do it well.

Delivering papers took me down into the valley in a winding route that ended at Boeing Field. There, my work finished, I'd lean my blue Elgin bicycle against the low fence and watch aviation history unfold.

Mail planes and airliners, military bombers and pursuit ships—I pretty much saw every "mystery ship" that Boeing rolled out in the latter 1920s and all through the 1930s. They had all been biplanes in the '20s, but that began to change with the coming of a new decade.

In May 1930, Boeing rolled out the model 200 Monomail, its first airplane to employ semimonocoque construction. The Monomail was strikingly different from any other Boeing airplane I'd ever seen. For one thing, it was a monoplane and its single low wing was fully canti-levered, which means that it didn't need external bracing struts or wires. For another, it was made entirely of metal.

There were already all-metal airplanes in service in the United States, of course, one example being the Ford Tri-Motor of the late 1920s. A workhorse in its day, the Tri-Motor was in fact too heavy for real commercial success because it was built pretty much the same way that wood-and-fabric airplanes had been before it. It had a full internal skeleton surrounded by a non–load-bearing skin.

In contrast, the Monomail and other semimonocoque airplanes have just a partial internal skeleton over which sheet metal is stretched and riveted. The result is a very strong, very light airframe in which the skin itself carries much of the structural load. This type of con-struction revolutionized aviation and is how Boeing airplanes are still built today.

Since the Monomail was a commercial design, it fell to Boeing's next airplane—which looked to me like a flying cigar—to demon-strate the virtues of semimonocoque construction to the military. This was the Boeing B-9, a twin-engine bomber for the U.S. Army that flew in April 1931. With its sleek fuselage and fully cantilevered wings, the prototype bomber ran away from the fastest fighters of its day. Boeing was now in the forefront of aeronautical design.

In March 1932, even as Boeing was delivering biplane fighters to the army and navy, a very different military single-seater caught my eye on the company's ramp. This was the P-26 Peashooter, the army's first monoplane fighter. The Peashooter fascinated me because it was a technological missing link between biplanes and monoplanes. It combined typical biplane features like an open cockpit, fixed landing gear, and external bracing wires with the single low wing that would soon be the standard for fighter planes.

I critiqued all of these Boeing types against my growing but still largely intuitive knowledge of aeronautical design. I had a pretty good feel for what did what on an airplane, because from an early age I understood that air is a fluid medium, one that airplanes "swim" through. That's why designers streamline them and lay them out so they balance in flight. It's also why planes have wings like birds and tails like the feathers of an arrow, and why those tails have rudders like a ship and elevators like the flukes of a whale.

If it looks right, it flies right goes the old aviation adage. While I learned that it's pretty much true, it didn't really satisfy me. I wanted *real* knowledge and *hard* answers. Why exactly did airplanes fly? How much of aeronautical design was art and how much science?

Finding out became a personal quest that claimed ever more of my time as I grew older. I studied eagles riding the wind, took notes on airplanes flying overhead from the seat of my bike, and hung on the words of my factory-worker neighbors as they groused about their workdays at Boeing. I also read everything I could get my hands on. Whenever the cover of *Popular Mechanics* showed an airplane, I immediately plunked down 25 cents of my hard-earned paper-route money to buy it at the local drugstore.

My friends still wanted to be pilots. *G-8 and His Battle Aces*, *Tailspin Tommy*, and *Ace Drummond* entertained us in print or on the screen at the local movie theater. Flying tales such as *The Air Adventures of Jimmy Allen* came right into our living rooms thanks to radio. Glamorous as they made it seem to be a pilot, though, I knew it wasn't for me. I wanted something else from the field of aviation but I couldn't put my finger on what it was.

———————

The answer came the day I watched Seattle's next wonder, the model 247, take off from Boeing Field. It was February 1933 and I was

Boeing 247

11 years old. Sleek and elegant with a low wing and two radial engines, the Boeing 247 was the world's first modern airliner. It had seats for 10 passengers and wheels that retracted in flight. In comparison, all other airplanes looked obsolete.

As I watched this captivating vision of aviation's future dwindle in the distance, I knew at last what I wanted to do in life. I would become an airplane designer. I saw with great clarity that multiengine machines like the Boeing 247 were aviation's future, and I wanted to be part of it.

In a sense, I was already an airplane designer. Flying machines sprang forth from my youthful imagination. I sketched them by the hour and sometimes built models from scratch that I hung from the ceiling of my room.

My ceiling was already crowded with kit models I'd built and hung on fishing line that was almost invisible. If you squinted, it looked almost as if those airplanes were really flying. I'm still grateful to my mother for surprising me with those airplane kits. Knowing how much aviation meant to me, she'd come home every so often with one or two more of them.

Those were balsa models you covered with doped tissue paper. Their propellers were powered by rubber bands. Being good with my hands, I built and painted them carefully and then went out and flew them until they cracked up. When their flying days were through, I did cosmetic repairs and retired them to the ceiling.

Working on my own designs, I kept coming back to one aeronautical concept that intrigued me more than any other. This was the idea of a huge long-range airliner that, following the trail blazed by Lindbergh, would take off and not touch down again until a distant continent loomed beneath its keel. The great commercial transports I dreamed of would pamper passengers even as they conquered the world's oceans.

This was pretty heady stuff back in the early 1930s, an era when nobody really expected to fly except for the occasional hop in a barnstormer's patched-up Jenny. But the Depression was now in full swing, and my family didn't even have the money for that. Besides, the era of the barnstormer was passing. Aviation was becoming serious business.

The 247 was a technological marvel but a commercial disappointment. Within just a few years, it was overshadowed by the legendary Douglas DC-3, which had twice as many seats and was a better airplane. So good was the DC-3, in fact, that it let airlines make a profit for the first time without air-mail subsidies. It put the world airline industry on its feet.

I was in my early teens when Boeing rolled out an utterly amazing airplane in the summer of 1935. This was the Boeing model 299, a prototype army bomber and at the time the largest land plane in the world. The 299 had no fewer than four engines on wings that stretched more than a hundred feet from tip to tip.

The sheer size of this airplane intrigued me. Its wheels were almost as tall as the men working around it. I and my friends gaped at it in awe when we read it had superchargers to carry it high into the substratosphere. All it needed was a name, and a Tacoma newspaperman soon took care of that. He took one look at this warplane's bristling gun positions and dubbed it the Flying Fortress. The name stuck.

Model 299

I personally witnessed a test in which the model 299's brakes locked up, throwing the plane forward on its nose. That accident led to a flurry of speculation in the press that Boeing's new bomber might be too much airplane for any pilot to handle. Ironically, I'd hear almost exactly the same fears expressed all over again three decades later as we readied the 747 for its first flight.

Les Tower flew the Boeing 299 one hot day in July 1935. Tragically, the 299 was lost a few months later in a takeoff crash at Wright Field, the U.S. Army Air Corps' flight test center in Dayton, Ohio. It was pilot error because military personnel took off with the airplane's control surfaces locked. Les Tower, Boeing's chief test pilot and a boyhood hero of mine, was in the cockpit but not at the controls at the time. He died as a result of injuries sustained in the crash.

Despite this devastating setback, the type survived, evolving into the famous Boeing B-17 Flying Fortress of World War II fame. As redesigned by Boeing engineer Ed Wells and his team, the B-17 became

Boeing 314 Clipper at Plant 1

a war-winning weapon and remains one of the legendary airplanes of that conflict. Almost 13,000 Flying Fortresses would be built by Boeing, Douglas, and Lockheed.

Two events of the late 1930s intensified my desire to design airplanes. The first was the testing of Boeing's model 314 Clipper, a flying-boat airliner developed for Pan American Airways (flying boats are boat-hulled airplanes that take off and set down again on water). The biggest and best of Pan Am's "flying clipper ships" of the 1930s, the ocean-spanning Boeing 314 was an enormous airplane for its day with a wingspan half again greater than that of the B-17.

The Clippers were the last airplanes to be built entirely at Plant 1. Because of their size, Boeing had to complete them outdoors. I watched the first one come together and was part of a large crowd on hand when Boeing towed it down the Duwamish River and tied it up at a barge in Elliot Bay, the part of Puget Sound that fronts Seattle.

From the far end of Beacon Hill, my friends and I saw the model 314 being put through its initial water taxi tests. On June 7, 1938, word came that famous Boeing test pilot Edmund T. Allen—another boyhood hero of mine—was about to fly the Clipper, so we hurried to our lofty neighborhood vantage point. When the time came, I heard the distant roar of powerful engines. A white wake formed behind the airplane as it gathered speed. Its boat hull lifted to skim the water "on the step," and then it was free.

It climbed out to the northwest and entered a gentle but continuing bank to the right that took it inland. Perplexed, I watched it disappear on a southerly heading toward Tacoma and Olympia. *Why are they flying that direction?* I wondered. *You'd think they'd want to stay over the water in case they have to set down.*

It turned out that Eddie Allen had little say in the matter. He had hardly any control over what direction his airplane flew. I learned from newspaper accounts that this first flight had ended safely on Lake Washington, which borders Seattle on the other side. I knew they hadn't planned to land the Clipper on the lake because there was no dock for it there.

Soon afterward we learned that Boeing's designers were modifying the tail of the model 314 to make it controllable. It had made its first flight with just a single vertical stabilizer and rudder. This was removed and replaced with two vertical stabilizers and rudders mounted out near the tips of its horizontal tail. Boeing tested the revised 314 and then modified it yet again, adding a middle stabilizer so that the airplane now had *three* vertical tails. Only then did the Clipper fly what looked like a normal flight-test program.

Clearly there was a lot more to designing airplanes than just sitting down and sketching at a drawing board, and even Boeing's professional engineers didn't have all the answers. This realization intrigued me.

The tragic loss of the first Boeing model 307 Stratoliner was the second event that intensified my interest in aircraft design during the late 1930s. A beautiful new design, the Stratoliner flew on the last day of 1938 and would enter commercial service in 1940 as the world's first pressurized airliner. As 1939 started, I frequently saw the first prototype flying overhead being tested.

On March 18, a few days shy of my eighteenth birthday, I got back

Boeing 314 Clipper

from high school and was doing my chores around the house. It was getting dark. Through the windows I noticed our next-door neighbors, the Zipps, gathered on their porch. The dad, a Boeing factory worker, was talking excitedly and the rest of them looked sober. His voice was loud enough that I caught the words *crash* and *Stratoliner*. It filled me with dread.

Soon the whole neighborhood was out on porches buzzing with the news. The airplane had crashed while flying out near Mount Rainier. Everybody aboard had reportedly been killed.

"New Craft Crumples on Routine Test Flight," proclaimed the headlines. The *Seattle Times* called the crash the "worst airplane disaster in the history of the Pacific Northwest." Boeing had lost seven people: three test pilots, a shop foreman, and several aeronautical engineers, including the company's chief engineer. Also killed were some would-be airline customers from KLM in Holland and the chief pilot for Transcontinental & Western Air, as TWA was then known.

I pored over the newspaper accounts trying to glean clues as to what had gone wrong. Witnesses had seen the Stratoliner cruising serenely along when suddenly it plunged into an unrecoverable spin. As the crew struggled to regain control, it broke apart in the air.

Model 307 Stratoliner

It had something to do with the tail, I suspected. From the start, the Stratoliner hadn't looked quite right to me. *Its vertical tail is too small*, I had thought when Boeing first rolled it out.

Solidifying my suspicions, the company had made a similar error with the model 314 Clipper just the year before. Airplanes with insufficient tail area are not sufficiently controllable in flight; that could certainly explain the crash. But as the weeks and months passed with nothing in the papers about it, I began to doubt myself.

But when later-production Stratoliners rolled out with a redesigned tail that was considerably bigger, I realized I had been right. The knowledge brought no sense of vindication, just more questions. How could Boeing get it wrong? Why were things done the way they were and what was the underlying basis of aeronautical knowledge? Just how precise a science was airplane design anyway?

Boeing built nine more Stratoliners. Three entered service with Pan Am and five with TWA. One went to billionaire Howard Hughes, who then controlled TWA, as his personal airplane. With their

Stratoliner with redesigned tail

pressurized cabins and supercharged engines, these luxurious high-altitude transports were technological marvels. They could cruise comfortably above most of the weather at 20,000 feet.

Like the development of instrument flight, the emergence of pressurization marked a key breakthrough in commercial aviation. Other airliners of the day—for example, the Douglas DC-3—were not pressurized, so they flew *through* the weather instead of above it. People today have forgotten what that was like or how intimidating air travel could be.

Let me take you along on a DC-3 flight to show you what I mean. The stewardess—there was just one and they were always female back then—issued chewing gum to help her passengers clear their ears when the unpressurized plane climbed or descended. On summer days when fluffy cumulus clouds dotted the sky, flying involved running the gauntlet through a never-ending series of updrafts and downdrafts. It felt like being on the string of a slow-motion yo-yo with occasional jolts, yaws, and shakes thrown in for good measure.

Douglas DC-3

Passengers would gasp or cry out loud when the DC-3 hit a particularly bad "air pocket," as downdrafts were misnamed back then. It kept people reaching for the sick sack. But at night or on those days when the air was still, the DC-3 flew smoothly except for the vibration of its two 1,200-horsepower radial engines. It was very much the luck of the draw.

Pilots really earned their pay when an embedded squall line straddled the flight route. There was no going around a squall line the way you could a single storm, so DC-3 crews became adept at picking their way through the worst of the thunder cells. Rain lashed and pelted the windows. Lightning flashed all around, further terrifying the passengers. In the cockpit, the crew donned rain slickers because the DC-3's front windows invariably leaked.

Flying through the weather instead of above it also had its moments in the winter. Ice would build up on the wings and propellers, forcing pilots to change altitude trying to find safer conditions as the plane's deicer boots and propeller anti-ice systems worked overtime. Few "normal" events in the history of air travel were more alarming than when a DC-3's propeller suddenly shed its ice with a god-awful clatter as it struck the fuselage.

Compared with the Douglas DC-3, the Boeing Stratoliner must have seemed positively miraculous when TWA and Pan Am introduced theirs in transcontinental services in July 1940. With its smooth high-altitude cruise, the Stratoliner launched the era of *comfortable* flying. I think it would have been a huge success if World War II hadn't come along when it did. That war so greatly accelerated the development of flight-related technologies that the Stratoliner was obsolete by the time that conflict ended in 1945.

Back in March 1939, the Stratoliner tragedy lent a more compelling focus to my dreams of being an airplane designer. I vowed that the airplanes I would someday create would be as safe as human minds could possibly make them.

All that lay in the future, of course. First I needed a college education.

2

UNIVERSITY AND WAR

I applied to and was accepted by the University of Washington. Except for my half brother John, I was the first member of my family to attend college. Like so many families at the tail end of the Depression, we Sutters didn't have much money, but my parents still managed to pay my way through school, for which I am forever grateful.

They were always totally supportive of my dreams. My dad died unexpectedly during the war. Mom missed him terribly and followed not too many years afterward. That happened fairly early in my Boeing career. I wish very much that they could have lived to see the 747. After they had put up with my drawing all those sketches and had hit their heads many times on the models hanging from the ceiling of my room, it would have thrilled them to see me realize my boyhood dreams.

I showed up at the University of Washington at the age of 18 in the fall of 1939. It was a heady time and a scary one. World War II had broken out in Europe on September 3, casting a huge cloud of uncertainty over those of us in our teens or twenties. World events were a frequent topic of conversation as I carpooled to and from campus with friends in an old De Soto.

The UW's College of Aeronautical Engineering had fine instructors such as Professors Eastman and Martin and Dr. Kirsten. One of my teachers was a young assistant professor named Robert Hage who would serve with the U.S. Army Air Forces during World War II and join Boeing on his return. Bob and I worked together on the 707 program before he jumped ship to McDonnell Aircraft back in 1958. Hage later led the development of the McDonnell Douglas DC-10, the 747's most successful competitor.

I loved math and physics, so the work at the UW was easy for me. We were a highly competitive group, and I strove for the highest marks in the program. I consistently led in academic standings except for the time that Dale Myers, a good friend and excellent engineer, beat me in advanced aeronautics. Dale would later be the second in command at NASA.

All in all, it was a very fine education and I enjoyed every minute of it. The fact that I soaked it up like a sponge told me I was on the right path. This was what I should be doing with my life.

During my final two years of schooling, I took a summer job at Boeing. Working as a mechanic in the subassembly area helped me to pay my way through school. My Boeing salary was a princely 62.5 cents an hour!

Before graduating from Cleveland High School, we senior boys had been given presentations by the army and navy for their college reserve officer training programs. The army's program was just two years long and didn't seem all that exciting. In contrast, the navy's was four years and chock-full of interesting subjects, so I enrolled in the Naval Reserve Officers Training Corps on arrival at the UW.

Naval ROTC was a classy outfit. It paid me 25 cents a day, which went a long way in those long-gone days. Better still, I learned celestial navigation, which was then an essential aviation skill. Between my college studies and ROTC during the school year, and my summer job with Boeing, life was pretty full until I graduated.

Fortunately, those demands didn't prevent me from meeting a lovely young woman named Nancy French! Nancy was a year ahead of me at the UW, where she majored in home economics. I met her at an NROTC dance in my junior year and we began dating. We fell in love pretty quickly. She was very attractive and had a special bearing, a way of speaking, and highly polished manners—traits that back in those days were summarized as "a lot of class."

Against this backdrop, events continued to worsen in Europe. The Low Countries and France fell to Hitler in 1940, and the Battle of Britain began. England survived by the skin of its teeth, in part because of Lend-Lease aid provided by the United States. It was increasingly clear that we as a nation could not remain neutral in the face of spreading fascism.

I was a junior at the UW when the Japanese bombed Pearl Harbor. That shocking event of December 7, 1941, propelled the United States into a two-front global conflict for which we were unprepared. Because of America's traditional antipathy to standing armies, we were a hell of a long way from mobilizing large forces and being able to equip them. Our industries hadn't yet geared up to produce all the airplanes, ships, tanks, and other weapons of war that we and our allies suddenly needed.

I clearly remember the sobering weight of those challenges settling on me as I listened to President Roosevelt address Congress and the nation on December 8, when he announced that we were at war. Like so many young Americans, I was ready and willing to do my part, whatever that might be. I postponed all thoughts of a career and prepared instead for a call to arms.

Senior year was downright crazy. Bittersweet and hectic, really, because I knew that all too soon my classmates and I would scatter to help fight a global war. Many friends had already been drafted or had dropped out of school, eager to enlist. Campus life had become very strange.

One cold day in February 1943, the prototype B-29 Superfortress roared low over the campus heading south toward Boeing Field. One of its engines was fiercely ablaze. Smoke poured back, leaving a long trail in the sky. Later as we carpooled home, a pall of smoke brought my first inkling of disaster. It drew our eyes to the flashing lights of emergency vehicles down at the Duwamish flats.

Stricken by an uncontrollable engine fire, that prototype Boeing B-29 had crashed into a meatpacking plant short of Boeing Field's runway. Famed test pilot Edmund T. Allen and several others were dead. Allen's loss was a profound blow to the company. In addition to testing the B-29, the MIT-trained engineer had piloted the first flights of the 307 Stratoliner and 314 Clipper before the war. Everybody had admired and would miss Eddie, including me.

Our graduation was moved forward so that we could meet the call to war. In the span of two days that eventful spring of 1943, I received my bachelor of science degree in aeronautical engineering, Nancy and I were married in West Seattle, and my orders arrived to report for duty with the U.S. Navy. I was a newly minted ensign.

Nancy and I were wed at the Alki Congregational Church near the beach in West Seattle. My brother Lou and Ray Oliver, a UW classmate, were my best men. The reception was at the home of Nancy's parents, a large colonial house overlooking Puget Sound. It was a bittersweet event. With a war on and military orders in my pocket, I was excited and more than a little nervous.

I reported to the navy's Sub Chaser Training Center in Miami. Fortunately, being married, I could take Nancy with me. We traveled by train and had a berth as far as Chicago, where we transferred in bitter cold weather. From that point forward, there were only seats— no berths—for the rest of the three-day trip.

Those trains were full of U.S. servicemen and a lot of them were drunk. I spent the trip running interference to keep them from making passes at Nancy. Military police at the stations frisked everyone in uniform every time we boarded a train, but that didn't put a dent in the number of booze bottles floating around.

Coming from Seattle, I didn't like Miami. It was hot and muggy and had cockroaches that the locals called palmetto bugs. After a few days, Nancy and I found a nice place to live and began settling in. Transition to military life was rapid for me. My training took me till the end of the year, at which time I took up operational duties in the wartime navy.

It saddened me that there would be no naval aviation for me. That had been my goal but circumstances conspired against it. Despite my studies in celestial navigation, that Naval ROTC training in the "art of seamanship" destined me for sea duty. Although I was advised not to, I did fill out an application for pilot training while still at the UW. My ROTC commander had called me in and chewed me out. "We trained you to be a deck officer, damn it, and that's what you will be," he informed me in no uncertain terms. "You will serve your country on the deck of a destroyer."

———

It actually turned out to be a destroyer escort. Mine was the USS *Edward H. Allen* (DE-531), a brand-new vessel just completed by the Boston navy Yard. Destined for the Atlantic Fleet, it was named for a decorated naval aviator who had given his life in the Battle of the Coral Sea in May 1942.

Low slung and fast, DE-531, as we called her, had two powerful geared-turbine engines that could propel her through the water at the remarkable speed of 24 knots. Just over 300 feet long, she carried 14 officers (I was the most junior) and nearly 200 enlisted men. Our weapons were depth charges and another antisubmarine system called the hedgehog, a single tube for launching torpedoes, anti-aircraft guns, and one "five-inch gun" fore and aft.

We took this new warship to Bermuda for a month-long shakedown cruise in January 1944. When it was over, we returned to Boston, where the deficiencies we had identified would be addressed. (There were a lot of fixes—perhaps because of wartime pressures, those DEs weren't very well built.)

We left Bermuda late one 70-degree day, steaming north with no inkling of trouble. Out on the high seas, the temperature and barometric pressure both began falling precipitously. As the officer with the least seniority, I generally drew the midnight-to-4-AM watch. It was ordinarily a quiet time and a struggle to stay awake. But that night was very different. When the orderly woke me shortly before midnight, the ship was heaving and plunging. "Mr. Sutter," he advised me, "you'd better pull on all the cold-weather gear you've got."

I donned everything I had—the navy issued good cold-weather gear—and went up on the pitching deck to assume the watch. A 70-mile-per-hour wind was blowing and the temperature was clearly below freezing. The waves were having their tops blown off and the spray was flash-freezing wherever it landed.

I saw that ice was building on the guardrails, stanchions, and every other projection of our ship. By four bells—2 AM—so much ice had accumulated that I awoke the captain and informed him of the situation. I recall his arrival on deck that dark night and how he surveyed the situation. "Yeah," he said, "collecting this ice is . . ." He frowned, leaving the thought unfinished. "We're going to be losing stability. Go below and get the *First Lieutenant's Manual*."

I did so and on his orders went into the pilothouse. Switching on a small light, I read the section about our ship's stability. The manual said how long it should take our ship to roll from one side to the other. This natural oscillation is called the ship's *period*. The manual went on to say that if this period doubled (that is, if the rate of our side-to-side roll slowed to twice as long), the ship was entering a "severe condition."

We were actually rolling through 50 degrees to either side. That doesn't sound all that alarming in print, but if you were there it was truly frightening. In fact, it looked like our smokestack was slicing into the waves on one side and then the other. I put all fear out of my mind and concentrated on timing the ship's period through three or four roll oscillations.

I did this several times and kept coming up with a number closer to *three* times normal. We had advanced way past *severe* to a condition not even described in the manual.

The ship was really struggling. We would roll far to one side, hesitate there and shudder, then finally start back, going all the way over until the other side of our ship wallowed and shuddered in the roiling sea.

Bracing myself for balance, I left the pilot house and reported my findings to Commander Graves, who consulted with the captain. There was really nothing any of us could do except keep DE-531's nose straight into the waves and hope that our power never dropped. If those engines had faltered, we would have capsized.

Time passed with agonizing slowness. There was no hope of working on that slippery deck, no possibility of removing the thickening ice. As dawn broke, our situation was dire and continued to worsen throughout the day. Very late that afternoon, miraculously and precariously, we managed to limp into Boston Harbor and made the navy Yard. We were *safe!*

Shock greeted our arrival. It looked like an iceberg had sailed in and tied up at the wharf. From our superstructure on down, we were a mass of ice decorated with spiky icicles extending back where the wind had blown them. The ship was so thoroughly encased that I couldn't even make out the big gun turret on the foredeck—it was just a formless blob.

Navy crews with steam hoses worked almost a week to clear off all the ice. When done, they determined that DE-531's junction boxes, switches, and all other above-deck electrical gear had all been irreparably damaged by seawater and expanding ice. With the entire topside needing to be rewired, it was a month before we could reclaim our ship and begin operations.

———

World War II made my generation grow up fast. From it I drew lessons that stood me in good stead later in my career, particularly during the 747 program. More than just teaching me about leadership, my navy service reinforced the value of teamwork, keeping a cool head at all times, and working on the problem—whatever it might be—to the best of my ability.

Ironically, it was that ice storm on our shakedown cruise that taught me the most valuable lesson of all. Reflecting back on our total helplessness in its fierce grip, I vowed to design airplanes that—to the greatest degree humanly possible—would continue to provide options and remain controllable for the crew despite unforeseen circumstances.

The rest of the war seemed almost tame by comparison. Operating out of Miami and Key West, Florida, and Norfolk, Virginia, we escorted convoys up and down the U.S. East Coast to keep them safe from the U-boat menace. Once we helped shepherd a convoy halfway across the Atlantic before being relieved by other navy escort vessels and turning for home.

That entire period was a happy time for Nancy and me, although the war made for an odd honeymoon. She followed me up to Boston when we picked up our new ship. Later she joined me at Norfolk, when we were assigned temporarily to the navy base there before returning to Miami. Despite the housing challenges, she successfully followed me up and down the East Coast.

A hurricane worked its way up the East Coast while we were at Norfolk. The storm was supposed to miss Chesapeake Bay, so the navy kept us at anchor even though the bay is too shallow for big ships to safely weather such events. When the meteorologists finally realized the hurricane was bearing straight down on us, we made a belated dash for the open Atlantic in rapidly deteriorating weather conditions.

I had a front-row seat to events. We were taking the full brunt of the storm when another navy vessel got blown sideways and blocked the channel, bottling us in. All we could do at that point was ride the hurricane out, steaming in minimal visibility, veering hard at the last minute to avoid collisions with other ships caught in the same predicament. So violent was this storm that the wind actually exposed the bottom of the bay more than once. I wouldn't have believed it if I hadn't seen it with my own eyes.

There were humorous moments to the war as well. One of the six vessels in our DE squadron at Key West was commanded by one of President Roosevelt's sons. This younger Roosevelt owned a Scottie that was a littermate of Fala, FDR's famous dog at the White House.

The younger Roosevelt's ship frequently seemed to have trouble leaving port. We were often called on to take up the slack. Needless to say, the crew of DE-531 was none too happy about having to give up our hard-earned liberty to do somebody else's job. We were out on one of these extra missions when radio silence was broken by an urgent message from Norfolk. Had we seen this dog, and was it by any chance aboard our ship, they wanted to know.

Joe on Eniwetok
(AUTHOR'S PERSONAL COLLECTION)

No one on the crew reported seeing it, yet when we returned to port five or six days later, the missing Scottie miraculously reappeared the moment we docked. The enlisted ranks have their own sense of justice and it's often sprinkled with humor. I'm sure the message was not lost on young Roosevelt and his crew.

———

After my tour in the DE, the navy ordered me to Memphis for training as an aviation engineer. Nancy followed me there but not beyond; we wouldn't see each other again until peacetime. Finishing this training, I reported to Floyd Bennett Field at New York City to learn my new posting. That's where I was on V-J Day in August 1945 when World War II officially ended.

The winter of 1945–46 found me posted to Eniwetok, a tropical atoll in the Marshall Islands, where I finished up my service at the rank of lieutenant as an aviation engineer. Eniwetok had been the site of a major naval battle in February 1944. That pounding had blown off most of the vegetation, so instead of a tropical paradise I found a bare island.

While I liked my aviation duties, there was little flying activity to support at that point and I was more than ready to come home. I returned by troop ship via Hawaii, excited by the prospect of at last beginning a career as an airplane designer.

3

DOUGLAS, BOEING, AND
THE STRATOCRUISER

While still in uniform on Eniwetok Atoll, I was flattered to receive two overtures from aircraft companies asking me to come work for them. One was from Boeing and the other from Douglas.

I gave those letters a great deal of thought. "You know," I recall writing to Nancy, "we're young and we haven't traveled much, so maybe I should take the Douglas job. We could get to know California and return to the Northwest later." She agreed with this proposal, so that's what we decided together.

Douglas offered me $210 per month in salary whereas Boeing offered just $200 a month. That doesn't sound like much nowadays, but an extra $120 per year went a long way in the immediate postwar era.

I was all of 24 years old when I returned to Seattle in January 1946. Nancy was well along with her first pregnancy by then. She suggested we hold off on moving to California until after the baby came and we had adjusted to being a family. Having already accepted Douglas's offer, I wrote to them explaining the situation and asking if they could defer my start date by a few months.

I received a kind reply saying they understood and asking that I let them know as soon as I was ready to come to Los Angeles. Meantime, needing a job, I went to Boeing and told them I was interested in working there on a short-term basis.

When I explained my situation, Boeing wasn't happy about being second on my list of potential employers. They suggested that I look more closely at the excellent opportunities they could offer me. This surprised me because of the vast difference in the two companies' fortunes back then.

The world's premier manufacturer of airliners before the war, Douglas continued to pursue long-range transport development during the war. The four-engine R5D cargo planes that had taken me from the United States to the Marshall Islands via Hawaii had been Douglas products. That airplane type—which the Army Air Forces called the C-54—became the DC-4 commercial airliner at war's end. It was the best transport plane in the world and Douglas was already at work on its pressurized successor, the DC-6.

Boeing, in contrast, had no commercial business to fall back on when the war ended. Wartime developments had rendered its pre-war model 307 Stratoliner obsolete. By fostering the construction of military airfields around the world, the war also effectively eliminated the need for any more flying boats like the model 314 Clipper. Those former military airfields provided a ready-made global infrastructure for air travel to resume in the postwar era using land planes.

Boeing's remaining military orders were summarily canceled and thousands of workers were laid off. How could Boeing survive such a precipitous decline in production levels, I wondered. What future could this company in my backyard hope to offer me?

Such were my thoughts as I reported for a job interview with Boeing's chief of flight test. I had applied to that department because I wanted to work hands-on with real airplanes. A job in flight test would combine my engineering degree with the practical knowledge I had gained late in the war.

Boeing Flight Test had an opening for me, but they requested that I first go over and speak with George Schairer, who ran Boeing's technical staff and was the company's chief aerodynamicist. A brilliant engineer, Schairer was a person of very strong opinions. When I explained my interest in flight test, he made me a counterproposal. "Do you really want to learn the business?" he asked. "If so, you'd do better to work in the aerodynamics arena and I think we might have a place for you."

Schairer made a good case. I walked out of that room convinced that aerodynamics would be the most interesting of all jobs; it would be aero or nothing for me at Boeing. Accordingly, I signed up with that department for what I thought would be only a few months before Nancy and I—and by then our new baby—headed off to Douglas in sunny Southern California.

———————

In February 1946, Nancy gave birth to a beautiful baby girl we named Gabrielle. On a rainy day that same month, I hired into Boeing's aerodynamics group and immediately found myself assigned to work on the Boeing model 377 Stratocruiser, a big propeller airliner that would enter commercial service early in 1949.

Big and blunt nosed, the Stratocruiser would be the most spacious, complex, and powerful piston-engine airliner of all time. Together with the postwar four-engine propeller airliners of Douglas and Lockheed, the Stratocruiser would span the oceans and help lay down the global aviation infrastructure that we take for granted today.

This new Boeing commercial transport was about 90% designed when I hired in, but it was plagued from stem to stern with problems. I was amazed to find that fixing these troubles immediately became *my* responsibility and that of a few other equally young and inexperienced newcomers to Boeing's engineering ranks.

This will make for an interesting temporary assignment, I thought. I didn't suspect that it would instead launch many decades of challenges and learning with Boeing. As for the mighty Stratocruiser

itself, it provided me with the best graduate course in airplane design that I could possibly have wished for.

My boss in Boeing's small aerodynamics group was Jack Steiner, a
gifted engineer who would rise to national prominence in the 1960s
for leading the design of the workhorse Boeing 727. Back in 1946,
Steiner was heading up the aerodynamic design and development of
the piston-powered Stratocruiser.

The Stratocruiser was a high priority for Boeing, which hoped for
commercial orders to offset the precipitous drop in military business
it suffered at war's end. Douglas and Lockheed had a head start, of
course. Douglas was beginning to deliver DC-4s to the world's airlines and would soon unveil the stretched and pressurized DC-6, the
most successful propeller airliner of the postwar era.

Lockheed was likewise introducing a new airliner series that, like
the DC-4, first flew as a wartime military transport. Slender and
beautiful, the Lockheed Constellation had greyhound lines and a distinctive triple tail. Lockheed's "Connie" was as sleek as the Boeing
Stratocruiser was ponderous but it was no faster.

Coming to market last, Boeing had never had a solid commercial
success in the airliner arena, so there was little for it to build on. But
Boeing had two trump cards up its sleeve.

The first was the B-29 Superfortress, the most technologically advanced airplane to emerge from World War II. A comparison of cruise
altitudes hints at this technological supremacy. Whereas the Douglas
DC-6 and Lockheed Constellation could cruise as high as 22,000
feet (and the unpressurized DC-4 half that high), the Stratocruiser—
thanks to its B-17, Stratoliner, and B-29 ancestry—could cruise at
35,000 feet while its cabin remained at a comfortable 8,000 feet or
so. No other piston airliner was ever certified to those high cruise altitudes, which are typical of jet travel today.

The second Boeing advantage was a promising concept the company had first tried with the model 307 Stratoliner back in 1938. This
was to combine the wings, tail, engines, landing gear, and systems of

an existing military airplane with a more capacious fuselage suited to airline needs. The Stratoliner was essentially a B-17 Flying Fortress with a fat new fuselage for commercial service.

Fortunately for Boeing, the military had already paid to give the B-29 a fat new fuselage. A wartime contract created the Boeing model 367, which would serve the postwar air force as the C-97 Strato-freighter and KC-97 Stratotanker. The former was used to transport cargo and troops and the latter for aerial refueling.

In 1946, Boeing was also improving the B-29 for use as a stopgap strategic bomber at the start of the Cold War. Called the B-50, this "better B-29" of the late 1940s featured more powerful engines, a taller tail, and other significant changes.

The Stratocruiser program took advantage of both these military-funded B-29 developments to create a propeller airliner promising unmatched capability and performance. However, this airliner was riddled with problems stemming from its excessive complexity. The B-29 was by far the most sophisticated airplane produced by any nation during the war, and the model 377—with its new engines and propellers—was even more of a handful.

Unfortunately, Jack Steiner really was not interested in solving the Stratocruiser's problems. His attention was focused on how to adapt jet propulsion, which was then a military technology, to meet the needs of commercial aviation.

During World War II, Germany pioneered the operational use of jet aircraft like the Messerschmitt Me 262 fighter and Arado Ar 234 bomber. Although the United States flew prototype jets during the war using British-supplied turbine-engine technology, we were already doing well with conventional airplanes, so we didn't pursue jets aggressively until just after the war.

Germany and Japan lay defeated, and the Soviet Union—an uncomfortable ally during the conflict—was emerging as a potential threat on the European continent, setting the stage for the Cold War. Technology was advancing rapidly, and several U.S. jet fighters and bombers were now flying or under development.

The Stratocruiser was the state of the art in commercial

transportation. However, next to the radical B-47, which Boeing was then developing for the air force, it looked ancient and lumbering. Jets were clearly the wave of the future, and it was no surprise that Steiner and other well-established engineers in aero were all angling to get onto jet programs.

That's why fixing up Boeing's troubled propeller airliner, getting it certified, and seeing it safely into the hands of its airline customers was left to newcomers like me and Lynn Olason, a lifelong friend who was my classmate at the University of Washington and who joined Boeing about the same time I did.

The senior members of our aero group, Steiner included, thought we new guys were working at a dead end. However, there's no doubt in my mind that the old Stratocruiser did Lynn and me a world of good. It was our responsibility and we ran with it.

My fingerprints could be found all over the company as I hurriedly came up to speed on the 377's design and construction. Fixing the Stratocruiser's systems required me to delve deeply into why it had been designed the way it was and why it wasn't working right. It required a lot of fact finding and creative head scratching.

On July 8, 1947, the Stratocruiser made its first flight. Watching a new Boeing airplane take to the skies was old hat, but this time I was observing it as an insider instead of as a kid taking time from his paper route to hang on the company fence. It was a funny feeling—and a very good one—to be there in an official capacity.

Whatever pride I felt was overshadowed by a mushrooming workload, because flight testing quickly revealed lots more things needing to be fixed. The test pilots found that the controls were too light in small turns and too heavy in large ones. There was also no feeling of "centering" in the control wheel to tell you when the control surfaces were at neutral and not deflecting the airstream.

Control surfaces are those movable surfaces used to guide and maneuver an airplane. They consist of *ailerons*, the *elevator*, and the *rudder*. Located outboard on the wings, the ailerons control movement around the roll axis. When the wheel is turned to the left, the aileron on that side goes up and the one on the right side of the airplane goes down. The result is a deflection of the slipstream that tilts the airplane.

Similarly, pulling or pushing on the control wheel deflects the elevator to pitch the nose up and down, and depressing the left or right rudder pedal yaws the nose from side to side. The elevators are attached to the tail's horizontal stabilizer, and the rudder is mounted on its vertical stabilizer.

The Stratocruiser had manually operated control surfaces boosted with servo tabs. These are small tabs on the control surfaces that deflect in the opposite direction, making the airflow help the pilot move the surface to its new position. The result from the pilot's point of view is lighter controls that need considerably less muscle power.

To fix the Stratocruiser's poor flight-control characteristics, we added variable springs in the control system here and changed servo-tab hinge lines there to get more desirable results. Every time we made a change, the airplane had to be flown again to evaluate the results.

This empirical process couldn't have made me happier, because it meant lots of flying in an amazing airplane. While I tried out the controls myself from time to time, I lacked the expertise to interpret what they were telling me, so I left that to the engineering test pilots. We eventually got the airplane flying beautifully and turned our attention to its other challenges.

Another problem I recall was the Stratocruiser's airspeed indicating system. We thought this would be an easy fix. It was anything but, because of that big airplane's blunt nose. Airplanes sense their speed through the air by comparing *static air pressure* with *ram air pressure*. The former is sensed through an opening that is flush on the side of the airplane perpendicular to the airflow. The latter is sensed through an opening directed straight into the airflow. The difference between these two pressures shows up on your airspeed indicator as the airplane's speed through the air.

To make sure that this ram air pressure measurement is accurate, it is sensed from the end of an angled tube called a Pitot (PEE-toe) tube. The Pitot tube allows the ambient air to be sensed away from the disturbed airflow passing around the fuselage.

Airliners actually have more than one Pitot tube and static port, the locations of which are carefully chosen to provide as accurate a reading as possible throughout the airplane's speed range. Although the shape of the Stratocruiser's forward fuselage made it very difficult, we finally found, by trial and error, a combination of Pitot and static locations that yielded good results.

By far the most challenging Stratocruiser issues were propulsion related. This airplane was powered by the air-cooled Pratt & Whitney R-4360, which is the most powerful piston aircraft engine ever produced. Rated at 3,500 horsepower, it was bigger and more powerful than the engines powering the competing Douglas and Constellation airliners.

Each of the Stratocruiser's R-4360s had 28 cylinders arranged in four banks of seven cylinders each. When this engine was uncowled, there were so many cylinder heads that it kind of looked like kernels on a cob, leading to the nickname "corncob engine."

If the Boeing Stratocruiser idled for too long on the ground, its spark plugs fouled and had to be changed. That doesn't sound so bad until you realize that each Stratocruiser had 224 spark plugs.

We worked very hard to integrate this troubled engine into the Stratocruiser. No matter how we arranged its cooling baffles, though, we could never get enough air through the cowlings to properly cool that last row of cylinders. This led to frequent failures in flight, an issue never solved throughout the Stratocruiser's career with the airlines.

The reliability of the P&W R-4360 was a real disappointment. Reciprocating engine technology had reached its zenith during World War II, as exemplified by Pratt & Whitney's superb R-2800 radial engine, which was rated at 2,000 horsepower or more. But by the latter 1940s, this technology had been pushed beyond its limits to the point of diminishing returns. Reliability really suffered, challenging airlines in the postwar era.

Boeing 377 Stratocruiser

The same was true of the Stratocruiser's four huge propellers, which were subject to extreme stresses. If the engine didn't fail in flight, very often the propeller would, adding to the propulsion challenges we faced. We worked on this with Curtiss and Hamilton Standard, the manufacturers of propellers for the Stratocruiser and its military cousin, the C-97.

Next I tackled the stalling of the compressed airflow in the internal ducting for the engine turbo-superchargers. I worked on this issue by adjusting the shape of this ducting and playing around with internal guides and baffles. It seemed that the propulsion-related issues with this airplane would never end.

———

The only time I was really scared in a Stratocruiser was when our number 3 engine quit. Oil from that failed engine entered the supercharger duct and caught fire, belching flames and smoke out the engine's exhaust. I was at my data recording station in the airplane's empty passenger cabin. I heard a warning bell from the open cockpit door and described what I was seeing over the intercom. Declaring an emergency, the crew banked us toward Boeing Field for an expedited landing.

There was some question as to whether we'd make it. I couldn't help thinking of Eddie Allen, Boeing's famous test pilot, who lost his life to an engine fire in that prototype B-29 a half-dozen years before. I was also thinking of Nancy and baby Gabrielle. It wasn't just me anymore; I had my family to provide for.

Another fellow and I removed the overwing escape hatch. We tightened our parachute harnesses and waited for the bail-out command even though we were pretty low by then. I nearly had one foot out on the wing and was imagining how I would dive over it when the fire ended as suddenly as it had begun. I reported this with relief and we landed a minute later.

The Boeing 377 Stratocruiser was a safe airplane except for those engines and propellers. They were the Achilles' heel of a great ocean-spanning airliner that was a real workhorse for the airlines before the jet age.

———

I was never again afraid aboard an airplane, not even during the aerodynamic stall tests we performed to satisfy Federal Aviation Administration requirements. You really had to love airplanes a whole lot to go through those Stratocruiser stall tests.

When the pilot pulled the Stratocruiser up into a full stall, the airplane would mush and then start shaking itself to pieces. Everything rattled and clanged in a very alarming fashion. Then the stall broke and the bottom dropped out of the world. The ground rushed up to fill the cockpit windows. Engines roared as the flight crew brought the power back up. Being careful not to overstress the airframe, they gingerly pulled our big ship out of its dive.

Aerodynamic stalls occur when the airflow separates from the wings. This happens if you pull the nose up without sufficient engine power to keep you moving forward. As the stall approaches, the airplane warns you by shaking as the airflow over the wings and tail becomes turbulent. The stall breaks when the airplane quits flying and starts falling.

Recovery from this stalled condition is simple. The pilot simply releases backpressure on the wheel and lets the airplane pick up flying speed again. If it's a big ship, you have to be careful not to let it pick up too much speed during the dive. You also have to make sure you stall high up so that there's plenty of altitude for your recovery.

There are several kinds of stalls, including power-off and acceler- ated stalls. Pilots generally practice these in small airplanes but not in large ones, where they can be hairy. That's particularly true if one wing stalls before the other. Then you get a violent roll that can flip your airplane over on its back.

It was unnerving as hell to do this sort of thing in the lumbering Stratocruiser. I'll never forget how violently the airplane shook, but we had to do it to make sure we were delivering a truly robust air- plane with good characteristics from one extreme end of the flight envelope to the other. Of course, neither extreme is ever encountered in airline operations, where pilots keep things as gentle as possible for the passengers' sake.

We junior engineers resolved the Stratocruiser's troubles in fairly short order. I thrived on the technical challenges and consider it one of the best learning experiences of my life. And because of all the fly- ing that this work required, I ended up getting my flight-test experi- ence after all.

Debugging the model 377 also brought me my first Boeing experi- ence with disciplines beyond engineering. In particular, it required me to work directly with the company's airline customers. As an engineer representing Boeing, I would sit down with their technical people, take them through the design, and show them how we were progressing in our efforts to achieve our *performance guarantees*. This term refers to the airplane's range, payload, economics, and other targets stipulated in the contracts Boeing has signed with its customers.

To be honest, the Stratocruiser's performance was marginal

because of insufficient engine power, aviation's perennial limiting factor. Since the time of the Wright brothers, propulsion technology has lagged behind what we designers have wanted to do with our increasingly capable airframes.

Pan Am, BOAC (British Overseas Airways Corporation), and Northwest planned to fly some pretty long overwater routes with their Stratocruisers. With this in mind, they were always pressing us for more airplane performance than we felt we could deliver. They could get pretty heated when we didn't see our way clear to giving them what they wanted.

This was great training for me in how to represent my employer's position. I had always tried to listen well and comport myself in a fair and honest manner. Now I devoted myself to understanding our customers and trying my best to see that they ultimately got an airplane that did the job safely and profitably.

———

John Borger of Pan American Airways was a true engineer who had been with Pan Am since the flying boat days in the 1930s. He was already an old hand when I got to know him during those Stratocruiser discussions. Borger knew what it took to operate an airline, what sort of equipment was required, and how to press airplane and engine manufacturers to get it.

Borger was a *very* forceful and intimidating personality. Built like a linebacker, he had the aggressive look and personality of a bulldog. Nobody who dealt with him was ever likely to forget it. He took us to task, challenging and berating us to secure for his airline the safest and best equipment and performance possible.

Borger's overpowering demeanor and frequent tongue lashings left countless people in the commercial aviation industry dreading their dealings with him. Many refused outright to do so, finding it too stressful. For some reason, though, I held up pretty well under his full frontal assault. We had plenty of lively discussions about the Stratocruiser.

Pan American had launched the Boeing 314 Clipper that so amazed me as a child. After sponsoring the Stratocruiser, this great airline would go on to spearhead the development of the 707 and 747. Representing Juan Trippe, the airline's legendary leader, Borger would play a huge role in defining both those airplanes.

I learned very quickly in our Stratocruiser discussions that Borger knew his stuff. I developed a lot of respect for the guy. Although many Boeing people felt he was too hard-nosed, I saw him as simply doing his job. We developed a close friendship that lasted throughout my Boeing career and continues to this day.

Finally, the Stratocruiser gave me my first experience working with the Civil Aeronautics Authority (CAA), predecessor of today's FAA. For me, it was the beginning of a long and very detailed practical education in the critical area of regulatory guidance and oversight.

Our young team successfully saw the Boeing 377 Stratocruiser through government certification. Pan Am introduced it to service between San Francisco and Hawaii in April 1949. Sporting the colors of Pan Am and Northwest Airlines, Stratocruisers were soon flying all the way to Tokyo, although like all airliners in the propeller era, they required a refueling stop in Hawaii or Alaska. Northwest chose the latter, having gained far northerly operating experience supporting U.S. operations in World War II.

Pan Am also flew Stratocruisers in European services across the North Atlantic. American Overseas and BOAC joined in with European Stratocruiser services of their own. United operated this big Boeing airliner domestically and to Hawaii in competition with Pan Am.

The Boeing 377 Stratocruiser was without question the best airplane of its day from the passenger's standpoint—very comfortable to fly. Popular features of the Stratocruiser included a lavishly stocked galley and railroad-style Pullman sleeping berths that added to the comfort of long overwater flights. Passengers liked falling asleep to the deep reassuring drone of those engines. They also liked the separate gold-toned dressing rooms for men and women and the

Boeing 377 Stratocruiser

lower-level cocktail lounge that could accommodate a dozen or more passengers.

The Stratocruiser did a very good job for the airlines. Although it wasn't the most efficient airplane in the world, it kept operators like Northwest and Pan Am going. Some competing airliners had groundings imposed for safety reasons—for example, the Douglas DC-7C with its Wright turbo-compound engines—but the old 377 never did.

Boeing delivered only 55 Stratocruisers to the airlines versus nearly 900 C-97 tankers and cargo planes to the military. While this last gasp of B-29 technology was a success, the commercial side of it definitely was not. It was clear to us that the future of Boeing as a commercial manufacturer couldn't rest on conventional airplanes like the Strato-cruiser.

I feel great affection for Boeing's last propeller airliner. It had a magic to it and nothing else ever sounded quite so powerful. That airplane gave me the priceless gift of a rapid, intensive education in integrating a total design. Through practical experience—always the best teacher—I learned that the "whole" of airplane design is more than the sum of its parts. It isn't just aerodynamics, structures, or propulsion—you have to make them all work together.

On the home front, Gabrielle—whom we nicknamed Gai—got a little brother named Jonathan in 1948. Adrienne came along in 1950, completing the Sutter family. I was in my late twenties and didn't know how life could be any better.

———

In June 1950, shortly after the C-97 Stratofreighter entered U.S. Air Force service, the Korean War broke out. The U.S. Air Force (USAF) Military Air Transport Service (MATS) found itself tasked with evacuating injured troops for treatment in Hawaii or the mainland United States.

Long flights aboard unpressurized C-54s quickly proved detrimental to the health of troops with lung injuries. Consequently, the Air Force delegated the task of returning those soldiers with chest wounds to the C-97, its only pressurized transport.

I soon found myself working the military side of the fence, preparing operational performance charts for the C-97. That airplane had barely enough range to fly from Tokyo nonstop to Hawaii in the first place, and air force flight crews were experiencing a high number of engine problems. Consequently, Dick Rouzie, Art Curran, and I were dispatched to Tokyo to observe the MATS operations and determine whether we could improve them.

Flying along on those military medical evacuations, I was amazed to see how differently each air force flight crew operated its C-97. None of them followed the existing Boeing performance operation manual. They fixated on the tendency of the P&W R-4360 engines to overheat and fail in flight, a worry that led them to improvise in their attempts to baby those engines.

They made a number of mistakes. They kept the cowl flaps open extra long to maximize the flow of cooling air to the cylinders. Unfortunately, the added aerodynamic drag of those open cowl flaps actually had made the engines strain harder, shortening their lives and increasing the probability of in-flight failures.

They also frequently climbed at higher-than-recommended airspeeds. This kept the cylinder-head temperatures lower during the initial climb, but unfortunately it extended the total climbing time, resulting in higher engine operating temperatures at cruising altitude. Again, the result was more wear and tear on those big Pratt & Whitneys.

I'll never forget one takeoff from Honolulu to San Francisco. Because of the two ill-advised procedures mentioned above, the C-97 I was on flew so low past the Aloha Tower Building that I found myself looking *up* to see its clock.

This field experience taught me that engineers had better make sure their designs fit with the way the airplane will be used in the real world. Being a navy man, I also got my first taste of air force culture, and I can't say I liked it. Those pilots were treated almost like gods. It went to their heads, judging by the poor way they treated the hardworking flight nurses tending the wounded.

By the time the Korean War ended in 1953, I felt I could probably design a piston airliner by myself. The first phase of my Boeing education was finished and a very different one was about to begin.

4

THE JET AGE

When I hired in, Boeing was developing the B-47 Stratojet, an airplane so audacious that it seemed the stuff of pure science fiction. The first large production airplane with jet engines and swept wings, the B-47 marked a huge leap forward and shocked the world when it was unveiled in 1947.

Interestingly, this strategic bomber for the air force started out with a conventional design featuring straight wings. Before my arrival, though, Boeing revised it with slender wings angled sharply backward. It looked like and truly was an arrow to the future.

Thus began a burst of jet-age creativity that would catapult Boeing to the forefront of aeronautical design and keep it there. It was this thrilling vision of swept-wing jets that caused me to give up any thoughts of jumping ship for Douglas. For a young aeronautical engineer, Boeing was definitely the most exciting place to be.

———

Boeing's quantum leap had an interesting genesis. When the war in Europe ended on May 8, 1945, George Schairer, Boeing's chief aerodynamicist, was already in Germany helping the U.S. government conduct a survey of that nation's aviation technology. At an aeronautical research center in Volkenrode, this technical intelligence team came across wind-tunnel data that confirmed the value of wing sweep to high-speed flight.

It was a timely find. By war's end, the challenges of flying faster—and the heady possibility of exceeding the speed of sound—were at the forefront of aeronautical thinking. But high-speed flight was chock-full of unknowns.

Many World War II propeller fighter planes had crashed in power dives, their pilots lost to inexplicable instabilities encountered above 70% of the speed of sound. The few who managed to bail out described how their airplanes had suddenly become possessed by forces seemingly intent on their destruction. They described dives where pullouts were impossible because the stick became locked in a vise, control reversals, and other baffling phenomena.

Scientists called these manifestations *Mach phenomena* after Ernst Mach, the Austrian physicist who first examined the ratio between the speed of an object passing through the air and the speed of sound. The press and general public had a different name for this faceless killer stalking the heavens. It was the *sound barrier*, an invisible stone wall in the sky that would shatter airplanes if they flew too fast.

What was actually happening? As an airplane approaches the speed of sound, the air can no longer get out of its way fast enough, so it bunches up and shockwaves begin to form. We call this airflow inelasticity at high speeds *compressibility*.

Compressibility is the reason that jets have swept wings. Angling the wings back delays the onset of compressibility and its associated Mach phenomena, thus allowing the airplane to cruise efficiently at higher speeds.

At Volkenrode, Schairer and the rest of the U.S. technical intelligence team found papers hastily dumped in a dry well to prevent their capture. Reviewing these technical documents, Schairer's excitement soared. The data showed clearly that swept wings combined with turbine engines was the way to go.

This was very good news, because airplanes with piston engines had inherent speed limitations imposed on them by their propellers. At high subsonic speeds, the propeller tips were already encountering transonic or supersonic flow. The propellers lost efficiency, so more power did not translate into more speed. In contrast, airplanes with jet engines had no such limitation.

On May 10, 1945, Schairer wrote a seven-page letter to his Boeing colleagues in Seattle in which he detailed these findings and his thoughts. As a result, the B-47 was promptly redesigned to incorporate 35 degrees of wing sweep. For maximum efficiency at high speeds, Boeing designers elected to make these wings very thin.

The B-47 design team evaluated different propulsion configurations, because nobody yet knew the best way to marry jet engines to airframes. A spectrum of possibilities was studied, including housing the engines entirely within the aircraft's fuselage. It was finally decided to place the B-47's turbojets in nacelle pods mounted below and forward of the wings on struts. The B-47 would have two engines in each inboard nacelle pod and one in each outboard pod, for a grand total of six engines.

Locating the jet engines *away* from the wings, not in them or in the fuselage, turned out to be an enormously important design advancement on Boeing's part. Together with the wing sweep, it would put Boeing at the forefront of designing large jets.

The B-47's thin wings brought two challenges. The first was their flexibility, which allowed them to flap and twist in flight. When ailerons were used to try to turn the airplane, the outboard wings twisted in opposition to the control input. Boeing solved this problem through the use of spoilers.

Spoilers are panels atop the wings that extend into the airflow to spoil some of the wing's lift. They can be used together to help a jet kill speed and descend, or differentially to help tilt it into a turn.

The second challenge was where to store the landing gear, since the B-47's very thin wings had no room for wheels. The Stratojet's designers addressed this problem by housing the landing gear in the fuselage. The B-47 ended up with a centerline gear with two wheels forward under the jet's belly and two aft. This arrangement dictated a fixed attitude, so the B-47 was designed to sit on the ground at just the right nose-high attitude for takeoffs and landings. Small outrigger wheels extended from the inboard engine nacelles to keep the bomber from tipping to either side.

The XB-47 prototype flew on December 17, 1947, 44 years to the day after the Wright brothers made history at Kitty Hawk. To me it was truly like something out of a science-fiction movie. Orville Wright was still alive at the time (he died the following year at age 76), and I remember wondering what he must have thought of the Stratojet. More than any other aircraft of its day, it symbolized the astounding pace of human progress in flight.

Another U.S. manufacturer actually beat us to the punch, manufacturing the first U.S. jet with swept wings. This was North American Aviation, a military manufacturer in California, which applied the findings of that technical survey in Germany to its XP-86 jet fighter. It flew on September 1, 1947, and gave rise to the famous F-86 series of Korean War fame.

Between North American's first swept-wing flight and ours, Chuck Yeager broke the sound barrier on October 14, 1947, in the Bell X-1 rocket plane. That research ship had straight wings because the National Advisory Committee for Aeronautics (NACA), the predecessor of today's National Aeronautics and Space Administration (NASA), did not want to introduce additional variables as it systematically probed the unknowns of supersonic flight. Also for this reason, the bright-orange X-1 did not have a "stepped" canopy that projected into the slipstream. Instead, its windows simply wrapped around its fuselage, following its contours.

Less than six months separated the first flight of the Boeing Stratocruiser airliner in July 1947 from that of the Boeing XB-47 bomber that December. Whereas the Stratocruiser had broken ground quickly, the XB-47 took forever to accelerate down Boeing Field's long runway. It climbed out with a flaring, ear-splitting roar and turned east toward the Cascade Mountains, disappearing quickly from sight.

I couldn't help thinking that those two Boeing airplanes were worlds apart and *this* one was the future. Yes, I badly wanted to work on jets, but not military ones; I wanted to work on jet transports.

———

Boeing next developed the larger and more capable B-52 Strato-fortress, the world's first long-range, swept-wing heavy bomber. It flew in April 1952 (it's pure coincidence that the B-47 flew in '47 and the B-52 in '52), and operational Stratofortresses began displacing Stratojets in Strategic Air Command service by the end of the decade. Boeing built 744 B-52s, nearly a hundred of which have been modernized and remain in first-line U.S. Air Force service.

By keeping my ear to the wall, I began picking up rudiments of designing large swept-wing jet aircraft. Those military programs dangled the intriguing possibility that Boeing might at last be poised to find the commercial success that had long eluded it in the airliner arena.

As the 1950s started, all of us at Boeing sensed that if things went right, we could play a significant role in the coming "commercial jet age." But I'm sure none of us suspected just how dominant Boeing would be, or to what degree our technological prowess would change the world.

———

By 1952, my success as an all-around aerodynamicist on the Strato-cruiser program won me the chance to head up the detailed aerodynamics work for a company-funded vision of what a jetliner should be. This was the Boeing model 367-80, or simply Dash 80. It would be ready to fly in the summer of 1954.

William M. Allen, Jr., a former lawyer, was then at Boeing's helm. A true gentleman and one of American industry's visionary leaders, Allen set a tone of tremendous integrity and the highest ethical standards in business dealings.

On the basis of answers his senior technical people gave him, Bill

Allen decided that jets were where the airline business was headed. He decided to invest whatever was required to ensure that Boeing was a part of this future.

At that time, Douglas Aircraft was the world's undisputed leader in the design and manufacture of commercial airliners. The California company was a formidable powerhouse, to say the least. Allen's decision to take Douglas on in head-to-head competition was daring and, if we missed the mark, fraught with peril. We had just one chance to get it right.

With the approval of Boeing's board of directors, Allen committed $16 million—a huge sum in those days—to designing and building a company-funded prototype that would show the world that Boeing could create a *good* commercial jetliner, not just jet bombers for the air force. This new transport would have the same 35-degree wing sweep as the B-47 and B-52 but would otherwise be an entirely new design.

Wisely, Boeing decided at the outset that its demonstrator airplane would be a proof-of-concept vehicle and not a production prototype. This meant we wouldn't be certifying the Dash 80, which simplified matters considerably. We would have latitude to be creative and learn by doing. This was shaping up to be an aeronautical engineer's dream project.

As the 367-80 designation suggests, the Dash 80 was actually a distant design derivative of the model 367 (C-97), although it was funded by Boeing and not the U.S. Air Force. Specifically, the Dash 80 inherited the fuselage cross section of the C-97 and Stratocruiser. It was longer than those blunt-nosed propeller types, so it looked more slender, and its sides were smoothed over to eliminate their familiar crease line.

The Dash 80 was launched just a week after the B-52's first flight in April 1952. Less than two weeks after that came a huge milestone in the history of aviation: on May 2, 1952, BOAC introduced the de Havilland DH-106 Comet I jetliner to service between London and Johannesburg via Rome, Cairo, Khartoum, Entebbe, and Livingstone. Sleek and beautiful, the Comet was a product of Great Britain's de

Havilland Aircraft, which had built the legendary wooden Mosquito fighter-bomber of World War II. Unfortunately, the de Havilland team didn't get the jetliner formula quite right with the Comet. Two design shortcomings in particular suggest to me that the British, in their haste to get a jump on the United States in postwar airliner sales, perhaps didn't quite think things through as well as they might have.

First, the Comet featured only a modest degree of wing sweep. It was faster than that last generation of piston airliners, including the Boeing Stratocruiser. However, the Dash 80 was much faster still. By way of comparison, the DC-7C—Douglas's last propeller airliner— cruised at about 350 miles per hour, the de Havilland Comet 1 at about 450 miles per hour, and the Boeing 367-80 at about 550 miles per hour. The Boeing 707, which would evolve directly from the Dash 80, would be even faster, cruising at about 600 miles per hour.

Second, the Comet had its turbojet engines buried within its wings. Piston-era practices started all big-jet designers off on the wrong foot, Boeing included. Propeller airliners had their engines in line with the wing and actually faired into it, so by default that was where people thought jets should have their engines. This unques- tioned assumption—a good example of the tyranny of a reigning paradigm—led de Havilland's talented designers to place the Com- et's four engines inside its wings.

The Russians made this same mistake in the *second* commercial jetliner to enter service. The twin-engine Tupolev Tu-104, which in- augurated the world's first *sustained* passenger jet operations behind the Iron Curtain in 1956, likewise had its engines buried in its wing roots.

Going this route has a few problems. First, it tends to make the jet airplane's engines difficult to access and maintain. Second and more important, it can endanger the entire airplane if something goes wrong with one of its engines.

Turbine engines spin at thousands of revolutions per minute. Par- ticularly in the early days when the metallurgy wasn't as advanced as today, those engines could spontaneously fail in an "uncontained failure" that could shoot high-energy metal fragments through the surrounding airplane structure, perhaps puncturing fuel tanks and damaging the other engines.

If this self-made flak didn't claim the jetliner, the rest of the failed engine could, simply by spinning out of balance. The resulting vibrations could be severe enough to cause a catastrophic failure of the airplane's structural integrity.

Another concern was engine fires, which were not unknown at the start of the jet age. All these possibilities made mounting jet engines within the wings a poor design choice, yet that was the industry's point of departure based on prior practices.

I hasten to add that those early jet engines were at least 10 times more reliable than the big piston engines they would soon replace. Two things explain the relative reliability of turbine engines. First, they are far simpler than piston engines. Second, they feature smooth, continuous combustion and rotation, unlike reciprocating engines with their individual explosions in cylinders and back-and-forth motions.

———————

Boeing was the first company to correctly assess jet-age safety concerns and come up with the optimal solution: strut mounting. Mounting the engines on struts *below* the wings distanced any propulsion-related threats to safety. Cleverly, Boeing designers attached the turbine engines to their struts by means of *fuse pins*. In the event of an out-of-balance condition, the fuse pins would shear and the damaged engine would fall away, sparing the airplane.

The Boeing B-47 first flew in December 1947. The de Havilland Comet didn't fly until the middle of 1949. Thus, the British had plenty of time to take advantage of this proven Boeing approach. Why didn't they? The answer to that question came when I met Ronald Bishop, who led the Comet's development at de Havilland Aircraft. Bishop was personally and passionately opposed to strut mounting, which he dismissed as "beastly podded engines!"

Dash 80

The most important thing to know about the Boeing 367-80 is that it truly defined the jetliner when it rolled out in 1954. In this very broad sense, it's the ancestor of *all* the commercial jet transports we take for granted today, not just the Boeing 707 or later Boeing jets. The Dash 80 is the granddaddy of them all, right up to the latest Airbus products and today's Boeing 787 Dreamliner.

Of course, being a junior designer at that time, I didn't actually have a hand in defining the Dash 80's configuration and characteristics. That task fell to senior Boeing engineers, including George Schairer, Ed Wells, Bill Hamilton, Jack Steiner, and Bob Withington, all of whom brought experience gained from Boeing's military jet programs.

My job was to head up the nine-person aerodynamics unit assigned to perform detailed aerodynamic testing and then finalize the Dash 80's wing characteristics. Needless to say, we had our hands full because the airplane had so many new features.

My aero team and I focused most heavily on the 367-80's takeoff and landing characteristics. We looked not just at its landing and take-off speeds but also at its handling characteristics and degree of controllability during these periods of slower flight.

We were more than a little concerned that a sleek, high-performance jet optimized to high-speed cruising wouldn't be able to stop in a decent length of runway. The B-47 bomber used drogue chutes to slow it down on landing, but that wasn't a viable option for commercial operations. There would be far too many landings on the nation's busy runways, and it wouldn't be practical for airline personnel to retrieve and repack those chutes even if the airlines had the money for all this extra labor.

Consequently, we worked the Dash 80's low-speed capabilities and characteristics *very* hard, particularly in the design of the wing flaps. The flaps are those surfaces that extend aft and downward from the rear edge of a wing. By increasing its total area and camber, they turn a high-speed airfoil into one geared to lower speeds. When combined with leading-edge devices, which produce a similar but smaller effect at the front of the wing, wing flaps can dramatically lower takeoff and landing speeds, and thus how much runway the jet needs.

The Boeing 367-80 rolled out on May 14, 1954. It was a thing of beauty and just looked *right*. Bill Boeing, then 72 and retired from his company for two decades, came back for this event. Bertha, his wife, christened the Dash 80 with champagne. All our hopes were pinned to the new jet, of course, and we knew it was a huge gamble.

I was there when this prototype jet transport flew for the first time on July 15, 1954, at Renton Field, the airport alongside Boeing's B-29 plant on the south end of Lake Washington where it had been built. Low fog caused the Dash 80's takeoff to be delayed from 7 AM until 2:14 PM, giving us all time to become very nervous.

With Tex Johnston and Dix Loesch at the controls, the lightly loaded Dash 80 broke ground after just 2,100 feet of runway and climbed effortlessly away. Of course, with straight turbojet engines instead of turbofans, it was a hell of a noisy airplane. I've heard the early jet age referred to as the "blowtorch era," and that name pretty well sums it up. Those turbojet engines also drew dark trails of soot in the sky. Nevertheless, we all knew it was the start of something important.

Bill Allen called the Dash 80's aerial debut "the most beautiful first-flight takeoff I've ever witnessed." I felt the same way, but I was more interested in this prototype's landing than its takeoff, because that concept prototype's low-speed flight characteristics were my team's primary focus. I climbed into my car and drove the short distance to Boeing Field, where the Dash 80 would be landing. After 1 hour 24 minutes aloft, it touched down on the 10,000-foot runway. I was highly gratified to see it come to an easy stop well short of the midpoint.

Now that the Dash 80 was flying, we kept it busy in two different roles. The first was as a research prototype undergoing flight testing. The second was as a concept demonstrator to share with airlines our vision for what a commercial jetliner should be.

Airline executives, pilots, and engineers came to Seattle from around the world to inspect and evaluate our jet, and I accompanied many of them on demonstration flights. That experience fostered relationships and friendships with many Boeing customers worldwide.

It was entertaining to go along on those flights and witness their reactions to jet speeds and comfort. When they saw how much more the Dash 80 could do compared with their propeller airliners, every single one of them left Seattle convinced that jets built to our formula were the wave of the future.

Douglas was then bringing out the DC-7C, the last and mightiest of its famous Douglas Commercial propeller airliners going back to the DC-2 of 1934. Lockheed also brought out its last piston-powered model about that time. The L-1649G Starliner was an ultimate Constellation with an entirely new wing. For all their capabilities, those airliners were in the Stone Age compared with our Dash 80.

In the half-century since the Boeing 367-80 first flew, Boeing alone has delivered more than 15,000 commercial jet transports built to this winning formula. The Dash 80 truly defined the category of airplane that has done the most to serve humanity. For this reason, many historians consider it second in historical significance only to the Wright 1903 Flyer itself. Today beautifully restored by Boeing volunteers, the Dash 80 is displayed at the National Air and Space Museum/Smithsonian Institution's Steven F. Udvar-Hazy Center at Washington Dulles International Airport.

As for me, I consider my 367-80 development experience to have been a very, very lucky stroke in my ongoing education. It got me in on the ground floor in the field of jet transport design.

———

On October 26, 1958, Pan Am introduced the brand-new Boeing 707 to service across the North Atlantic. It was a *huge* success and marks a milestone in the history of flight. The 707 was the third jet transport in service, but it got the formula right and paved the way for the world to travel a new way. This airplane opened the floodgates to jet travel, spearheading a rapid transition to jets during the 1960s.

The third time was indeed the charm for Boeing, which had seen its commercial hopes dashed on two prior occasions. Boeing was the technological leader with its model 247 of 1933, the world's first modern airliner. It led again with the Boeing 307 Stratoliner of 1938, the world's first pressurized airliner. Both those programs had been commercial disappointments. Now in 1958, Boeing had again combined vision with technological prowess, and this time the orders came flooding in.

I have long wondered what makes this U.S. company so innovative compared with other aerospace firms. Bill Boeing founded the company on his conviction that we could and should build the world's safest and finest airplanes. "Leave no stone unturned," he said. His successors, notably Bill Allen, nurtured this vision, fostering an environment that continues to attract the finest aerospace engineers and other professionals.

The 707 closely resembled the Dash 80 but was actually a larger and more powerful jet with a wider fuselage. Before designing it, though, Boeing created a Dash 80 derivative for the U.S. Air Force

Boeing 707

called the C-135. This military transport, and a tanker version called the KC-135, featured a slightly larger fuselage diameter than the Dash 80.

Boeing planned to use this revised fuselage for its commercial jetliner, but Juan Trippe of Pan Am had other ideas. By far the most powerful and influential figure in the airline industry, Trippe wanted his Boeing jetliners to have an even wider cabin. The cost of accommodating him was so high that our leaders were not inclined to agree, particularly since we had already widened the Dash 80's fuselage once for the air force.

As always, Trippe knew how to get his way. When Pan Am launched the 707 with a historic order for 20 airplanes in October 1955, it also ordered 25 DC-8s from Douglas! That split order was a wakeup call of seismic proportions. It told us that we weren't listening well enough to our customers.

Needless to say, we bit the bullet and revised the 707's evolving design with a cabin that was wider than that of the DC-8, a jet that Douglas was just beginning to develop to the Boeing formula. The 707 fuselage cross section has served the world well, having been used not just in the 707 but also in Boeing's subsequent single-aisle models, the 727, 737, and 757. This fuselage cross section is still used today by the Next-Generation 737 family of twinjets.

The Douglas DC-8 entered domestic service in September 1959 and joined the 707 in transatlantic service the following year. The DC-8 had 30 degrees of wing sweep (5 degrees less than the 707) and was a very fine airplane.

But for once Douglas was playing catch-up. Its jetliner was an also-ran that followed our lead and was built extremely closely to the formula we had defined with the Dash 80. This time around, it was Boeing that garnered the lion's share of business. The world's airlines beat a path to our door, ultimately ordering more than a thousand 707s versus half as many DC-8s.

This was an astounding reversal because Douglas was the overwhelming industry leader back then. Our total production of airliners in the propeller era after World War II was those 55 Stratocruisers we delivered. In contrast, thousands of Douglas DC-4s, DC-6s, and DC-7s entered service. Some were delivered as airliners. Others were built by Douglas for wartime military use and were converted to commercial use following the war.

I attribute Boeing's innovation at the start of the jet age to three things: The first was the amazing vision of Bill Allen, Ed Wells, George Schairer, Maynard Pennell, and other top Boeing people. They saw the potential of jet transports and willingly gambled all to realize this dream.

The second was Boeing's willingness to invest whatever it took to be the technological leader. This total commitment to R&D led our management to build a transonic wind tunnel, a huge commitment of funds that proved invaluable as we pioneered wide-scale jet operations.

The third and final factor was Douglas Aircraft itself. They ridiculed and dismissed us as a bunch of rosy-cheeked engineers who didn't have a clue about building airliners. This derision spurred us on and fostered a tremendous rivalry. Trumping Douglas became something we were all very enthusiastic about in Seattle. All these factors coalesced to create a very exciting work environment.

———

And what of the de Havilland Comet? Two years after inaugurating the world's first passenger jet services in 1952, the Comet was grounded by several fatal crashes. After two Comets disintegrated spontaneously in flight over the Mediterranean, it was belatedly realized that a third such event in India—previously attributed to a thunderstorm—might also have been the result of an inexplicable structural failure.

Thus began one of the most fascinating aviation investigations on record. Metal fatigue was soon identified as the culprit. It was initially believed that a square escape hatch in the cockpit roof had failed, unzipping the whole airplane. Wreckage recovered by a fishing boat subsequently suggested it might have been a passenger window. Exactly where this failure had occurred didn't matter, though; the killer had been unmasked.

Neither de Havilland nor the British Civil Aviation Authority, which certified the pioneering airliner as safe, was at fault in this notorious case. They had labored in good faith, but not enough was known back then about the effects of repeated pressurization cycles on the structure of an airplane that cruised twice as high as most propeller airliners.

Fortunately, we at Boeing had significantly more experience with pressurization than the rest of the world. The 707 built further on knowledge gained with the Stratoliner, B-29, B-50, Stratocruiser, and Stratojet, all of which were pressurized for high-altitude cruise. The de Havilland Comet had square windows and hatches. In contrast, we designed these components with rounded corners so as not to concentrate fatiguing stresses at any one point, the way square corners do.

De Havilland extensively redesigned the Comet over the next four years, stretching and revising it to create the Comet 4, which had round side windows instead of square windows. With great fanfare,

BOAC introduced the Comet 4 to service across the Atlantic on October 4, 1958, three weeks ahead of the 707. However, it proved no match for the vastly superior performance, capacity, and operating economics of the Boeing product. Great Britain's once-bright hopes for a dominant role in postwar commercial aviation faded quickly.

My role on the 707 program paralleled my Dash 80 involvement. I once again ran the aerodynamics unit, but the job was a bit different this time around. In addition to performing detailed design work, my team and I had to see the airplane through government certification and develop the detailed performance data that airlines would need to operate the 707.

Supporting the certification of the 707 was probably the most important of my duties. We worked with the CAA, which would become the FAA in 1958.

Back in the mid- to late 1950s, the CAA had nobody with jet experience. This led to an unusual situation whereby we at Boeing had to help our own regulatory authority by taking what we knew about big jets and fitting it into their existing civil certification framework and processes.

This is how we at Boeing came to author the basic U.S. certification rules for jet transports. That first set of jetliner regulations was called SR 422 (the *SR* stood for "Special Regulation"). Most of its contents were drafted by me and others in the technical staff.

It was quite a challenge. We had to understand the full intent of the existing FAA requirements for piston-powered airliners and develop an equivalent set of rules that would fully ensure the safety of jet transports. We worked closely with the CAA/FAA, the Civil Aeronautics Board (CAB), the airlines, and the Air Line Pilots Association (ALPA). Safety was always foremost in our minds, because these were the standards to which all subsequent U.S. jetliners—Boeing and others—would be developed.

It's usually a very bad idea from a public safety standpoint for any industry to write its own regulatory guidelines. Too much of that has happened in recent years and the American people are the losers. I'm personally against it, but there was no alternative back in the late 1950s. I take aviation's sterling record since then as evidence that we did our parts selflessly and well.

I still recall the many meetings I attended where these regulatory proposals were put on the table for discussion. Regulation must be in step with technology or it can hinder the safety it's supposed to protect. Heated arguments often sprang up in Washington, DC, as we discussed the gamut of certification issues.

How do you properly define a jetliner's landing performance? What should its climb limits be with one engine inoperative? What are the characteristics of a jetliner nearing its Mach limits, and at what point do you deem them unacceptable? And when a jetliner enters a rapid dive, as when cabin pressure has suddenly been lost and the crew needs to get down to denser air, what design features will help preclude the possibility of the airplane inadvertently rolling inverted?

I enjoyed this full education in government regulation, which is an area beyond the traditional boundaries of the duties taken up by airplane designers. Airplane safety has always been my strong focus, and this unexpected experience had me living and breathing it. I learned more every day.

Meantime, my aero team and I methodically supported the 707's development. It was a straightforward process, and the airplane went together fairly easily because we had already resolved many potential challenges on the Dash 80.

Just two issues of any consequence remained to be resolved after the 707 entered service in the fall of 1958. The first was insufficient low-speed controllability with one engine out. We addressed this concern with a redesign of the jet's vertical tail and the addition of rudder boost.

The second problem was that the 707 was very noisy. The turbojet engines that powered it and all the other first-generation jetliners were painfully loud. We fitted noise suppressors to those engines, but they did little to alleviate the flaring roar that left your ears ringing.

The promise of a meaningful solution came at the start of the 1960s when the engine manufacturers began replacing their "straight turbojets" with low-bypass-ratio turbofans. The Rolls-Royce Conway was the first fanjet engine in commercial service, followed almost immediately by the superior Pratt & Whitney JT3D. Both debuted on 707s in 1960. Thus began a dramatic ongoing reduction in jetliner noise that continues to this day and is one of aviation's greatest success stories.

The Boeing 707 caused a veritable sensation when it entered service. Sleek and quiet, at least from the passenger's perspective, it was also extremely comfortable. Gone was the fatiguing drone and vibration of those big reciprocating engines of the propeller era.

The 707 was also fast. Compared with the prop planes then in service, it cruised nearly twice as fast and carried more payload. It had about 140 passenger seats. In contrast, the DC-6B—the most successful of the postwar piston airliners—had 66 seats, the DC-7C had about 110, and the Lockheed Super Constellation and Stratocruiser (when not fitted with sleeper berths) each had just under 100.

This combination of greater speed and greater payload gave the 707 four or five times the productivity of propeller airliners. Needless to say, this astonishing jump in productivity made the 707 a very, very popular airplane with the world's airlines!

So well did the 707 sell that it single-handedly established Boeing as one of the world's premier manufacturers of airliners. The success that we dreamed of in commercial aviation was suddenly at hand.

———

After the 707 had been in service for a few years, the airlines placed increasing pressure on us for a follow-on airliner. The 707 was designed for long-haul operations. "Can't you make a *medium*-range jetliner?" our salespeople heard over and over.

In Europe, the French Caravelle had entered service and the British Trident was in development. Both were short- to medium-range jetliners. At Boeing, we determined that we couldn't live on just one program. Management felt we should also get into this medium-haul arena.

Jack Steiner was put in charge of this second Boeing jet transport program. I was asked to lead the aerodynamics unit as before, and also to head up the technical staff. This meant that in addition to my aero people, I would have propulsion, structures, and systems people reporting to me. It was a big step forward in my career, and one that required me to learn a great deal more about these other disciplines.

Building on the success of the 707, Boeing marketing people selected 727 as the designation for this follow-on airplane. Thus began the practice of giving Boeing jets designations that start and end with the number 7. The 737, 747, 757, 767, and 777 have all contributed luster to this famous naming convention, a prestigious Boeing brand recently updated with the 787 Dreamliner.

The 727 would again push the state of the art because it had to combine excellent high-speed performance with the ability to operate in and out of smaller airports not designed with jets in mind, such as LaGuardia Airport at New York and Midway at Chicago. That was something the 707 could not do.

The runways at LaGuardia and Midway were quite short for jet operations. I think they were only about 5,500 feet long. This challenged us to create a more capable flap system that let the airplane approach slowly and with excellent stability and control. The design solution turned out to be slats for the entire leading edge of the wing, and powerful trailing-edge flaps with three segments each—the triple-slotted flap, as we called it.

To further reduce pilot workload at touchdown, we gave the 727 extremely effective braking systems. Jetliners actually have three separate and independent systems for this purpose: *wheel brakes, thrust reversers*, and *ground spoilers*. The wheel brakes are like those on your car and can be activated automatically. Reverse thrust—that bellowing you hear when the plane is rolling out after landing—deflects most of the engine thrust forward to further slow the plane. As for the ground spoilers, they deploy automatically at touchdown, popping up from the tops of the wings to create drag and kill their remaining lift.

This 727 program was an exciting education all over again. We were largely working with a different set of customers—domestic operators, not international carriers—so it also gave me the opportunity to get to know more airline people. I dealt with the FAA and ALPA. Both organizations were very concerned about the suitability of jetliners to smaller airfields worldwide. They were dubious that we had the ability to produce such a jet.

Those doubts weren't limited to external organizations. A couple of senior people I reported to at Boeing were also doubtful that the 727 would be practical for short airfields, even though the numbers told us we could do it. So the onus was very much on Jack Steiner and his design team to prove out the concept, initially with our engineering data and then in the air with the airplane itself.

Early in the 727 flight test program, we took the number 4 airplane on a tour around the country to show what it could do. I went along on some of those displays. Boeing also sent that jet overseas for demonstrations in Japan and other parts of the world.

In the United States, LaGuardia Airport was the most important demonstration we flew. Located in Queens just eight miles from Midtown Manhattan, LaGuardia was managed by the Port Authority of New York and New Jersey. That meant that we needed the approval of the "borough masters" of the communities around LaGuardia to stage our demonstration.

These communities were so assaulted by airplane noise that they didn't even want to let us demonstrate the 727. However, pressure from the airlines and other interested parties finally got us our chance to show what it could do. We were granted permission for one flight only.

At that time, our 727 demo ship was in another part of the country. The moment our team got the news, we flew straight to LaGuardia. I occupied the cockpit jump seat right behind the pilots. We arrived late in the morning to find miserable weather and turbulence that jolted us in our seats. LaGuardia was reporting heavy rain and strong gusting crosswinds.

Airliners were stacked up in holding patterns waiting to get into New York. The approach controller put us into this stack, instructing us to descend until we were handed off to LaGuardia Tower. Switching frequencies, we listened to the new controller calling on pilots to expedite their approaches because there were so many flights waiting to land.

It was finally our turn. We flew LaGuardia's traffic pattern behind a Convair propeller airliner and knew that another—a TWA Constellation, according to the controller—was following us. "Please accelerate your approach into the airport," we heard the tower controller instruct the Connie.

"Well, I would if you'd get that big slow jet out of my way!" its pilot replied.

The Boeing test pilots and I grinned like kids. That comment tickled us because it meant that the 727, despite the jet engines and high-speed cruise, fit right in and was just another airplane on landing. No disruption and no special handling required.

We lucked out when we touched down. The wind was blowing so hard that the borough masters, who were stationed out near the end of the runway, hardly heard our airplane. As a result, the 727 got good marks on noise and won airlines the right to operate it at La-Guardia. I must admit I felt a twinge of guilt, because it was not a quiet airplane. Today's Boeing jets make only a fraction of the noise, and tomorrow's will be much quieter still, thanks to new technologies in the works.

Midway and Washington National also welcomed the 727. Pretty soon it was flying everywhere, bringing jet speeds and convenience to travel within the United States. If the 727 hadn't been available, turboprops like the Vickers Viscount and Lockheed Electra would have played a much bigger role in the evolution of U.S. domestic operations.

All of this was a significant triumph for us. We had worked very hard and succeeded beyond our expectations. Pretty soon the 727 was selling itself. Its acceptance didn't depend on Boeing doing some big song and dance in the way of marketing. Instead we let the airplane show what it could do and orders flowed in.

The Boeing 727 entered service in 1964. Following on the heels of the first version, the 727-100, Boeing introduced the longer 727-200 in 1967. Unfortunately, that stretched model traded too much performance for greater capacity and consequently wasn't popular with the airlines. Boeing bit the bullet and funded the 727-200 Advanced, a major derivative with upgraded capabilities that entered service in 1972 and was a huge hit. With its availability, the 727 program became Boeing's cash cow. The company delivered more than 1,800 727s to customers before production ended in 1984.

I wasn't involved with the 727 beyond its initial development. But that participation was extremely satisfying. Devising and validating solutions to new design requirements is what gives aeronautical engineers the greatest pleasure.

———————

With the 727 entering service to complement the 707, a "family of jetliners" concept took hold at Boeing. Instead of offering just one or two jetliner models, our leaders saw that our goal as a company should probably be to build an entire family of commercial transports that would cover the spectrum of existing markets and perhaps even open up a new market or two.

What weren't we building yet? A requirement had emerged for an even smaller, shorter-range airplane than the medium-haul 727. Over in Europe, France's Caravelle had been in service since 1959 and Great Britain's BAC-111 was then in flight test. In the United States, Douglas Aircraft—which had lost out in the lucrative 727 market— was developing a small twinjet called the DC-9. Like the BAC-111, the initial DC-9 would carry about 80 passengers on routes up to 500 miles long.

There were many people at Boeing—Jack Steiner among them— who felt strongly that Boeing should compete in this little-jetliner arena. Jack was a pretty good promoter and he kept pressing for it with our upper management. I recall a meeting held in 1964 to discuss whether Boeing should spend the money to go head to head in competition with those other jets, particularly the DC-9. Douglas had about a two-year jump on us at that time.

As you can imagine, it was a very divisive issue. Only half of us at the meeting said yes. A decision was deferred and Steiner was asked simply to keep working on the concept. I returned to my group and everyone was naturally eager for a firm answer one way or the other. "Are we going to do it or not?" I was asked.

"Well," I replied, giving my read of the situation, "they told Jack to go back and study it some more. But I know Steiner. He's not going to study anything—he's going to get it launched. You guys had better assume we're building this small jetliner."

Sure enough, that's what happened. The story's been told of how Jack, a very persuasive fellow, did an end run around Bill Allen to personally lobby members of Boeing's board on behalf of this new jet. Boeing's chairman wasn't at all happy about it even though he supported the 737.

History would show how right they were. Launched in early 1965, the 737 is by far the most successful commercial jetliner of all time. Total orders have topped 6,000 at the time of this writing. Today's version is the Next-Generation 737 family, which has many models and is actually the third generation of Boeing 737s.

With the 737 launched, we set about defining our DC-9 competitor. The approach that everybody used for small jets was to mount the engines on the aft fuselage. The French Caravelle, British BAC-111, and American DC-9 twinjets all went this route. So did the Trident and 727 trijets.

Designing with aft-mounted engines usually means going to a T-tail configuration to keep the jet's horizontal tail out of the engine exhaust. Horizontal tails have two main components: the *stabilizers* at front that slice through the air, and movable surfaces called *elevators* that are attached to the stabilizers by hinges. When the pilot pulls or pushes the jet's control wheel, these elevators deflect up or down, raising or lowering the airplane's nose.

All of the twinjets and trijets I named have T-tails (i.e., the horizontal tail on top of the vertical tail) except the Caravelle. That French jet's horizontal tail is mounted just partway up the vertical tail in a cruciform configuration.

As our initial studies progressed, we found ourselves starting to design yet another airplane to this same basic configuration of aft-mounted engines and a T-tail. Steiner and I worked pretty closely during the initial definition of the 737. It was here that each of us came up with concepts that led the 737's design down a different and better path.

"You know," Steiner remarked, "those other twins all have four or five seats abreast per row. Since we've got the 707 fuselage to work with, why don't we consider going to six-abreast economy seating? It'll look like a flying football and there may be some drag issues, but it'll give the airlines real economic efficiencies."

That's how we came to evaluate the 707 cross section for the 737. It looked fine and we went with it. But when I looked at the resulting airplane, I couldn't see a good aerodynamics solution for the new problem this introduced: namely, where to put the engines.

Steiner's point of departure was having pylon-mounted engines on the aft fuselage like every other small jetliner. But because the 737 would be short and wide, the intakes of these aft-mounted engines would be close to the trailing edge of the wing and thus subject to its disturbed airflow. Those engines would also have to be spaced wide apart to keep them out of the affected airflow of the fat fuselage. That in turn brought the penalties of a heavy mounting structure and large drag-producing fairings.

There has to be a more elegant design solution. With that thought in mind, I took line drawings of our proposed jet up to my office. Sitting at my desk, I pulled scissors out of a drawer and cut out that beginning design's aft-mounted engines. I began sliding them around the 737 line drawings to see where else we might place them.

Why don't we go back to putting the engines on the wings? I wondered. It was an intriguing idea, but I saw at once that we couldn't do it the way we did on the 707. Holding the engines below and ahead of the wing in strut-supported pods would block access for boarding stairs to the door of the 737-100, which was a very short airplane. Strut-mounting the engines beneath the wings would also require the 737 to sit high off the ground on long landing-gear struts to give the engine nacelles sufficient ground clearance.

I frowned. The airlines wouldn't like that. From my fact-finding discussions with them, I knew how important this issue of airplane height is to short-haul flight operations. Small jets typically make short flights on routes a few hundred miles long or less. They can log up to six or seven of these per day. The less time they spend on the ground between flights, the more time they can be in the air generating revenue for their operators.

If I kept the design of the 737 low to the ground, it would turn around more quickly and be back in the air sooner. Why? Because no time would be wasted retrieving, positioning, and removing ladders and maintenance stands. Airline mechanics could walk right up and perform needed line maintenance on the engines and other systems from ground level. And when late-arriving passengers showed up at the gate, airline employees could simply take those last-minute bags out to the jet, pop open its cargo hold, and toss them in.

I considered other factors as I moved that paper engine around the drawing. The secret to success in any business is to properly define and meet customer requirements. It's all the more important in commercial aviation, because jets are so enormously costly to develop that mistakes carry heavy penalties.

Aft-mounted engines on pylons and wing-mounted engines on struts were both problematic. Was there a third configuration providing a better solution?

I slid that cutout tight under the wing and felt a sudden flash of excitement. Instead of mounting the engines away from the wing on struts, why not mount them hard against the underside of the wing itself?

Was it possible? Was it desirable from a safety standpoint?

The answer to the first question was yes. Looking at it critically, I saw that the answer to the second was also yes, provided we placed the engine far enough back on the wing so that its turbine section was *behind* the rear spar. That would alleviate a key safety concern by preventing turbine bursts from penetrating the fuel tanks.

A jet's wing has two main *spars* that converge outward from the fuselage toward the tip of the wing. Mounted transversely on these beefy structural members are *ribs* that further increase structural strength and give the wing its airfoil shape. The space between the front and rear wing spars is largely reserved for fuel. As laid out, my design met the certification requirement that this area not be exposed to flying shrapnel should an engine disintegrate in flight.

Mounting the engine directly to the bottom of the wing solved the height issue. It also provided the engines with good airflow undisturbed by the airframe. It looked workable to me, so I took my sketch down to Jack Steiner. "Well, you know," he commented, "maybe that's a good idea."

To find out for sure, he launched two parallel 737 parametric design reviews. The Red Team would evaluate the original configuration with engines at the rear, and the Blue Team would look at engines hard-mounted beneath the wings. Each of these teams had two members.

Because the original configuration was Steiner's, he and an engineer reporting to him became the Red Team. For my Blue Team, Steiner lent me one of the designers in his group and we set about configuring the airplane as I had proposed. Although we allowed a couple of months for the exercise, a clear winner emerged within just two weeks.

Our studies showed that having the engines beneath the wings meant we could carry six more passengers. In a 100-seat baseline airplane, that meant 6% more revenue and probably 100% more profit for the airlines. Although those initial figures were crude, they confirmed that this was indeed the way to go.

Late in 1964, we locked in the 737 configuration with the engines positioned under the wings so that their turbine sections were aft of the rear spars. Also called the hot section, this is the part of the engine where combusted gases expand through a series of turbines to drive the engine. If there's an uncontained failure, it's generally here because this is where the temperatures and stress are greatest.

This engine installation proved fairly straightforward to engineer and was enormously successful in service. Nevertheless, the 737 did have engineering challenges elsewhere. Fitting systems like flight controls into an airframe is proportionately more difficult in small jetliners, for example, and we thrived on finding creative, elegant solutions.

By far the biggest lesson I learned from the 737 was never to take an initial design configuration as a given. It's human nature to do just that and go charging ahead to work within an existing framework. However, that doesn't necessarily lead to great airplanes.

Engineers love to dive right in and analyze the hell out of reams of data. Very often, though, they can't see the forest for the trees because they haven't done the simple work up front to be sure they're starting down the right path. The time for detailed work with massed computing power is *after* the basic concept has been properly defined.

Jack Steiner and I share the patent on the 737, he for its wider cabin and I for the placement of the engines. Both were novel concepts for a short-haul twinjet. We each received the then-standard payment of $50 from Boeing for that patent. It was a satisfying moment. While aerospace isn't a field where people make a lot of money, I still felt I was working for a company that valued initiative and independent thinking.

The 737 taught me to step back at the outset of any program and take a clear, simple look at the basic physical problems that need to be addressed. The more brain power you apply up front, the greater the likelihood that you'll find the design path that solves your challenges and meets your customers' requirements.

By the summer of 1965, I was deep into the demands of the 737 program. Since the jet wasn't scheduled to fly until 1967 or enter service until late 1968, I fully expected Boeing's littlest jet to keep me busy for the next few years. But as it turned out, Boeing had different plans for me.

5

I GET THE 747

In August 1965, Nancy and I headed out of town for an entire week off. I really needed the vacation; I was 44 years old, had been working very hard, and had never taken much time off from Boeing in the nearly two decades I'd worked there.

Our three kids were at camp or elsewhere, so it would just be Nancy and I at our cabin on Hood Canal. Situated right on the water, this cabin is surrounded by wooded hills. Hood Canal looks like a river but is estuarial and rich in oysters, which like a mix of fresh and salt water. The shore of our beach is littered with their shells. To the west of Hood Canal is the Olympic Peninsula with its high mountains.

Our cabin has been the scene of countless happy hours for several generations of Sutters. Buying and building on the property was Nancy's idea. She knew and loved Hood Canal from her childhood and had taken the initiative in finding the perfect summer retreat for us as a family.

The cabin we built has a large and very welcoming common room with an open kitchen and a fireplace built from water-rounded stones we gathered ourselves. The front of the cabin opens out onto a sloping lawn and the beach. At the back are a bedroom and a bathroom beneath an open loft so big a dozen people can sleep there. You get to it by climbing a vertical staircase ladder, which gives the loft a nautical feel that kids love.

Back in 1965, the cabin was still unfinished. The floor was bare cement, the walls were uninsulated, and the exterior siding wasn't yet in place. The kitchen had a temporary shiplap countertop and an equally temporary utility sink.

We didn't yet have a phone, so I'd given Ruth Howland—my devoted Boeing secretary of many years—the telephone number of our nearest neighbor. "Don't call unless it's an emergency," I remember telling her.

The weather at Hood Canal was beautiful. The air was fragrant, the sun warm. Nancy and I spent most of our time outside, she tending to her garden and I checking the fruit trees I'd planted. They weren't doing well because the deer kept coming down from the hills and eating their leaves. It didn't look like we'd ever have an orchard.

I also checked my strawberry patch. Thinking that a strawberry and rhubarb pie would be nice, I'd planted them in a large box I filled with good soil. One week those strawberries were green, the next yellow, and the next *gone*—the deer had eaten them too! Fortunately the hills all around are full of berry bushes, so later that summer Nancy made us blackberry pies instead.

A couple of days into that vacation, Nancy went back into town to play bridge with her friends. I was alone and wandered outside to enjoy the sunshine and salt air. I considered digging for clams but decided instead to cut up some driftwood. Without insulation, the cabin could be cold even in the summertime, and I needed firewood.

I was busy with an axe, thinking about all that firewood my brothers and I had cut and stacked during my childhood, when my neighbor showed up unexpectedly. "Hey, Sutter," he informed me, "they're calling you on my phone!" This neighbor was ordinarily a friendly enough guy but aloof. He took his privacy seriously and didn't appreciate being bothered with other people's problems. I followed him back to his cabin, apologizing for the inconvenience.

It was Dick Rouzie, chief engineer of the Boeing Commercial Airplane Division. We had been studying how we could improve the 707, which was becoming too small in light of the fast-rising global demand for intercontinental air travel. We kept looking at stretching our flagship jet the way Douglas did the competing DC-8, but to do so we'd have to give it a longer landing gear. Otherwise the tail would scrape the runway on takeoff and landing.

Unfortunately, revising the landing gear would be horrendously expensive because it meant a major redesign of the wings and fuselage where they meet. Looking at this, we all recognized that we'd pretty much reached the point of diminishing returns on the 707. It just didn't make sense to pour that much money into a short-term solution.

On the phone, Rouzie broke the news to me that Pan American World Airways was pressing Boeing hard for an all-new airplane much larger than the 707. Would I like to leave the 737 program, he asked, and head up the company's studies for this bigger jet?

I said yes. I had no way of knowing where this new assignment might lead or even whether it was a good career move. But a request like that from your boss at Boeing was effectively an order. Still, even if it hadn't been, I would have agreed because it meant a program of my own. And not just any program. This one was for a large long-range airliner—precisely what I'd dreamed of ever since I was a kid.

I thanked my neighbor and wandered back to my cabin, my mind racing. How big an airplane were we talking about? What would it look like? What features should it have? Fortunately, the usual constraint of limited engine power would not be a factor so I could think as big as the airlines wanted.

At that time, people on the military side of Boeing were competing to build the C-5, a big new cargo jet for the U.S. Air Force. While I wasn't involved in that engineering effort, I understood from colleagues that the Boeing team had come up with a sophisticated design that we felt outperformed Lockheed's entry.

The military C-5 program was doing something extremely important for commercial aviation: fostering the development of *high-bypass-ratio turbofan engines*, a new technology that promised much larger, more powerful, and more fuel-efficient engines than the low-bypass-ratio fanjets then powering the world commercial jetliner fleet.

A jet engine works by compressing air, mixing in fuel, and feeding this fuel–air mixture into combustion chambers, where it ignites. The exploding exhaust gases vent to the rear past curved metal blades on rows of turbine discs. This hot, high-pressure efflux pushes on those curved blades, spinning the turbines on a central shaft running the length of the engine. This rotational energy in turn powers the compressor at the front of the engine so that it pushes more air through the engine, continuing the continuous combustion cycle.

What I've just described is a *turbojet* engine. Its advantages are simplicity and reliability, but it also has key disadvantages, these being high fuel consumption and poor acceleration on takeoff. A turbojet accelerates a small amount of air to a very high speed. It's like trying to start a bicycle in high gear.

To this formula, the *turbofan* engine adds a *fan unit* at the front. This is a wide compressor that passes only some of the air it pressurizes through the engine's core. The rest of the air passes around the core in a nozzle-shaped path through the engine that produces net thrust. This *bypass* air does not get mixed with fuel and is not combusted.

Turbofans have three advantages over turbojets. First, they accelerate a larger volume of air to a lower velocity so that takeoff acceleration is improved. It's like switching your bicycle into a more efficient gear ratio. Second, they use less fuel. Third, they are quieter because the hot exhaust gases from the engine's core are shielded by the bypass air instead of being exposed to the cold air beyond the engine. This eliminates the flaring blowtorch hiss so characteristic of early jets.

U.S. jet engine manufacturers Pratt & Whitney and General Electric competed in the 1960s to power the C-5 transport. GE won this coveted government business with its proposal for a large fanjet with a bypass ratio of 8 to 1 (that is, eight times as much air would be ducted around the core of the engine as passed through it). Pratt's losing bid was for a big proposed fanjet with a bypass ratio of about 5.5 to 1.

While no large high-bypass-ratio fanjets had yet been built, this emerging technology was like money in the bank for my new airplane program. The imminent availability of such engines meant I could probably think as big as I liked and still have engines to power it.

Here was a situation unprecedented in the annals of aviation. Power plants usually lagged *behind* airframes and systems, limiting what designers could do. Boeing's XB-15 had been a giant airplane rendered impotent by tiny engines. So was Douglas's wartime XB-19. For all their might, both the B-29 and the Stratocruiser had been underpowered.

After working on Boeing's smallest jetliner, here I was suddenly heading up the development of its largest in the first commercial application of those big fanjets. The prospect was downright thrilling.

Boeing would learn in October 1965 that we had lost the C-5 military competition. Located in California, the most populous U.S. state, Lockheed benefited from much better representation in Washington, DC, and we couldn't help but think that political clout had snatched the C-5 contract away from us.

I should add that fostering large high-bypass engines was *all* that the USAF C-5 competition contributed to the Boeing 747, as my new airplane would be called. Time and again there appears in print the logical but false assumption that Boeing took its losing military C-5 bid and revamped it as the commercial 747. In fact, the 747 would be an entirely original design that owes nothing to the C-5.

Excitement had me wandering absentmindedly around the cabin, knocking aimlessly about, unable to think of anything but the challenges ahead. When Nancy returned from Seattle, I told her all about the telephone call. We spent the next couple of days trying to relax at the cabin, but I couldn't get this new assignment out of my head. Finally—to my neighbor's relief, I'm sure, since I kept receiving calls from people at Boeing—I gave up and we headed back to town.

Friday of that abandoned vacation week, I met with Rouzie and other Boeing people affected by this sudden turn of events. They described in very general terms what they envisioned and authorized me to begin assembling a team for my big-airplane study. I started with a staff of 20 or so and won approval by the end of August to increase the head count to 100. This was the start of the Boeing 747.

Why was I picked to lead the engineering development? I suspect I was about the only qualified person available. Maynard Pennell, Bill Cook, Bob Withington, and many other more senior engineers were all tied up designing a supersonic transport (SST) for the United States—Boeing's flagship program in 1965, an all-out, government-funded engineering effort to deliver a supersonic airliner called the Boeing 2707.

It seemed everyone back then believed SSTs were commercial aviation's future. The British and French certainly thought so. They launched SST programs of their own and then threw in together when their efforts became too expensive for each country individually. The result of that collaboration was the Concorde. The Soviets also thought SSTs were the way to go and developed the Tupolev Tu-144, the first supersonic airliner in service.

The Boeing 2707 was far more ambitious than either of those two other SSTs. From its delta wings to its titanium structure and its 66,000-pound-thrust straight turbojet engines, this U.S. SST program was probing deep into engineering unknowns. It promised to advance the technology of flight on many fronts.

Everyone at Boeing wanted in on the 2707 program. Almost all the top engineering leaders were there, with the notable exception of Jack Steiner, who was still heading up the 737. So who was left when Boeing needed someone for the big subsonic jetliner Pan Am suddenly wanted? Yes, I believe I was simply at the right place at the right time and I consider myself hugely fortunate.

I was also very fortunate that there were no ground rules established from above for my big-airplane study. It was entirely up to me and my team to define Boeing's new subsonic jet. We would do that by working closely with our airline customers, Pan American first and foremost.

Pan American was by far the most influential international airline back then. It had launched the 707 and would also launch the 747, as our new airplane would be known when the program was started— that is, *if* we could come up with something that Pan Am liked.

I initiated discussions with Pan Am and immediately realized they wanted a really *big* jet. The numbers they quoted sounded enormous, in terms of both airplane size and desired performance. Could they be right? Did the world really want intercontinental airliners that carry upwards of 400 passengers at one time?

Juan Trippe's vision of a big airplane was enough of a challenge. To make matters even more interesting, he wanted this big new airplane *now*. His business instincts were telling him that Pan Am's intercontinental routes could use the added capacity of bigger airplanes as soon as he could get them.

Starting with Pan Am's data points, I set my team to work doing preliminary parametric studies to generate airplane weight, size, and performance figures. Of course, we also asked TWA, British Airways, Japan Airlines, and many other international carriers what they felt they needed in the way of a big jet, but this sort of pie-in-the-sky question rarely generates meaningful answers, and our request was no different.

It was enormously important for us to find out what customers besides Pan Am wanted in a new jetliner. To elicit meaningful inputs, we proposed three different airplane sizes to them and asked which they wanted us to build. Specifically, we identified a 250-seater, a 300-seater, and a 350-seater and supplied basic weights, performance parameters, and operating economics for each of these options.

This approach worked and the results were surprising. I was amazed to see that every single one of those other international carriers voted for 350 seats, the largest size. By way of comparison, the

707 and DC-8—the two largest airliners then in service—each carried about 140 passengers. This meant that the airlines wanted us to build an airplane *two and a half times bigger than anything in existence.* By comparison, today's Airbus A380 (550 seats) is one third bigger than the 747-400 (416 seats).

While those results endorsed Pan Am's vision, it was sobering if not outright scary for those of us on the design front, because it took us into an entirely different region of airplane sizing. We set to work trying to determine what such a big airplane would look like. It was at this early juncture in the program that we reached what would be a turning point in my career and a major milestone in airplane design: an entirely new airplane configuration.

―――――――

At that time, when you discussed the concept of very big airliners with people, they immediately and invariably thought double-decker. Going to two interconnected decks (like London's famous double-decker buses) was the obvious way to immediately double the capacity of any airplane. You could only stretch an airliner so far, of course, so going to two full-length decks seemed the logical way to increase passenger counts.

Boeing's losing C-5 proposal had actually been a double-decker, which further consolidated this two-level concept within Boeing. Lockheed's winning bid also specified two full decks. Still in service today, USAF Lockheed C-5 Galaxy transports carry oversize vehicles, heavy equipment, and other military cargoes on their lower deck, and military troops and personnel on the upper.

Our airline customers likewise thought in terms of a double-decker 747. This was particularly true of Pan Am. A naval aviator in World War I, Juan Trippe had successfully adopted ocean liners as the paradigm for his ocean-spanning air services of the 1930s. He called his boat-hulled Sikorsky, Martin, and Boeing airliners *flying clipper ships* and staffed them with captains, first and second officers, stewards, and pursers. Pan Am continued using this maritime motif right into the jet age.

It was obvious to me that Pan Am's chairman wanted the new Boeing 747 to be an aerial ocean liner with tall sides punctuated by two parallel rows of windows like portholes. If he had his way, passengers viewing the 747 from the airport terminal would look out and see something suggestive of a ship.

Thus, the double-decker was quite naturally my study group's point of departure. My people began drawing up double-decker fuselages. As a result, considerable friction arose when I let it be known that I did not believe we had done enough studies to lock into any one configuration yet.

Fresh in my mind was the lesson of the 737 program, where my up-front reconsideration of the spectrum of engine-placement options led us to an unsuspected but ultimately better design approach. It seemed to me that we should take a bit of time for similar reflection on the 747. This thought started us down the road to a winning configuration for the 747.

It was a muggy summer day in Washington, DC. I was on a solo business trip and had been in meetings with the FAA to discuss 747 certification issues. I dragged myself back to my hotel after a long day and ran into 20 or so colleagues from Boeing.

Whereas I was alone on my 747-related trip, they were there in force to brief the FAA on the Boeing 2707, our SST. I saw lots of star power in that high-level Boeing delegation. I was hot, sticky, and tired. All I wanted was to go up to my room, have a shower, and get some rest, but they were in high spirits and had other ideas.

They bought me a cocktail in the hotel bar and asked me how I was doing. After bringing them up to date on my progress, I listened to elated descriptions of how well their SST presentations had gone at the FAA. One member of that group put his arm around my shoulder and said, "You know, Joe, you do a good job on this big airplane of yours, and we'll save you a place on the SST program!"

As much as any single event, that revealing encounter shows what I contended with on the 747 program. They had enough funding for

20 people to travel at one time, whereas I had to go it alone. For all its later success and impact, the 747 was *not* considered the next big thing at Boeing or even an area where technology was at the forefront. Instead, people viewed it as an interim conventional airliner, useful only until SSTs took over long-haul air travel.

Consequently, I had trouble getting everything from good people to facilities to priority in the wind tunnel. I had to fight city hall, as it were, every step of the way to get the 747 designed, built, certified, and into service.

The people that Boeing gave me for the program were all good and experienced individuals, although they were not the stellar types who were considered to be Boeing's future engineering leaders. Brought up on subsonic jets like the 707 and the 727, they were fine and competent engineers, managers, and other professionals who for one reason or other hadn't made the cut for the SST.

Nobody likes being passed over or consigned to a backwater, and morale probably wasn't all that great initially. I knew I would have to change that. I began by letting my team know that I believed in them and that I valued the skills and knowledge they brought to the table. We had a big job to do and they saw how confident I was that we would get it done.

———

It wasn't just the aviation manufacturers who were taken in by the enticing vision of SSTs in our collective future. In fact, almost every airline I talked with as a committed or possible 747 customer was also ordering either Boeing 2707s or Concordes.

Different though they were in size and performance, the 747 and those SSTs actually competed head to head for airline orders and dollars. There are two ways to make an airliner more productive in revenue service. The first is to make it carry more payload (that is, more passengers and cargo), which is the route we took with the 747. The second is to make it faster so that it can fly more times in a given time frame. That, of course, was the whole idea behind the SST, which promised to dramatically reduce travel times.

It was universally assumed that the 747 would be an *interim* subsonic jetliner until the SSTs took over the intercontinental air routes. That's what Boeing's marketing people thought; they estimated we'd probably sell 50 or so 747s for passenger use. But even after the SSTs siphoned off the passengers, airlines would still need a large *cargo* jet with intercontinental range. It was this anticipated alternate use that made the 747 program economically viable from the company's point of view.

Consequently, I decided to configure the 747 airplane from the very start for passenger *and* freighter use. This "dual mission" program goal would greatly influence the definition of the 747 airplane and accounts in large measure for its subsequent popularity and success.

This doesn't mean that the 747 program wasn't seen as important by Boeing's leaders. It most certainly was, if only for the vast amounts of money we would spend to develop it. Because of the focus on SSTs, though, at times it seemed the company's unwanted stepchild.

———

Boeing's board of directors formally launched the 747 program in March 1966, and Pan Am signed a contract for 747s the following month. At that time, my product-development study became the fourth committed airplane program under way at Boeing Commercial Airplanes. In line ahead of us for our company's limited resources were the SST, the 737, and a stretched reworking of the 727 known as the 727-200.

Boeing was already overextended before we began work on the 747. This was troubling, because even with government funding, the SST was consuming more resources than had been anticipated. So was the 737, which got off to a rocky start in airline service with wheel shimmy, ineffectual thrust reversers, and other issues needing attention.

Other Boeing divisions were also draining away company reserves, notably the giant *Saturn V* first stage that Boeing was developing to take NASA astronauts to the Moon. Consequently, my team and I found ourselves last in line for resources at a difficult time for Boeing.

A slowing economy dipping toward recession promised to aggravate the situation.

If ever a program seemed set up for failure, it was mine. Even so, I can honestly say that it was the high point in my career and I relished almost every minute of it. Here I was creating a product that with any luck would have a production run measured in decades and an even longer life in service.

Needless to say, few, if any, products in this world are as expensive to develop as new jetliners. With literally billions of dollars at stake, you have to get it right. The consequences of bringing the wrong airliner to market are dire and long lasting. It was one hell of a responsibility. By all rights, I should have felt weighted down. But I didn't. This was what I'd been hoping and working for all my life. It was a good program and it fit my skills and personality. It's in my nature to assess issues and tackle problems as they arise, trusting that solutions will be found down the line to what I can't solve right away.

———

As we sat down to design the 747, my team and I knew the airlines wanted us to think really big. We also knew that it had to be a good passenger airplane *and* a good freighter. This latter requirement led us to ask, "How do you carry freight?" It would obviously be harder to fill a double-decker with air freight than to fill a single-deck airplane. Even with special equipment, loading and unloading an upper deck high off the ground would be tricky and take time.

Our knowledge of real-world airline operations told us that some air freight carriers would want to move cargo through their systems in shipping containers. What kind of a shipping container could we come up with that would work on both levels of a double-decker without sacrificing too much of the plane's available internal volume?

There seemed to be no good answers to our growing list of questions. Trying to come up with them, Rowland "Row" Brown, a superb Boeing engineer, drew up one double-decker after another—probably hundreds in all—but none satisfied him or me from a configuration standpoint. Nor did they satisfy Milton Heinemann, a payloads engineer from way back whose expertise in designing airplane interiors was without equal.

Furthermore, Milt and I shared a concern about double-deckers in the passenger role. FAA regulations require that the design allow the maximum number of passengers that the airplane is certified to carry to evacuate safely within 90 seconds, in case of emergencies occurring on the ground, such as a jet running off a runway or otherwise being damaged. This is an extremely important requirement. I didn't see how we could meet it on a double-decker.

Double-deckers are short relative to their weight, so the wing is very broad relative to the fuselage length. This characteristic makes it difficult for there to be sufficient emergency upper-deck escape slides to the ground that clear the wing. Moreover, this deck is so high off the ground that there is a very real possibility passengers will balk at using them.

All these concerns started us thinking along heretical lines: *Why not put a very wide single-deck fuselage onto the drawing board by way of comparison?* When I communicated this intriguing idea to the team, I encountered a surprising amount of resistance. We faced severe time constraints and people were anxious to get on with the design work. They had already locked their thinking into two passenger decks, one above the other.

Since Pan Am wanted its airplane yesterday, I knew we had to arrive at a decision *quickly*. Consequently, I had Row Brown start drawing up single-deck cross sections. There was no time for formal analyses and comprehensive evaluations. Instead we did rapid studies of the "cut to the chase" variety, with a healthy dose of horse sense factored in. In this respect, the 747's development process perhaps more closely resembled that from the colorful early days of aviation than from modern times. For all the sophistication of today's modern tools, it probably takes longer now to develop an all-new airliner than it did in the past. Aviation might have lost something when rules of thumb and "quick and dirty" determinations went by the wayside.

As I looked at Row Brown's single-deck alternative, it didn't take me long to see that—radical as the idea seemed—a very wide single deck was indeed the way to go. The fuselage we settled on was wide enough for 10 economy-class seats lined up side by side across two aisles. This was the configuration we locked in for the 747.

Those studies also led us to arrive at another distinctive 747 feature: the bulge at the top of the fuselage. It was necessary for loadability in the freighter role. With our jet expected to do double duty as a main-deck cargo hauler, we felt a large freight door on the side of the airplane might not always be enough. To ensure cargo operators the flexibility to meet their customers' needs, we decided to also provide for straight-in loading through the airplane's nose.

This idea in turn led us to locate the flight deck *above* the main deck instead of in line with it, as was the case with earlier airliners. Combined with a hinged nose that would lift up and out of the way, this high flight-deck location would permit cargoes to slide right in. For aerodynamic reasons, a fairing was added aft of the flight deck, giving the 747 its famous hump.

There were other gross configurational details to work out, of course. One was the wing, which we swept back 37.5 degrees for a fast and efficient cruise. Another was the landing gear. My team defined a four-post main gear with four wheels per post. Two of these four-wheel landing gears are mounted on the wings and the other two on the fuselage. Having 18 tires, including the 2 on the nose gear, spread the weight of the huge 747 sufficiently to allow it to operate on the same concrete surfaces as smaller and lighter jets.

Designing a high-capacity transport suddenly became a hell of a lot easier now that we were looking at a single deck. Cargo capacity and loading, passenger boarding and deplaning, the in-flight cabin environment, flight attendant services, and emergency passenger evacuations all became more manageable.

With its large fuselage diameter, our wide-single-deck airplane would weigh a bit more than the double-decker we had abandoned. However, the overwhelming advantages of this alternative configuration more than offset the issue of increased airframe weight. One of my challenges would be to make Pan Am understand this, since they were very concerned—and rightly so—with keeping weight down so that performance wasn't compromised.

Amazingly, we accomplished all the above in just a month or so, not the six months that might have been more reasonable. Here was another example of what I had learned from cutting out those paper engines and moving them around that 737 line drawing: The simplest and fastest approach often works best.

In the drawings before me was the world's first airliner passenger cabin with two aisles instead of one. We had just invented the wide-body jetliner, a concept with evident rightness. Looking at it, I knew it would change people's perceptions of air travel for the better.

It was truly a collaborative achievement. While not every engineer in my study group was happy about giving up on the double-decker, my key people—Row Brown, Milt Heinemann, Everette Webb, and many others—were on the same page with me about this. The benefits spoke for themselves.

If I made an individual contribution, it was my insistence that we take stock before charging out of the starting blocks. Before gambling Boeing's future, we needed to know for sure what was best.

Veterans of the C-5 program had been arriving on my team since the latter half of 1965. I needed every person I could get and was glad to have them. Row Brown and Jim Norman, two of my lead engineers, came to me this way.

With time on their hands between assignments, many of these newcomers had been playing with ideas for salvaging their losing proposal. They didn't want to see all that work on the C-5 go to waste. It was only natural for them to see my big-airplane study as the perfect opportunity to recycle their efforts. Since the proposed Boeing C-5 would have been a double-decker, that's what they were thinking the 747 should be.

Dick Rouzie, our vice president of engineering, called me about that time to say that another C-5 person was being sent over to be my assistant. He added that this assignment was being made at the request of Ed Wells, one of Boeing's most senior people. When this newcomer arrived, he surprised me by informing me that Wells had suggested he should design the airplane while I instead worked with Sales on our external dealings with customers for the 747.

Some kind of a power play appeared to be under way. Keeping calm, I replied that this was not my understanding. My refusal to go along didn't slow the fellow down any, though. The next thing I knew, he had my people drawing up double-deckers all over again even though we had abandoned that configuration. Not wasting a moment, he also held a closed-door meeting with my chief engineers to tell them what he wanted done.

I learned all this when they came to me afterward in confusion. "Who's running this program, anyway?" they asked, understandably bewildered.

I saw Dick Rouzie and filled him in on what was happening. "There's only room for one director of engineering on the 747 program," I pointed out, "and you've got to decide who that is."

Boeing's management must have decided that I was that person, because very shortly thereafter my self-proclaimed successor was gone.

The Vietnam War was raging in the late 1960s. The Beatles flooded the airwaves, NASA was taking aim at the Moon, and Pan American World Airways utterly dominated international air travel. TWA and other U.S. carriers also flew international routes back then, but their services were very limited. As for the non-U.S. airlines, they were still playing catch-up from World War II and had a long way to go.

In short, Pan Am was king of the hill and Juan Trippe *was* Pan American. He had a lot of good people working for him, and a few who weren't so good, but what Boeing received in the way of airplane requirements always came directly from him. He was autocratic, and his people lined up and followed orders.

Juan Trippe actually tried hard to get Lockheed to build a very large airliner for him. He felt that the company, having won the air force's C-5 program, was well positioned to build it, but Lockheed declined the business.

Lockheed's caution didn't surprise me. Every U.S. airplane manufacturer knew how brutal business dealings with Pan Am could be. That reputation arose in the 1930s, when a young Juan Trippe—intent on conquering the world's oceans by air—ordered flying boats from Sikorsky, Martin, and Boeing. In each case, he promised the company big orders to secure lower per-airplane pricing, then reneged and went to the next company, where he pulled the same stunt all over again.

Sikorsky, Martin, and Boeing all lost huge sums of money as a result of Trippe's cutthroat business practices. Martin actually went into bankruptcy for a while but recovered. Of course, World War II ended flying-boat operations so we'll never know how many Boeing 314 Clippers Trippe would actually have purchased.

With Lockheed not playing this time around, Douglas was Boeing's only competition. The California company pushed hard to sell Pan Am a much-stretched version of the single-aisle DC-8 jetliner. That put us at Boeing over a barrel. All of us recalled how Trippe, to force us to widen the 707's fuselage, had ordered 25 DC-8s from Douglas at the same time that he launched the 707 with an order for 20 airplanes. One thing was certain: Juan Trippe knew how to play hardball.

If I could have changed any aspect of the 747 program, it would have been our schedule. More than once I wondered what had possessed our management to commit to having the 747 completed in two thirds the amount of time it ordinarily takes to develop an all-new jet.

Our challenging schedule wasn't entirely Pan Am's fault, of course. It was pretty well agreed between Pan Am's chairman and ours, and Bill Allen certainly didn't have to commit to his friend's desire for an early service introduction. But I suspect Allen probably wanted this big new Boeing airplane just as much as Trippe did, and for very human reasons.

Boeing's chairman turned 65 on September 1, 1965. He would soon be retiring and probably saw this last collaboration with Pan Am, and the big airplane it would produce, as a parting legacy. Trippe, who was just a year or so older, probably had similar thoughts.

Whatever the reason, Pan Am insisted that it had to take delivery of its first 747 by the end of 1969. That gave us just 28 months to design the airplane from scratch, despite its being a major challenge in terms of size and technology. My group was under tremendous pressure to define the airplane and begin the detail design work that would culminate in the release of manufacturing drawings.

You might think that my people might have responded in a negative manner, but that was never the case. In all my years at Boeing, I've never met a gang that pulled together as well as my 747 team. We seemed to have the same can-do attitude that was even then putting Americans on the Moon.

I can't look at a 747 without seeing it as a living piece of technological sculpture, a winged trophy dedicated to the men and women who put their hearts and souls into conceiving and building it.

———————

Even as Boeing and Pan Am were firming up the contractual specifications for the "new technology airplane," as the 747 was called before program launch, I was wondering how best to announce within the company that we had changed our design to a single-decker. I knew this would be a bombshell and was a bit apprehensive about dropping it, but there was no avoiding the issue.

I told Tex Boullioun, the leader of Boeing Commercial Airplanes, and Mal Stamper, head of the overall 747 program, of our baseline design change. I also informed our sales and contracts departments. I can only describe their collective reaction as a state of shock.

High agitation reigned in the halls of Boeing's sales and contracts communities. They felt I had thrown a truck-sized monkey wrench into the delicate ongoing negotiations with Pan American World Airways. Juan Trippe expected a double-decker, they told me, and this was what we should deliver.

As word spread, a lot of very senior Boeing people became afraid of what might happen when our most powerful customer found out we were designing a single-main-deck airplane. Trippe will file suit against us, many of them predicted. He'll jump ship and get Douglas or Lockheed to build him his double-decker.

The 747's configuration was my call as director of engineering. I wasn't about to change it back just to placate a galloping case of nerves. I have no idea how my explanations were received at high levels but I commend Boeing's leadership for respecting my decision.

This situation posed a ticklish question: Who should fly out to New York and break the news to Juan Trippe and Pan American? Ordinarily it would have been me, but politics dictated otherwise.

I am a plain-spoken person with strong views. Such being the case, it was felt that if I attempted to explain our alternative configuration to Juan Trippe, he might react negatively to my convictions and feel we weren't following the path he had specified for us. After all, he was the bill-paying customer and arguably knew more about the airline business than anyone else in the world.

I recognized the wisdom of not letting this engineering change be associated too closely with me. The last thing I wanted was for Juan Trippe to see this as a competition between *his* vision for the 747 airplane and Joe Sutter's.

Accordingly, I was pleased when Milt Heinemann was chosen to fly to New York and meet with Pan Am. At that time, Milt and his people were gearing up to create an interior for our new jet in collaboration with the industrial design firm of Walter Dorwin Teague Associates. Today known as Teague Associates, this firm has participated in the development of every Boeing airliner interior since the Stratocruiser back in the late 1940s.

More than anyone back then, Milt knew how to combine passenger comfort, efficient operation, and safety in an airliner cabin and see it all through certification. He had a superb reputation from the 707 and 727 programs and was held in universally high regard by the airlines. These credentials made him the ideal choice for breaking the news to Pan Am.

As Milt prepared for this all-important meeting over the weekend, he racked his brains for a way to present our widebody concept to customers who were wanting and expecting a double-decker. He knew that engineering reviews didn't always cut it; sometimes you need something simpler and more fundamental. Something dramatic. He hit on a brilliant solution.

Milt cut some clothesline to a length of 20 feet, the width of our single-deck 747 cabin. Coiling this cord, he snapped it shut in his briefcase and took it with him to New York. Arriving early for his appointment at Pan Am, he found the airline's main conference room vacant. Before anyone showed up, he hastily measured the room with his cord. With a jolt of surprise, he found that it happened to be exactly the length of the cord—that spacious conference room was exactly 20 feet wide!

Juan Trippe arrived with John Borger, his chief engineer, and other high-level Pan Am executives. They all took their seats, not happy that Boeing had kept the purpose of this requested meeting a secret. It implied bad news.

This was probably as tough an audience as Milt ever faced. After perfunctory greetings, he launched into the reason for his visit. Growing consternation met his words as people around the table realized their double-decker concept was not what Boeing was developing for them. As Milt explained our rationale for going to a single deck, palpable unease and displeasure filled the room.

Pan Am's chairman watched with a scowl. The others shot worried glances his way as if expecting him to call a halt to the proceedings at any moment. But Trippe listened and so did Borger, an engineer who kept an open mind.

"You say you can get the full specified passenger load onto this single deck?" Trippe asked when Milt was done.

"Yes," Heinemann replied.

"Comfortably?" Pan Am's chairman said, unconvinced.

"Yes, it's a very *wide* cabin." Milt looked around. "In fact, it's as wide as this room."

Stunned silence met the statement. Milt pulled out the coiled clothesline. "This cord represents the inside width of the 747 passenger cabin," he said, handing one end to the nearest Pan Am person. Instructing the man to hold it to the wall, he unwound the cord as he backed the other way. When the far wall stopped him, he held out his end of the cord and it reached the wall.

Incredulity registered on the faces of Trippe and his people. The conference room was twice as wide as any airliner that had ever flown. Picturing it as a passenger cabin boggled the mind. As Milt had hoped, Pan Am's interest was piqued. Juan Trippe agreed to the Boeing proposal, as put forth by Milt, that we build comparative fuselage mock-ups for Pan Am to come evaluate.

In fact, work was already under way on two lumber and plywood mock-ups at Renton. The first depicted a section of the best of the double-decker fuselages we had drawn up. A tall, narrow tube, it had three floors, the lowest for cargo and the two above for passengers.

The second mock-up represented the forward fuselage of our alternative wide-single-deck configuration. This, of course, is the 747 that the world knows today. These mock-ups were very crude but they served their purpose.

———

Shortly after Milt Heinemann's trip east, Pan American World Airways reciprocated with a visit to Seattle. Juan Trippe led the high-level delegation, which included Sanford Kauffman, John Borger, and other key Pan Am people. They arrived with dubious expressions and were a bit less cordial than usual.

Milt's presentation in New York had come as a huge surprise. Despite his assurances about the benefits of our alternative 747 configuration, our actions smacked of "bait and switch," something no customer likes. And while they were intrigued by the idea of a single very wide passenger deck, this change introduced additional uncertainty into an important industrial agreement. Needless to say, they were very concerned.

Tensions ran equally high on our side of the fence. Bill Allen, Boeing's chairman and Juan Trippe's old friend, dropped everything to attend. So did Tex Boullioun, the head of our commercial airplanes division; Mal Stamper, chief of the 747 program; and Clancy Wilde, our excellent VP of commercial sales. All of us recognized we were at a critical juncture.

My people and I made an engineering presentation in the morning about the original double-decker configuration and our idea for a better alternative. After lunch, we went to the mock-up shop, which was in a factory building at Renton. I knew as we entered that we had arrived at the single most important moment of the entire 747 program. I should add that—in my opinion, at least—we were showing Pan Am these mock-ups not to give them a choice but instead to show them why we had made a decision that was already locked in.

There was no doubt in my mind that the 747 should have a wide single deck with two aisles, not two narrower decks, one on top of the other. Would Pan Am agree? If they didn't, what could Boeing and they do about it? Would we still have a contract? I took a deep breath and did what engineers so often do: relax and let the facts speak for themselves.

We crossed to the double-decker. Borger and others peered into the crude mock-up's lower hold. They knew already that double-deckers don't offer much room for passenger baggage and revenue cargo, but there's nothing like seeing it for yourself. I saw disappointment on their faces.

The group ascended the stairs of a somewhat rickety roll-up metal stand. The Pan Am contingent was accompanied by Bill Allen, Tex Boullioun, and Mal Stamper. I should mention that those metal stairs were not shaky on purpose, as some people have suggested. It was just a regular stand used by Boeing factory workers. Rickety stairs were not part of some master plan to sway Pan Am's thinking away from the double-decker.

I watched from below as the party inspected the lower passenger deck. Taking in the surroundings, they looked less than thrilled by the airplane's proportions. Without comment they proceeded up to the upper deck and looked even less happy, perhaps because the tapering crown of the fuselage made the sidewalls tilt claustrophobically in.

Trippe and Allen came forward and stood together at the railing of the open end of this upper deck. The factory floor was 25 feet down and probably looked farther. The true height of the double-decker apparently came as a shock to them. I saw dismay on their faces.

Borger also looked down and I could read his thoughts: *How are we going to get people down out of here in an emergency?*

The party descended with evident relief, and we entered the mock-up of the single-main-deck 747 configuration. Its amazing spaciousness was unlike anything that anybody ever expected to experience aboard an airliner. It was twice as wide as a 707 and felt like a *place*, not a conveyance.

We were in the forward fuselage where first-class passengers would sit. I had hoped one look around would convince Juan Trippe, but he made no comment. After inspecting the main deck, we proceeded to a side mock-up representing the upper level. "What's this for?" Trippe asked, looking around in the open area aft of the cockpit door.

Borger replied that he thought that space might make a good rest area for flight crews on long flights.

"Rest area?" Trippe replied. "This is going to be reserved for passengers!"

Relief flooded through me. The crisis was over. Juan Trippe, the titan of the airline industry, had just relinquished his cherished vision of a double-decker airliner and bought into our alternative.

With Trippe's insight about how to use that upper space under the aerodynamic fairing aft of the flight deck, the 747 *did* get two passenger levels, although it remains primarily a single-deck airliner. Today's 747-400 carries about 40 business-class passengers under that upper bulge, which has been extended since the 747 first entered service.

"You made the right decision," Trippe told me confidently as we exited the mock-up area.

———

This was an utterly unforgettable moment in my career. I went home feeling that we had come up with something new and important. Our key customer had agreed that it was the way to go, so we were free to proceed with a very different airplane than the world expected.

Selection of an airliner's cross section is probably the most important decision made in the development of any new airliner. You can revise an airplane configuration in many ways—modify its wings, replace its engines, lengthen the fuselage—but you can't change its fuselage cross section after the fact. The cost would be prohibitive.

In looking back over the 747 program, I don't believe Boeing would have manufactured well over 1,350 747s—or even 300 for that matter—if my design team had delivered that double-decker everyone expected us to create. It also seems to me that what my design group actually achieved has never been fully understood or appreciated within Boeing. My hope is that this book will redress this oversight.

I hasten to add that we did not *invent* the concept of a twin-aisle airplane. For example, the passenger cabin of the Boeing's SST was going to have two aisles. We *did* introduce the world's first twin-aisle jetliner and give it a very wide cabin.

Turning our backs on the double-decker also accomplished a de facto change in my status at Boeing. Before that decision, there were those outside the 747 program who saw me as young, unproven, and maybe needing guidance. Now with our bold adoption of this new configuration, those same senior Boeing engineers saw that I was calling the shots with authority and a clear vision for what the 747 should be. My reasoning must have impressed people at high levels, because I was never again bothered with outside attempts to steer the design of the 747.

————————

The large-airplane study group I formed in 1965 started out with capable and often fairly senior engineers who hadn't made the SST cut or been claimed by the 737 or 727 programs. At no time did I ever have enough people for the Herculean task before us, and conspicuously absent all along were the up-and-coming young hotshots and engineering superstars. Most of my people came from other programs in the Seattle area, but some came from other company activities around the country.

Boeing's top management felt that the people they gave me were adequate for defining another subsonic airplane of about the same level of technology as, say, the 707 or 727. In reality, though, the 747 would significantly exceed those earlier types on almost every technological front, which added further to the magnitude of the challenge before us.

As a result, practically all of my people in those formative years of the 747 program were older than me, often by a decade or more. I felt like a college kid attempting to direct those experienced engineers, and I'm sure that more than a few of them felt their leader was not yet dry behind the ears. It was definitely an uphill battle convincing them that I could manage the program and that together we could create a great airplane.

Back then, I thought not being able to get the attention of Boeing's senior management was a disadvantage. As I look back on it now, though, I have an entirely different take on the matter; my team had more autonomy and authority than would otherwise have been the case. Let the SST hog the limelight; there was freedom in the shadows and we took advantage of it.

My 747 team was the finest group of professionals I could possibly have wished for. They had been through many airplane programs in the past and understood what it takes to develop and certify an airliner that is safe and durable. They knew just how far you can stretch technology.

This team would routinely achieve the impossible under astoundingly challenging conditions. To this day, I am at a loss to express how much I value all their individual contributions. Space prevents me from doing more than just scratching the surface, so I'll introduce a few of my team's key members and let them stand in for countless others.

The head of my technical staff was Everette Webb, someone I thought of as "100% engineer." Sincere and straightforward, Everette was not a self-promoter and had no axe to grind. His entire focus was simply on getting the job done.

Everette's office was near mine and we worked closely together. His job was to help define and create an airplane that would meet its stated goals and could be completed within the allotted time and budget. He and I didn't always agree, but when we didn't, our differences didn't fester in memos, additional analyses, and deferred resolution. Instead, we got together and settled the matter—usually within a single meeting.

Al Webber was responsible for the structure of the 747. While he might not have been old enough to be my father, I'd guess he had 15 years on me. I still remember his dubious expression the day we met. "How did this young squirt get put in charge of the program?" it said.

But as Al and I worked together, we developed a strong rapport. Again, when differences arose, we thrashed them out in a single session with minimal loss of time. This was in fact a defining characteristic of our program.

Ralph Mason led the detailed design of the 747's fuselage. No matter how early I got to work or how late I left, I could look across our work area and see Ralph plugging away, deftly managing the 500 designers under him. Multiply that professionalism and dedication several thousand times over and you'll get a sense of the determined bedrock supporting the creation of the 747.

Milt Heinemann, who had visited Pan Am with that coiled length of clothesline, was in charge of payload systems. He was one of the key players in the close collaboration that brought us to our wide new cross section. Milt was also the person behind the unprecedented idea of double-wide doors for the 747, which make for faster boarding and deplaning and help ensure rapid emergency evacuations.

Ed Pfafman came on board as head of hydraulics and flight-control systems. A stubborn Dutchman, Pfafman knew his job inside out. He flogged his points over and over to make sure he had been understood. It kind of wore the rest of us down, so he wound up winning most of his arguments.

Any irritation on that score was more than offset by his singular expertise. For example, later on when baffling troubles were encountered with the hydraulic system of the 747 during flight test, Pfafman marched out to the test ship, stood under an open wheel well, and listened as the hydraulics were operated. "Change that pump," he ordered, "it's not working properly." We swapped it out, and the problem disappeared.

Jack Waddell was our chief project pilot. A strong-willed Montanan, he would be taking the 747 aloft for the first time. In his mid-forties, balding, and very self-assured, he was a former naval aviator who had flown Dauntlesses (a Douglas aircraft) and PBYs (patrol bombers made by Consolidated Aircraft) in the South Pacific during the war. Following test duties at North American flying F-86s, he came to Boeing in 1957 as a B-52 test pilot and had since tested every Boeing commercial jetliner.

Far from being the white-scarf test pilot of the movies, Waddell had a master's degree in aeronautical engineering from Cornell. His understanding of airplanes, FAA certification requirements, and what airline pilots would actually need in service was invaluable to us.

Waddell and Pfafman both had strong personalities, and they didn't get along at all. One example involved the 747's autothrottle system. Just as an autopilot controls the airplane when the crew isn't doing the flying, an autothrottle will automatically manage power settings.

Up to that time, autothrottle capability was available to pilots only during autopilot-coupled approaches and landings in bad weather. However, Jack Waddell felt strongly that it should be available to flight crews throughout the flight. As the sophistication of autopilot systems increased and flights became longer, he believed that this companion system needed to follow the autopilot's lead for fully auto-mated flight.

In contrast, Ed Pfafman was extremely leery of introducing new systems and technologies into airplanes. Being just as stubborn as he was conservative, he flatly rebuffed Waddell's efforts to see full-time autothrottle capability incorporated into the 747. As I did so many times with my people during the 747 program, I stepped in to make sure they really communicated and we ended up with the right solutions.

Jack Waddell was correct, but a simple decision in his favor by me would not have resolved the underlying issue of clashing personalities. These key people in my program needed to work together for the 747 to succeed, so I took it on myself to serve as a catalyst between them to ensure that they worked out their differences. It was worth the extra effort, because in the end they both felt they had been heard and Pfafman came to accept Waddell's approach.

Everette Webb and our stubborn Dutchman also had trouble work-ing together. Their personalities clashed so strongly that they wanted nothing to do with each other. To solve this impasse, I told them that if they did not work through their differences for the good of the 747 program, I would put them in side-by-side offices, have a doorway cut between them, and not allow a door to be installed. Eager to avoid such close proximity, and perhaps humiliation as well, they learned to collaborate.

Jim Norman, another of the engineering chiefs reporting to me, led the design of the 747's electrical and environmental systems. Jim had a heck of a lot on his plate, but being a first-rate engineer and popular manager, he knew exactly what needed doing and how to get it done. A quiet South Dakotan, Jim began working at Boeing on the eve of World War II. We met after the war on the Stratocruiser pro-gram because he designed that complex old bird's instrument panels. He also contributed to the B-47, Dash 80, 707, and 727 programs and had played a large role on the C-5 effort before joining my team in the fall of 1965. Whereas so many others are gone today, I'm glad to say that Jim is still going strong.

There were countless other 747 program contributors, of course. Two key ones were Lynn Olason and Roland "Row" Brown, who together worked 747 product development. Row and Lynn were always looking at alternative configurations and innovative uses for our big airplane beyond its roles as a basic passenger plane and main-deck freighter. It was this team of idea men who invented the 747 Convertible, a version airlines can quickly change back and forth between passenger and freighter use. They also came up with the 747 Combi (for *combination*), a model whose divided cabin carries passengers forward and freight aft.

Olason and Brown would constantly show up at my office with engineering proposals. Lively debates sprang up over their creative suggestions, some of which I adopted and others of which I threw out. If we had differences, I made sure we ironed them out on the spot.

My engineering leaders were a colorful bunch. I valued the fact that they brought vastly different personalities and perspectives to the table. John Morrison, chief of 747 propulsion, was irascible. Al Webber was of the old school and didn't understand some of the new methods we younger engineers had for tackling problems. Ed Pfafman was plodding and dogged. Ken Plewis, who helped on the administrative side, went strictly by the book.

Whatever our differences, we all shared the same dedication and brought keen intelligence and hard-won expertise to the project. I don't believe there was a more comprehensive knowledge base in commercial aviation to draw from in the world. Like me, the people on my team believed implicitly that with enough effort we could solve any problem our big-airplane development program could throw at us.

Also on my 747 team were a few non-Boeing experts from the airlines who worked quite closely with us. One key outsider helping us was John Borger, Pan American's chief engineer. Virtually a "program insider," Borger almost lived with us throughout the definition and design stages of the 747. His fingerprints are all over the airplane.

A good friend and a living legend in aviation, John Borger was a rock-solid technical expert who knew airplane design and his airline's requirements. As competent an engineer as ever worked that side of the fence, he was without a doubt also the most intimidating. When John Borger came to Boeing, the red carpet was rolled out for him. People treated him with kid gloves because everybody was afraid of him. He did his job full tilt and was unsparing of those who didn't give definitive answers to his probing questions.

Borger had the uncanny ability to see every problem associated with an airplane design. He wasn't the kind of person you could butter up or placate with blithe assurances. Back in the Stratocruiser days when we got to know each other, there'd been *plenty* of problems for him to see. But the Stratocruiser was Pan Am's premier airliner in the propeller era, so we made it work.

Working on those issues with John, I found him to be a 100% Pan Am guy who was not about to let Boeing get away with anything. There were plenty of times when he and I sat across the table with strongly differing viewpoints, but I was always square with him and he knew it. That was the start of a very, very close working relationship and a lifelong friendship based on mutual trust and respect.

Borger and I had known each other for two decades by the time we got into designing the 747. Here again, he knew what his airline needed, and he was out to make damn sure Boeing met those requirements. While more than a few of my people were leery of him, I knew it was a lucky break to have the benefits of his long experience and intelligence.

The 747 program would sorely test the Boeing–Pan Am business relationship. If I had been more confrontational and less constructive, I suspect that this strained business relationship would have ruptured well short of the finish line. It was really John's and my mutual commitment to solving problems that would see the 747 into service.

Borger wasn't the only airline representative to help shape the 747, of course. Eager to know what our customers wanted, we also invited other airline experts to come review our work and make suggestions. One I recall in particular was Charles Abel, the chief engineer of BOAC. Like Borger, Abel made certain that his airline—today called British Airways—got the airplane it wanted and needed. Engineers from Lufthansa, Japan Airlines, Qantas, and other intercontinental carriers also contributed suggestions and ideas while watching the 747 design evolve.

One of the great experiences of my life has been dealing with these airline people. They were all very fine individuals who were dedicated to getting the job done. They understood the challenges we faced as a manufacturer and were committed to helping us define and deliver an airplane that everyone could fly safely and successfully.

By having these non-Boeing experts working so closely with us, our program informally pioneered the winning Boeing practice of inviting airline technical experts inside to help us develop our new airplanes. The 777 program of the early 1990s took this concept to unprecedented heights. Pilots, cabin crews, maintenance technicians, and other end users lived with Boeing and participated on our 777 design-build teams to ensure that this great airplane is well thought out.

———————

Look at any Boeing program today, and you'll see that the whole organization generally occupies adjoining facilities so that it can work as a team. Engineers, production people, planners, finance people—all are housed in close proximity in modern, well-equipped facilities.

Unfortunately, that was *not* the case on the 747 program in its earlier days. Our swelling ranks were scattered all over the map. As detailed design began, my people could be found crammed into back corners or unused floors of buildings already occupied by other groups and programs. Of course, there was no voice mail or e-mail back then—not even fax machines—so our lack of unified and centralized facilities came close to being an insurmountable obstacle in its own right.

Our last-in-line commercial airplane program clearly played fourth fiddle when it came to the allocation of company resources. Nowhere was this more evident than in the facilities Boeing saw fit to provide us.

My group started out on the second floor of building 2-01, the infamous "Drop Hammer Shop," in a space originally set up for factory production planners. It was here that the initial definition of the 747 took place, and it wasn't made easier by the noise and vibration of the massive tooling down below, stamping out metal parts for airplanes.

We squeezed into that building before we really ramped up in personnel. Even so, not everyone on my team could fit. My powerplant people took up lodgings in a former Ford plant acquired by Boeing, and other parts of my 747 team were scattered throughout Renton and the Duwamish Valley.

As a result, I personally spent far too much time in my car going from one place to the next to work with the different engineering disciplines that were part of my team. Visiting all my people took me up and down Boeing Field, to Renton, and elsewhere within a radius of five miles or so.

As for staff meetings, I was extremely reluctant to call them regardless of how important they might be. My people didn't walk down a hall to attend a meeting; because of our situation, they had to drive. That often made the total cost of meetings too high in terms of lost productivity.

I spent a lot of time on the road because it was better for me to go see 20 people than to have them drop everything to come over to see me. I also relied more on the telephone than I ordinarily would have, and I tried in many other ways to ensure adequate coordination.

Fortunately, every time we changed something on the 747, our process was to issue a design decision memorandum. These DDMs kept my team up to speed on things they might have missed in all those meetings we didn't have.

In light of all we put up with, it really made my people grumble when they had occasion to go visit people in the SST camp. That airplane program was all housed in the Development Center, a huge new building with lavish engineering offices. Conveniently located just down the road from the main Boeing plant on East Marginal Way, the DC was so big that a full-scale, 300-seat SST mock-up (minus one wing) was constructed inside! There it sat for those privileged Boeing engineers to gaze down on and draw inspiration from.

Our SST colleagues were clearly the haves to our have-nots. But their affluence was now straining Boeing. So was the 747, which was a bigger and more expensive program than Boeing's leaders had initially thought. They knew it now; all of us from Bill Allen on down were well aware that it could break the company.

As work progressed, we got into doing developmental testing of the air-conditioning, hydraulics, flight controls, and other systems we were devising. This work was performed in scattered and scrounged facilities, most of them located around the north end of Boeing Field.

I still recall hoofing it over to those buildings time and again to observe those key tests. And more often than I care to remember, it involved slogging through the mud and soaking rain of our typical Seattle winters. It was not a happy situation.

The worst day for me was the time I visited John Morrison, who was running the 747 program's powerplant development. John's group was off by itself in an old Ford plant. You got there by driving down West Marginal Way and crossing a bunch of railroad tracks. Having lots of things on my mind this particular day, and being sleep deprived to boot, I wasn't paying enough attention and went right through a railroad stop signal.

I came extremely close to being struck by a frantically hooting Great Northern freight train. I cleared it only by stomping on the accelerator. Still shaken during my drive home that night, I couldn't help imagining what the newspapers would have said if my luck hadn't held out: "Boeing encountered another stumbling block in the development of the 747 when its chief engineer was run over by a freight train. . . ."

In short, conditions were not ideal. Later on, my engineers began moving north to new facilities at Everett, Washington. For a period of about four months, I was working face-to-face with people in building 2-01, the Ford plant a couple of miles away, and in Everett, 30 miles to the north, on an almost daily basis.

I made those trips to Everett very early in the morning. Without traffic, it took about an hour from my house. This let me get a good deal of work done and be back in the Drop Hammer Building—another hour's drive—late that night. After yet more work, I'd make the half-hour drive home to West Seattle with few other cars on the road.

Joe Sutter, age 3

With Nancy during WWII
(COURTESY MARCELLA OLASON)

Naval Aviation Training in Memphis, WWII (Joe is second from right in the back row)

Joe reclining on the lawn of the University of Washington campus

Nancy with Adrienne,
Jonathan, and Gabrielle, 1954

The cabin on Hood Canal

RA001, the first 747, and Joe in 1969
(COURTESY THE BOEING COMPANY)

OPPOSITE PAGE: Boeing 747 being tested in a wind tunnel

Boeing 747 interior mock-up
(COURTESY THE BOEING COMPANY)

First flight, February 9, 1969
(COURTESY THE BOEING COMPANY)

Boeing field flight test ramp in 1969; Mount Rainier in the background
(COURTESY THE BOEING COMPANY)

Bill Allen and Juan Trippe, 1970
(COURTESY THE BOEING COMPANY)

Production begins at Everett, Washington, 1969

747s awaiting engines at Everett, 1970

I remember countless drives down I-5 or across the West Seattle Freeway in fog, rain, and gloomy mist. Exhausted, struggling to stay alert, I knew another too-long day was just hours away, and then another and another without letup. That was the only way that an airplane like the 747 was going to get into the air on time. My team knew it too. We kept up the pace day after day.

Saturdays were sacrificed to work. So were too many Sundays, but at least Nancy and I had a little bit of time together in the evenings.

Even at the peak of the 747 program, we got out to our cabin on Hood Canal one Sunday a month or so, but it was unfinished and needed so much work that I found it hard to relax. We also managed occasionally to get together with friends. That was important, as it brought relief and perspective.

My workload was supportable because I could see the milestones ahead. The airplane would get designed. It would get built. It would roll out and then fly. We would test it, certify it, and deliver it to airlines. Delivery was the light at the end of the tunnel.

The 747 would be so big that no existing Boeing factory could accommodate it. An entirely new plant would have to be constructed in which to build our new jet.

Boeing's vice president in charge of facilities and planning did research on where to site the 747 factory. He rightly concluded that there wasn't space available in Seattle for a new plant, which had to be located on an airport with a long runway. It would have to be built elsewhere, and a team was chartered to figure out where.

This determination should have been a straightforward process. Unfortunately, politics took it in an unworkable direction and put me in conflict with key people in Boeing's senior management. It was the first of a number of times on the 747 program that I found myself at loggerheads with my higher-ups.

Those site-selection studies began as we roughed out the preliminary design of the 747. Many locations were evaluated. As 747 program director of engineering, I wasn't invited to attend most of them,
and those I did took more time than I had. But as the selection process
moved toward a decision, they brought the whole team into the picture, me included.

One finalist was Snohomish County Airport some 30 miles to the
north of Seattle. Better known as Paine Field, it was a former military
air base at the near edge of Everett, which was a sleepy little lumber
town back then. Another contender was down I-5 the other way past
Tacoma, where Boeing was eyeing a site adjacent to McChord Air
Force Base with access to its runways.

But it was the third option that caused all the grief: Walnut Creek,
California! Some very senior Boeing people were pushing very hard to
site our 747 factory there to benefit from that state's greater political
clout in Washington, DC. As the nation's most populous state, California had many more representatives in Congress than did Washington
State. This meant more affected constituencies, more elected officials
to speak at the national level on their behalf, and more opportunities for
paid lobbyists to successfully represent the interests of manufacturers.

Boeing's recent loss of the C-5 program to California-based Lockheed was a painful reminder of the consequences of inferior representation on Capitol Hill. Douglas, North American Rockwell, General
Dynamics, Northrop, and many other aerospace firms were also based
in California, the Walnut Creek faction pointed out, so siting the 747
factory there could offset to some degree the ongoing political advantages of many more Boeing commercial and military competitors than
just Lockheed.

Mal Stamper, the General Motors–trained vice president in charge
of the 747 program, led the committee making the decision on where to
site our new factory. Helping him was 747 Director of Facilities Bayne
Lamb, whose job it would be to spearhead the creation of this factory
and related program facilities. The remaining 747 program division
chiefs—including me as director of engineering—were told to refrain
from rendering judgments outside their own areas of responsibility.

In one of those meetings, however, I was asked what I thought of this Walnut Creek idea. Given this opening, I told 'em point-blank that I thought it would be an unmitigated disaster. If 747 production were sent down there, communications would slow, coordination would suffer, costs would rise, our overall logistical challenges would increase, and there was no way in hell that we would meet our schedule commitments to Pan Am.

The reaction on people's faces ranged from a startled *Why do you say that?* to a clearly angry *Who invited you to this meeting?!* Needless to say, the Walnut Creek crowd wasn't happy to have reality intrude on their political brilliance. While many people agreed with me in the ensuing discussion, though, the California faction stuck by its guns and took pretty strong verbal exception to my blunt statements.

I'm absolutely sure that if 747 manufacturing had been sent to Walnut Creek, we would never have gotten the airplane designed in the short time we were allotted. That would still have been true even if my engineers and I had relocated down to California along with the airplane, which would have been a huge and prohibitively costly disruption.

I was responsible for the engineering development of the 747 airplane. As I saw it, I wasn't doing my job if I didn't speak my convictions and voice important truths, however impolitic. If that made me unpopular with my management, so be it. They could always replace me if they wanted to. Until then, I'd do my job to the best of my ability.

———

As it turned out, the SSTs never materialized as a competitive challenge. Why didn't they catch on? The answer is fundamental physics. It simply takes too much fuel to fly faster than the speed of sound, because you're fighting shock waves that form when the airplane tries to push through the air faster than it can get out of the way. You have to power your way through, which means bigger engines that burn a lot more fuel.

The Concorde is a good case in point. The British and French

thought they'd sell at least 200 Concorde SSTs, but in fact 20 were
built and only 14 ever entered service. Why? Because the Concorde
used as much fuel to cross the North Atlantic with 100 passengers as
a 747 did with 400. For all its technological success, it was an economic white elephant.

A recession at the start of the 1970s got the Concorde program off
to a rocky start. Things only got worse later in the decade, which
saw Arab oil embargoes that made jet fuel much more expensive.
Consequently, the only airlines that ever flew the Concorde (aside
from occasional leases by other carriers) were Air France and British
Airways, the flag carriers of its two sponsoring governments.

And what of the Boeing 2707? North America's SST was progressing more slowly than Europe's, because it called for a more advanced
and capable airplane. Whereas the Concorde had barely enough range
to cross the Atlantic with 100 passengers, and its aluminum structure
limited it to a cruise speed of about Mach 2, the 2707 was designed to
span the Pacific nonstop with some 270 passengers at a cruise speed
approaching Mach 3.

In late May 1971, Congress cut funding for the Boeing SST, effectively killing the program. Whether it would have lived up to its performance goals will never be known, but Boeing already knew that its
economics were highly problematic. In fact, an internal Boeing study
had revealed that there was no way airlines could make a profit with
the Boeing 2707 SST if the price of jet fuel went up even 5% over
1960s levels.

Accordingly, while there were a lot of heartbroken people in Seattle when Congress pulled the plug in 1971, there were also a few au-
dible sighs of relief. These grew louder as the decade unfolded to
soaring crude-oil prices and long lines at gas stations (jet fuel is basi-
cally kerosene, which is derived from oil).

Of course, all that was still in the future.

To my immense relief, Boeing decided at the start of 1966 to build its
new plant at Everett. I suspect my blunt comments played a role in

this selection. Building the 747 factory would prove a Herculean task in its own right, one deftly led by Mal Stamper and Bayne Lamb.

Construction began in June 1966 with the grading and leveling of a 700-acre site, which required more soil to be moved than had been shifted for the Panama Canal and Washington State's Grand Coulee Dam combined. By the end of the year, some 2,500 construction workers were employed full time on this $200 million job, with others called in as their skills were needed.

Despite two months of relentless rain, creating endless mud and misery, the construction crew erected a factory building encompassing more than 200 million cubic feet. So big was it that Boeing workers would sometimes see clouds forming *inside* it. Since then, the Everett site—Boeing's largest plant—has grown to more than 1,025 acres while the factory building itself has more than doubled to 472 million cubic feet.

The Guinness Book of World Records lists this factory as the largest (but of course not the tallest) building in the world. Today the 767 and 777 are manufactured there alongside the 747. The new 787 Dreamliner will be assembled at Everett as well.

The master 747 program schedule said that before the factory was even finished, tooling would have to be laid down and a production line established. Our schedule was so tight that the first 747s would in fact be built as the factory was being closed in around them. I didn't know if this idea was even workable, but that was Stamper and Lamb's problem and I didn't worry about it; my hands were full just developing the airplane.

Our schedule also called for my team to begin relocating to Everett late in 1967 to brand-new engineering facilities near the factory. Good as this news was, it meant things would get worse for me before they got better. I would be dividing my days between Seattle and Everett, and that meant a hell of a lot of extra driving. Once my team completed this phased move, we would at last have centralized facilities for the tail end of the program.

But that was a long way off. In the meantime, my team and I had an airplane to design.

6

A GIANT TAKES SHAPE

Jack Steiner's 737 was halfway through its design development. He'd had a devil of a time getting his program staffed up to strength because of the SST, with its exorbitant demands on head count. Then along came the 747, and things got so bad for him that Steiner would accuse my program of "demanning" his.

My situation was, if anything, more challenging than his. My attempts early on to get people invariably triggered the same response. "Look, Joe, we know what you're doing is important," I'd be told, "but it's not an airplane under contract. The SST is under contract. So is the 737. Those jobs have to meet their schedule commitments, so you're just going to have to make do with what you've got."

Then in April 1966, Boeing and Pan Am signed the contract that officially launched the Boeing 747 airliner. We too became a committed program. Jack Steiner was livid that I could now invoke the same priority as he could on the 737, or for that matter the 727 team then developing a derivative of that trijet. We were all in the same boat and the size of the 747 threatened to swamp it.

It was in this environment that my team and I set about designing the 747 in detail. Having already decided to go to a single main deck, we needed to figure out just how wide our widebody jetliner should be. Getting it wrong could spell decades of lost business because jetliner programs have very long lives. The potential consequences of not doing our homework properly could literally cost Boeing billions of dollars.

The design requirements we defined with our airline customers provided answers to our questions, driving the design's evolution. The 747 had to be an excellent freighter, not just an excellent passenger plane, so we decided to try to accommodate *two* shipping containers side by side on its main deck. To help our customers, moreover, we determined that these containers should be eight feet by eight feet, the standard size used by the maritime, rail, and trucking industries. Although the 747's main-deck containers would differ because of aviation's stringent weight requirements, they would still simplify life for operators by accommodating standard-size loads.

A single column of containers didn't call for a very wide fuselage. It also didn't make for very good use of space. But when we placed *two* rows of containers side by side on a single main deck, things suddenly looked *much* better.

It was Row Brown who first sketched out this circular fuselage, and boy, was it wide! A bit more than 20 feet across, it was nearly twice the width of a 707, which was the most spacious airliner then in service. I'm sure all of us gulped; this was an audacious airplane!

Because our new fuselage was so large in diameter, the 747 passenger cabin would have relatively straight sidewalls. The more we looked at it, the more valuable this particular benefit seemed. In passenger service, straighter sidewalls provide roomlike proportions that enhance passenger comfort. In freighter service, they maximize usable volume because almost all the internal space is available to cargo in shipping containers or on pallets.

The benefits of this new configuration also extended below floor level. Going from the double-decker's deep but narrow proportions to a wide cross section meant much more spacious forward and aft cargo holds. Passenger airlines would have plenty of room left over after passenger bags were loaded for profit-enhancing air freight. Freight operators would be able to carry additional cargo in side-by-side belowdecks containers 64 inches high.

In freighter service, this design path provides the capacity, performance, and structural capability that operators need to carry high-density cargoes from stem to stern. It makes loading and unloading simple. Main-deck cargoes nearly 10 feet tall and 13 feet wide enter through a huge side door. Boeing-built 747 freighters (but not 747 passenger jets subsequently converted to freighter use) also have hinged noses for through-the-front loading. Today nearly half of the world's air freight travels aboard 747s.

In passenger service, our configuration allows very nearly the entire cabin length to be used for passenger seating. Although we elevated the flight deck to allow through-the-nose freight loading, it pays dividends in passenger service too, because revenue-generating floor space is opened up where the cockpit would ordinarily have been.

After the configuration of the 747's fuselage cross section, the next most important design decisions we made involved the definition of this airplane's wing. The wing determines how much weight you can lift off the ground, the efficiency and economy of the airplane in service, its takeoff and landing characteristics, and of course its basic flight characteristics.

In those days, commercial jet transport cruise speed had pretty much been defined by the 707. That jetliner built on what had been learned with the B-47 and B-52 by people such as Schairer, Cook, Hamilton, and Withington. Thanks to them, Boeing had learned how to put together a wing that would cruise efficiently at high speed.

The 707 was designed for a nominal cruise speed of Mach 0.82, which is 82% of the speed of sound. (What speed this actually is depends on the density of the air and thus the jet's altitude.) Without Boeing's hard-won knowledge, Douglas was leery of pushing the speed so high on the DC-8, its first jetliner. Worried about buffeting and other transonic effects, Douglas settled for a somewhat slower cruise speed to the detriment of that program.

Other jetliners of that period generally cruised at eight tenths or so the speed of sound. Notable exceptions were the hotrod Convair 880/990 series, which flew quite a bit faster but burned too much fuel (Convair jetliners borrowed perhaps too heavily from that company's jet fighters), and the de Havilland Comet at the other extreme, cruising at only about Mach 0.70 and thus 100 miles per hour slower than the 707.

As we set about to define the 747's wing, we found ourselves in a good position. Not only did Boeing possess world-leading expertise, but we also had our own transonic wind tunnel in which to evaluate our concepts and validate their performance. Boeing's willingness to invest in R&D was paying off handsomely.

We initially defined a generous wing of 5,200 square feet, which was soon increased to a full 5,500 square feet. This greater area meant a somewhat lower wing loading and a slightly slower airplane, but we felt that the benefits of this huge wing—improved low-speed characteristics, additional fuel volume, and future growth potential—made it desirable.

The low-speed regime of the 747's flight envelope got a great deal of attention during the design phase. We knew we had to have high-lift capabilities for the freighter version of the airplane, which would be landing with heavier payloads than passenger 747s. This requirement led us to do some innovative thinking.

The challenge is that jetliner wings are optimized to high-speed flight. This is great when you're cruising near the speed of sound, but not during takeoffs and landings when you instead want a wing that's geared to lower speeds. In general, the way to convert a high-speed wing into one suited to lower speeds is to increase its area and camber.

Increasing the wing's area reduces its *wing loading*, which is how much weight each square foot of wing supports. This has the effect of reducing the airplane's *stall speed*, which is the speed at which the airplane can no longer fly and instead begins to fall. Lower stall speeds are particularly desirable during landing, because they mean a slower touchdown, shorter stopping distance, and generally safer operations.

Changing the wing's *camber* (that is, how arched or curved it is) also helps reduce landing speeds. Wings are airfoils, and broadly speaking, low-speed airfoils are more cambered than high-speed ones.

So how do you change a wing in flight? If you've looked out the window during a jetliner flight, you may have seen the answer. Jets have flaps that extend aft and downward from the rear of the wing. In addition, they have "leading-edge devices" that extend from the front of the wing. These two modifications together significantly increase the wing's area and camber.

To meet our design goals, we developed a "triple-slotted flap" for the 747. This enormous three-segment flap system did the trick, yielding low approach and landing speeds as well as excellent flight characteristics throughout this critical phase of flight.

We gave the 747 something equally innovative at the front of its wings. Previous Boeing jetliners had used slats as the leading-edge device, but our aerodynamics people came up with something even better: the *Kruger flap*. This hinged segment folds out into the slipstream at the front of the wing to effectively increase its lift and camber.

Of all jetliners, the 747 remains one of the easiest to land in good weather or bad. The airplane takes severe gusting crosswinds in stride with lots of margin, giving flight crews a very high degree of confidence in the airplane. Passengers who fly aboard 747s know that you frequently don't even know it has touched down until a rumbling tells you the wheels are rolling on the runway.

Pan Am desired the fastest subsonic jetliner it could get. The airline wanted the 747 to cruise at about Mach 0.88. Meeting this requirement led us to push the state of the art in wing design. In particular, we would have to go to a sweep angle greater than the 35 degrees we'd employed so successfully on the B-47, B-52, Dash 80, and 707.

This customer requirement for greater speed caused great concern outside my program. Boeing's senior management worried that we'd tread too close to the point where wing buffet and other Mach phenomena set in, creating an airplane with undesirable high-speed flight characteristics. As we began our wind-tunnel testing, we found that a wing swept back 40 degrees would get us Mach 0.88, but that seemed a bit too audacious a leap for many of these senior people. As a result, the collective decision was made to explore wings that cruised in the 0.85 area.

The more Webb and his people learned in the wind tunnel, the more convinced we were that we could achieve Mach 0.85 with a wing swept 37.5 degrees, so we locked this value in. With that established, we proceeded to evaluate different airfoils and aerodynamic devices to find the most efficient high-speed cruise combination. I made sure that what we did at the high-speed end of the flight envelope did not compromise the jet's low-speed capabilities and handling.

Our wind tunnel studies told us we could actually achieve better high-speed flight characteristics than we'd expected. At this point, I felt very confident of our wing despite its being such a bold step forward. Another piece of the 747 design had fallen into place.

Later on, an unanticipated structural crisis would arise with our wing. Marked by high drama and strong personalities, it would come very close to derailing the 747 program.

———

Safety was paramount in all aspects of the 747 design. One example is the landing gear, a system often overlooked because it's tucked out of sight. Landing gears are enormously significant from a design standpoint because so much of the rest of the design is shaped by them.

Laying out a landing gear for any new airplane is a challenge. The wheels have to be in the proper position for weight distribution and airplane balance on the ground, and also for proper takeoff and landing characteristics. This gear must also be stowable within the airframe in such a way that it doesn't cause large increases in weight or aerodynamic drag. Above all, the gear must be durable and reliable despite the extreme loads to which it is subjected. This would be particularly true for the 747.

As a designer, you can't allow the airplane to be jeopardized by the damage that inevitably occurs to landing gears in service. Gears can hang up or fail structurally. Their brakes can seize and their tires can blow out. With this in mind, you have to position the gear so that when such things happen, the airplane isn't torn up, the fuel tanks are not ruptured, and debris isn't thrown into the engines.

There has not been a successful airliner yet whose initial "service entry" configuration was adequate for more than a few years. The reason is that the airlines immediately start asking for more payload and range out of the airplane, which in turn means later models with higher-thrust engines, more fuel carried, and higher gross weights. Thus, you need to design the landing gear for this weight growth. You do this by making it more robust than is initially needed and by designing to allow a more capable gear to be substituted down the line without the expense of major redesign.

In looking at the 707, 727, and 737 as well as competitor airplanes, you will see that they've all contended with growth demands. A basic landing gear configuration is needed that does not add a lot of built-in weight at the start but can be increased in capability as time goes on.

As we designed the 747's landing gear, we arrived at an excellent configuration quickly without a lot of computer time and tedious analysis. This arrangement employs four main gear posts and a nose gear, the former with four tires each and the latter with two. The 747 is thus an 18-wheeler whose weight is spread over a wide footprint to keep it from damaging airport ramps and taxiways.

This was an extremely elegant design solution that took into account the airplane's planned operating weights, particularly for the freighter, and included growth capability for heavier 747 models in the future. Two of the 747's main gear legs are mounted on the wings. The remaining two—those farther aft—are mounted on the fuselage. All four retract into a very compact shared space in the jet's belly.

We also designed this landing gear not to cause trouble if parts failed. Tire blowouts would have little ability to affect the engines. In the event of an accident or a collision, the gear legs themselves are designed to tear safely away without damaging the rear wing spar or piercing the fuel tanks.

There have been quite a few instances where 747 landing gears hit obstructions on runways and taxiways, or where a gear failure did occur, yet the 747 landed safely without much collateral damage.

———————

Uncertainty on the propulsion front introduced an enormous amount of risk into the 747 program. Never before in the history of commercial aviation had a new type of airliner been developed for a type of engine that didn't exist yet.

The state of the art in commercial jet engines in the 1960s was the low-bypass-ratio turbofan engine. These put out at most about 15,000 pounds of thrust, which is what each of the four engines of a long-range 707 and DC-8 produced. In contrast, the 747 was to be powered by four *high-bypass* turbofans, each generating more than 40,000 pounds of thrust.

The potential was certainly there for these new engines, which were very promising on paper. They would be much larger, quieter, and more fuel efficient than anything in service. Pratt & Whitney and General Electric had competed to develop large high-bypass fanjets for the air force's C-5 military transport, so development was under way. GE won the C-5 competition with an engine that featured a by-pass ratio of 8 to 1, which means that eight times as much air passes through the large fan at front than actually goes through the engine's core. Pratt & Whitney's losing proposal had a lower bypass ratio of about 5.5 to 1.

As we set to work, we were acutely aware that we were working with "paper engines." All our efforts and Boeing's heavy investment would count for nothing if working high-bypass fanjets failed to materialize in time for the 747. We prayed that no significant technical glitches would arise on the propulsion front.

The new engines presented one hell of a challenge for the engine manufacturers, who now entered an entirely new and particularly ticklish region of airflow control. Air passed through a combination of high-speed and low-speed compressors and turbines spinning on concentric shafts. The danger was that when the throttles were moved, these components would get out of sync.

If that happened, the airflow would be disrupted and internal stalling would occur. Fuel would continue pouring through an engine with insufficient airflow, causing a surge or a detonation that could burn up the turbine blades. One such hiccup could reduce millions of dollars' worth of jet engine into just so much junk. It was a tough design problem.

At the start of the 747 program, we solicited bids from GE and Pratt & Whitney for a high-bypass-ratio engine suitable for our big jetliner. GE responded by proposing to adapt its winning C-5 engine. Pratt instead proposed a new engine designed to the basic parameters of their losing bid.

The P&W engine was selected after our analyses revealed that it met our requirements and GE's did not. Lockheed's C-5 Galaxy was being designed for a low cruise speed of Mach 0.70, whereas our 747 would cruise at about Mach 0.85. As a result, we needed more thrust than GE's engine was capable of delivering.

The decision of which manufacturer's engine goes on a new airplane is traditionally made by the customer. What I didn't know back then was that Pan Am had on its board of directors a fellow who was also on GE's board. In a conflict of interest, this individual got Pan Am's board to push Boeing hard to adopt the GE engine for the 747.

That would have scuttled the 747 program because our data showed GE's modified C-5 engine would not allow the 747 to meet its performance commitments to Pan Am and other airlines. The resulting airplane would not have been able to take off at sufficiently high gross weights. It also could not have cruised at Mach 0.85 and would not have had sufficient range because it would have burned too much fuel.

I fought very hard to keep the GE engine off the 747. Boeing's management did finally endorse my recommendation and locked in the Pratt engine. But with so many nontechnical people at Boeing falling all over themselves to placate Pan Am's misguided push for GE engines, this critical decision was reached only after I'd been subjected to a hell of a lot of stress and pressure from inside my own company.

At that time, I had no idea why I was getting so much grief. Rude comments reached me about how uncooperative and pigheaded I was being. I didn't know until later about this incestuous board relationship, and I found it shocking that the data itself didn't deter my critics. If one engine could do the job and another couldn't, the decision should have been a no-brainer. That rude awakening was another lesson in how political a major airplane development program can be. Growing up the second youngest in a family of five very active children stood me in good stead, because I learned early in life to stick to my guns and not defer blindly to others.

The 747 would initially carry 350 to 375 people and later versions would carry more than 400. As I contemplated these requirements, the single overriding design imperatives for me were *safety* and *airworthiness*. Important as speed, operating economics, passenger comfort, and maintainability might be, they and all other considerations were secondary to delivering the safest long-range airplane the world had yet seen.

Safety is a broad and often abstract term. You don't design safety *into* an airplane; instead you design an airplane to have excellent airworthiness characteristics so that a pilot can handle it in good conditions and bad, including those unforeseeable occasions when damage is sustained, or the airplane must operate in severe atmospheric conditions, or when highly adverse conditions prevail during takeoff or landing. This in turn dictates a robust structure and engines that are reliable and powerful enough so that major events won't put the airplane into jeopardy. The airplane must be able to absorb punishment, and after it does, its pilot must be able to bring it in for a safe landing.

Boeing has an unmatched reputation for designing rugged airplanes. One way it does this is by producing a *Design Objectives and Criteria* book for each airplane type it develops. Several hundred pages of this book detail precisely how we engineers plan to meet or exceed FAA requirements, which are seen as the minimum acceptable standard rather than the design target. This book also formalizes Boeing's own internal safety requirements and how we plan to meet them. Boeing has produced these volumes for every airplane type from the earliest days onward. Each new airplane builds on the most recent one before it and benefits from everything learned up to that point. I helped draft the *Design Objectives and Criteria* book for the 707 and was a major contributor to those for the 727 and 737.

On the 747 program, I spent a great deal of time early on helping my engineers draft the requirements to which the 747 would be built. As the responsible engineer, it was my honor to sign off on the Boeing *747 Design Objectives and Criteria*. I still have my historic original copy of this thick book.

———————

When we designed the 747, the 707 was the most advanced long-range airliner in the world. The 707 lifted the industry to a higher plateau of safety because it spearheaded Boeing's *safe-design philosophy*, which reflected decades of hard-won knowledge.

One tenet of the Boeing safe-design philosophy is the idea of *no single failure modes*. In plain English, this means that airplanes shall be designed in such a way that no single system failure or structural failure can ever result in catastrophic consequences. Another tenet is the idea of *no uninspectable limited-life parts*. In other words, if a part isn't where an airline can get to it in order to check it, then it must be designed to last the entire life of the airplane.

One approach we use to achieve safety is *redundancy*. This is the term we engineers use to refer to safety enhancements achieved through the use of *backup systems or structure*. When a primary system or structure fails, prudent design ensures that there are backup systems and load paths available to take over, preserving the safety and integrity of the flight.

On the 747 program, I decided to take redundancy to a higher level. My team and I would be introducing the biggest airplane in the world. Here was our chance to also make it the safest.

I'll jump ahead to after the 747 entered service to give you a dramatic example of safety-enhancing redundancy at work. On the afternoon of July 30, 1971, Pan Am's *Clipper America*—a new 747-100—struck approach lights beyond the runway's end at San Francisco International Airport. The collision tore a broad swath through the fuselage underside, ripping away two main landing gears and severing three hydraulic systems. Amazed to find themselves still in the air and under control, the crew dumped fuel and evaluated the crippled ship's handling before coming in for an emergency landing on the remaining wheels. The plane touched down successfully and veered to a safe stop in a grassy area. As the passengers evacuated, the big airliner settled slowly back onto its tail, its nose pointing skyward.

The 747 has four main landing gear legs, and it was the aft pair that tore away, so the jet landed on its forward main landing gears. If that airplane's crew had talked with Boeing before landing, we would have advised them to move their passengers forward to keep the center of gravity (CG) of the airplane forward of those remaining gear legs.

That would have prevented the airplane from tilting back on its rump when it came to a standstill.

While there were some injuries among the passengers, Boeing and Pan Am were enormously thankful there were no fatalities. Boeing has always built the world's most rugged jetliners—it still does—but in this case, it was more than ruggedness that saved the day—it was redundancy that kept those passengers safe.

For example, we made the decision to give the 747 four separate and independent hydraulic systems. Back then, airliners generally had two hydraulic systems, a primary and a backup. We knew the 747 would need more than that. It would be the first airliner entirely dependent on hydraulic actuators, since muscle power alone couldn't deflect its control surfaces if the control boost failed.

We also increased redundancy by giving the 747 four separate main landing gear posts. Previous jetliners had two main gear posts. This four-post arrangement enhanced safety by permitting safe landings even if one gear leg sheared away in a collision. In fact, safe landings would be possible even if *two* main gear legs tore off, provided they were on opposite sides of the airplane.

Four hydraulic systems and four main landing gear legs together represented a huge leap in redundancy, but that was just the beginning. Because of the 747's size, we split its flight controls to create inboard and outboard elevators, inboard and outboard ailerons, and an upper and lower rudder. We made different combinations of our four hydraulic systems actuate the different halves of these split control surfaces, minimizing the chance that damage, jams, or the loss of some hydraulics would ever result in a total loss of controllability.

Like all jetliners, the 747 has spoilers on top of its wings to help with lateral control and provide aerodynamic braking. (Spoilers are those hinged, hydraulically actuated panels you see extending into the slipstream.) The 747 has several spoiler segments per wing. Each is powered by a mix of hydraulic systems so that if anything jams or disables some of the segments, the others remain functional.

My team and I also increased redundancy in the wing's leading-

and trailing-edge devices. For example, we powered each wing's inboard and outboard flaps separately so that a collision or other damaging event would not deprive the wing of its entire flap area. This increased prospects for a safe landing by reducing the potential for an asymmetry of drag sufficient to roll the airplane over.

In my mind, I called my team's pioneering efforts *quadruple redundancy* (for example, four hydraulic systems, four main gear legs, four flap arrays, four aileron and elevator segments). What led us to go this route? As I think back on it, I believe it was that winter ice storm I experienced on my ship in World War II. Steaming helplessly into the teeth of that storm and watching ice build up with no option but to pray we made it to port before capsizing left an indelible impression on me. I came away determined to design, to the best of my ability and the greatest degree humanly possible, airplanes that would never leave their flight crews without options or control.

As we locked the above-described features into the 747's design, I heard grumbling from outside our program. Some people considered my quadruple redundancy a case of overkill. They argued that it would never be needed and dismissed it as just so much extra weight and complexity. Three hydraulic systems would have done the job, they said.

Then a year and a half after the 747 entered service, Pan Am Flight 845 had its encounter with those approach lights at SFO, and all such criticisms abruptly stopped. Even with three hydraulic systems out of action and two main landing gears gone, that 747 landed safely. That event showed us we had made the right decisions.

At the time of Pan Am's accident, the world's next two widebodies—the Douglas DC-10 and Lockheed L-1011—were poised to enter airline service. They are both excellent machines but neither has more than three hydraulic systems.

The 747 has been in service for well over three decades now and has amassed a superb safety record. There have been quite a few more cases where airplanes came home safely despite failures caused by external factors. It's been highly gratifying to me to see other commercial transports following our lead with greater redundancy, although not always to the same degree.

———————

Trouble arose unexpectedly when Boeing's leadership concluded correctly that the 747 was too big for us to build all on our own. Thus the help of other U.S. and overseas aerospace manufacturers was enlisted in industrial agreements that subcontracted or farmed out the detail design and manufacture of many 747 parts. Northrop would produce most of the 747's body sections, Grumman the trailing-edge flaps, Ling-Temco-Vought (LTV) major parts of the empennage (that is, the tail section), and so on.

This was a new way of doing business for Boeing. Its promised benefits were on the manufacturing side, where it would yield components Boeing didn't have the space or staff to build. Unfortunately, it didn't make things easier for us. In addition to doing our own design work, we now had to define these subcontracted components, work up their basic engineering descriptions, and provide them to third parties to design in detail and produce. It also became our responsibility to coordinate with those parties, helping them when they asked for it and fixing their mistakes after the fact.

Had we been given a choice, I would have preferred to do the entire 747 design in-house and farm out only the manufacturing. It would have saved us the stresses of pioneering a new way of doing business for Boeing in the midst of a program with a compressed time frame.

The story of the 747's subcontracted entry doors provides a good example. We designed the 747 with five doors on the main deck for normal and emergency use. They were all type A double-wide doors, each mounting a double-width escape slide that would inflate automatically if the door was opened in an emergency.

Our design philosophy called for all these doors to operate alike so that cabin crews would not be confronted with different ways of opening and closing them or arming and disabling their automatically deploying emergency slides. Standardization of this sort is important for intuitive use.

Unfortunately, things went wrong when many suppliers with different detail design responsibilities took different design routes. Worse still, they farmed out some of their Boeing work to second-tier suppliers who likewise employed a wide mix of design methodologies.

The upshot was that not one of those five similarly sized 747 doors had its detail design performed by the same people! My people had provided overall design guidance for such aspects as the type of linkage, locks, slides, and so on; we thus expected similar doors. But when they began arriving, we were dismayed to find that these cabin doors were all different in just about every regard. Just as troubling, many of their features did not work well.

Under my direction, the engineering department straightened out this entire mess. In the midst of this crisis, there were 747 doors all over the factory floor as we identified changes to standardize them and, where necessary, make them more workable. We had to convey all this to our suppliers and see that the fixes were performed properly. It was a nightmare that took a real toll on my people.

I don't think any previous or subsequent program at Boeing ever went through that sort of trauma, but in the end it all worked out. And it was an important milestone for Boeing in that it set a precedent for the way we would do business in the future. The 747 paved the way for the teaming we did on the 767 program and the partnering on the 777 program. The new 787 will take this industrial collaboration to even greater heights.

Of course, Japan's superb aerospace industry played a major design and manufacturing role in the 767 and an even bigger one as risk-sharing partners on the 777. The result today is the most productive and envied intercontinental industrial collaboration in the world. Most people think Japan and Boeing's first industrial collaboration was on the 767, but in fact it was on the 747, or rather a shortened 747 model called the 747SP. Back in the early 1970s, Boeing contracted with Mitsubishi, Kawasaki, and Fuji—Japan's three heavies—to make that model's flaps, spoilers, ailerons, and parts of its rudder. Ironically, it was the one model of the 747 that Japan's airlines never flew.

———

World War II and two decades at Boeing had taught me what I knew about leadership. In life, though, there's always room to learn, and the 747 program was a good teacher. I found myself constantly learning leadership lessons that contributed to team spirit and helped me become a better manager.

One such lesson occurred early one evening after most of my people had gone home. I had something I wanted Al Webber to see as soon as he came in the next morning, so I walked over to his office. I was surprised to find Al still at work. He was pondering a problem with the titanium beam that supported the wing-mounted landing gear. I gave him the data and started to leave, when I noticed he seemed down in the dumps. He admitted that although he could see resolving the design problems he was wrestling with, he thought he was working on a loser.

It was late in the evening. My first thought was to let it go and just go home. But then it occurred to me that if Al saw the big picture, he might not be so down, so I decided to take the time to discuss the program with him. After filling him in on what I thought was the real situation, he told me he felt a *lot* better.

Thinking about it as I drove home, I realized that all of us on that incredibly complex and demanding program were so close to our own problems that we probably couldn't see the forest for the trees. I decided to fix that starting immediately. From that point forward, I worked hard to keep my 747 engineering team as broadly informed as I was myself. Sitting in on their meetings or visiting their locales for impromptu gatherings, I covered the sales picture, our engineering challenges and successes, pertinent events inside and outside the company, what we anticipated might happen in the future, and anything else that seemed relevant.

The time I spent with Al Webber that evening had important

effects on project morale. The first was immediate. Al was the senior project engineer and was well respected. His enthusiasm increased after our session, and that positive attitude transferred to the other project managers he dealt with.

My fuller communications with the troops helped us all to become a more cohesive and spirited team. I saw that the role of manager isn't simply to pass out instructions; it's also to *inform*. While I think I've always listened well (I believe in hearing people out politely and fully), the leadership lesson with Al that night taught me that people need to know where they stand. It's a psychological necessity, and morale suffers in the absence of such knowledge.

One day in 1968, Tex Boullioun surprised me with word that Juan Trippe was dispatching Charles Lindbergh to Seattle for a private briefing on the 747. Lindbergh—an extremely private man—would be traveling incognito as "Mr. Stewart."

I knew Lindbergh was Trippe's close personal friend and longtime aviation technical advisor. In Pan Am's exuberant early days well before World War II, Charles and Anne Morrow Lindbergh had spent their honeymoon conducting survey flights to map out overwater routes for Trippe. Lindbergh, a longtime board member of the airline, also provided Trippe with independent assessments of his airline's plans and operations.

Juan Trippe must be concerned about the 747, I thought.

Preparing to allay any concerns, I collected supporting data from my engineering team and instructed Ruth Howland, my administrative assistant, to show "Mr. Stewart" into my office without fanfare. When he arrived, we were not to be interrupted.

At the appointed time, Bill Del Valle, the local Pan Am representative, arrived with a visitor. He deposited "Mr. Stewart" in my office and left.

Tall and still slender in his mid-60s, Charles Lindbergh had aged well. He was bald, which was what allowed him to travel incognito.

His face had not changed all that much in 40 years, and his eyes really shook me up. Piercingly blue, they had the same "look of the eagle" I'd seen in newspaper photos when I was six.

For the next hour or more, Lindbergh asked insightful questions about the 747's high-speed characteristics, its safety features, and many other aspects of our evolving jet's design. It was obvious to me that he had a very good understanding of airplane systems, stability and control, and aero engineering in general.

The tone of this discussion was polite but serious, with lots of in-depth probing on his part. We talked at significant length until I had fully addressed his concerns. I left nothing out and even included some points that he hadn't brought up.

When we were through, Lindbergh rose and thanked me warmly. We shook hands and I walked him to the door. When I opened it, Bill Del Valle was right there.

Heads turned as Lindbergh walked out of our building. Security apparently wasn't as tight as I'd thought. I smiled as everybody pretended to work while sneaking peeks at the great man.

Should I tell my management about this visit? Or John Borger, Pan Am's chief engineer? Both might be a bit disconcerted by it, since it could imply Pan Am had reservations. I called Tex for guidance, and he told me to do nothing. If Trippe felt that action was needed, Boeing would hear from him. If not, there was no point alarming people.

Nobody contacted anyone, so apparently I had reassured Lindbergh. As for Juan Trippe, he retired later that same year from the airline he had founded. A chapter had closed and commercial aviation would never be the same.

I would meet Lindbergh just once more.

———

About the start of 1968, the U.S. government began reducing its military orders. With the cutbacks that followed, Boeing's senior management began looking for other things for those employees to do. Somebody up there looked my way.

The first I knew about it was when a Boeing vice president arrived with a large engineering team cut from these military programs. He told me that the company had assigned him and his people to devise a flight-test program for the 747.

The first flight of the 747 was more than a year away, and I was too busy to give any thought yet to that phase of my program. Nevertheless, I welcomed this VP and his people with open arms, giving them the run of the place and assuring them full access to my people for any data they might want.

This VP described in glowing terms what his team's military-style test program would do for us. It would be rigorous and scientific because of a process called PERT, the Program Evaluation and Review Technique. *PERT* was a reverently repeated buzzword.

This group set busily to work drawing up complex plans and cascading diagrams that didn't bear much resemblance to the flight testing we would need to perform. The more I learned about it, the more I saw that it would blow our schedule and not get us where we and our airline customers needed to be. I might have been concerned except that I'd learned a thing or two over the years about Boeing and how it works. The corporate world can be bizarre, so I knew to pick my battles and I didn't worry. This was a sizable group—somewhere between 50 and 100 individuals. I sure could have used their help with all the design work at hand, but unfortunately they weren't there to help us get the 747 finished on time. They were there to devise a PERT program, which they accomplished in four or five months.

Their efforts culminated in a visit by the VP and his top aides, who ceremoniously presented me with a book two inches thick. With equal formality, I thanked them for their expert help on our behalf. Highly pleased, they melted away into other jobs at Boeing, and my team and I were left once again to our own devices.

I thumbed through that report once and put it on a shelf, where it sat throughout the rest of my program, including the 747's testing and civil certification. That was the end of that. Of course it represented a hell of a lot of wasted money and effort that Boeing could have spent better anywhere else, but if I had tried to point that out, I would only have picked a needless and unwinnable political battle.

If there's one lesson I can pass along to people in situations like mine, it's that the best way to see a program through—and it took me a long time to learn this—is simply to accept the help, cooperate, and let others do what they think is worthwhile. In the meantime, continue racing toward the finish line.

———————

As we designed the 747, an odd request arrived at Boeing from the U.S. Department of State. Would a delegation from Boeing be willing to meet with one from the Soviet Union for an open exchange of technical information?

Boeing President Thornton "T" Wilson didn't know what to make of this request from high levels. The 1970s hadn't yet hit, bringing with it the thawing of U.S.–Soviet relations known as détente. This was still the late 1960s; the Cold War was in full swing with rampant suspicions on both sides of the Iron Curtain. It was a ticklish proposition for T Wilson. He might well have politely declined except that here, unexpectedly, was a chance to get some badly needed help with a critical issue challenging our SST program.

The issue was titanium, a strong and light metal used in jet engines, missiles, aircraft, and spacecraft. Because titanium has a high resistance to heat, the Boeing 2707 SST was going to have a titanium fuselage. This ambitious airplane was to cruise at Mach 2.7 or more at extremely high altitudes far above the regular jet lanes. Despite the coldness of the very thin air at those altitudes, the 2707 would have to contend with supersonic "skin friction" that would heat its hull to many hundreds of degrees Fahrenheit. Titanium was thus an essential ingredient in America's SST program.

The problem was that this metal is notoriously difficult to work with. While we used it in key places in our jetliners, we didn't know nearly enough about titanium to feel we could manufacture an entire fuselage out of it at an acceptable cost.

The same was true of the British and French, who steered entirely clear of titanium for the Concorde. Instead they gave it a conventional structure, which limited Europe's SST to a cruise speed of Mach 2.2 or so. Beyond that, skin friction would soften its aluminum hull too much.

In contrast, the Russians knew a great deal about titanium, which is found in abundance there. The Soviet aerospace industry was far ahead of the West in this regard. Accordingly, T Wilson accepted the State Department's request for a meeting in "neutral territory."

We soon learned that this meeting was to be held at a restaurant in Paris. I was told that the Soviets wanted to find out why we at Boeing placed the engines of our jets beneath the wings instead of on the aft fuselage like most other manufacturers. The Russians were also extremely curious about the evolving Boeing 747.

T Wilson asked me to go with him and speak about both these issues. In addition to the two of us and Mal Stamper, the Boeing delegation would include Bob Withington, a senior engineer who was deeply involved in the SST program, and Ken Luplow, the Boeing Commercial Airplanes sales executive responsible for Soviet-bloc countries.

T wanted Ken along to provide insights on a variety of cultural and technical fronts. Ken's position in BCA sales was not an enviable one, because the countries behind the Iron Curtain back then didn't buy Boeing. Lacking hard currency, they were pretty much obligated to fly Russian airliners, which were inferior to ours. It gave us peace of mind to know Ken would be there, although as it turned out, his expertise was not needed.

We flew to Paris and settled into our hotel. As the hour of our utterly unprecedented meeting drew near, I realized I didn't have a clue what to expect. How productive could our session be in light of Cold War tensions and the deep distrust between our two governments?

Accompanied by State Department officials acting as our hosts, we climbed into a fleet of Parisian taxicabs and were soon shooting across broad boulevards. I caught glimpses of Montmartre and the Eiffel Tower bathed in late-evening sunlight as we plunged through narrow, curving streets. I must admit to feeling more like a character in a spy novel than a Boeing engineer. Our taxis deposited us at the entrance to a restaurant that looked well established and altogether too normal for a face-to-face with the Soviets. What was I expecting, I asked myself, Checkpoint Charlie? Entering to savory aromas, we ascended to a private dining room on the second floor and took seats around a large table.

T Wilson had decided that we would ask our questions first. Afterward, if and only if we felt the Russians had been fully forthcoming, were we to return the favor and share Boeing's hard-won knowledge with equal candor. This plan was approved up front by the State Department, which hoped that a mutually beneficial exchange of information might help thaw relations between our two countries.

There were nontechnical people at that dinner, but we pretty well ignored them except for the translators. We quickly found kindred spirits in the Russian engineers sitting around the table. They were intelligent and gregarious and shared our great love of the subject.

Bob Withington peppered them with questions, initiating an animated and very enthusiastic exchange of knowledge about titanium and its fabrication. Finally, after at least an hour, he informed T that all his questions had been fully answered and that he considered the exchange valuable. By now we had finished the main course at our superb restaurant—although I have no memory of what we ate—and out came the vodka and other potables. These flowed pretty freely, which no doubt contributed to the collegial discussion.

By the time my turn came, it was close to 11 PM. T instructed me not to hold anything back. The Russians started by asking me why we hadn't mounted our engines on the aft fuselage like Great Britain's BAC-111 and Vickers VC-10, the French Caravelle, Douglas's DC-9, and their own Ilyushin IL-62, the Soviet Union's first intercontinental jetliner.

I explained the many advantages of wing-mounted engines, including such things as structural loads, airframe efficiency, drag and stall characteristics, usable cabin volume, and so on. The Russian engineers asked me to illustrate my answers to their eager and probing questions. A pen was found but there was no paper. Somebody suggested that I sketch on cloth napkins, which I did, and when those ran out, I drew charts, curves, and structural sketches on the tablecloth itself.

This went on for another hour until finally the Russians were satisfied. We stood, more than ready to return to our hotels and get some sleep. I noticed that the Russians carefully rolled up the napkins and tablecloth and took them away with them. A lot of valuable American technological know-how went to Russia courtesy of that French linen.

When we got home and word spread of this Russia–Boeing meeting, a lot of Boeing people felt that I had violated Boeing and U.S. security by giving away this hard-won Boeing engineering information to the Soviets. They didn't realize that T Wilson himself had ordered me point-blank to do so at the direct instigation of the U.S. government.

This misconception resurfaced a few times thereafter when Russian engineers visited Boeing for meetings in which I was not involved. As I ruefully learned each time, they tended to praise me so liberally for my "invaluable" contributions to Soviet aerospace that more than a few of my colleagues probably thought I should be led off in handcuffs.

It didn't help that Russia's first widebody jetliner, the IL-86, emerged with four engines under its wings like a 747. The first one entered service late in 1980 after a very protracted development. It is a poor airplane, though, and very few were built.

7

WILLING TO BE FIRED

In the late summer or early fall of 1967, I stood at the front of the BCA Management Control Center—a corporate war room—facing Boeing's chairman, president, chief financial officer, the head of our commercial airplanes division, the 747 program chief, and two dozen other senior executives. I was alone, way out on a limb, and there was nobody to back me up or take my side.

Well, I thought, steeling myself to say what they didn't want to hear, *today's as good a day as any to get fired!*

This was absolutely my worst day as an airplane designer. As the room fell silent, I considered the events that had brought us to this juncture.

My team's job was a hell of a lot bigger than the resources we had to complete it. We were tremendously under the gun and behind schedule, with a lot of our drawing releases running a couple of months late. All of us were working massive amounts of overtime trying to meet the 747 program's ever-expanding commitments.

At the same time, outside events were conspiring to make life more stressful. The world economy dipped into recession. Airline orders dried up, depriving Boeing of badly needed revenues for the 747 development and other programs. To make up this unexpected shortfall, the company had borrowed ever more heavily, until now the banks were worried. Some were so concerned that they were telling us no more money would be available.

An unprecedented reckoning loomed on the horizon. It looked like we were driving off a cliff. So bad did it get that as we left one meeting, Boeing Chief Financial Officer Hal Haynes—usually the picture of calm—said, "Sutter, do you realize that your engineers are spending five million dollars a day?" Having your company's CFO tell you something like that doesn't exactly give you a warm feeling. There was no answer, of course, and none was expected; Haynes had already left the room. *We'd be doing a better job*, I thought, *and maybe saving Boeing some money in the long run if we were spending six million dollars a day!*

The financial situation actually became so dire that Bill Allen ordered Tex Boullioun and Mal Stamper to drastically cut company expenditures. George Snyder, the Everett Division's vice president for engineering and my immediate boss, conveyed to me Stamper's idea for fulfilling Allen's desire: I was to drop 1,000 engineers from my program!

At that point I had 4,500 people reporting to me, some 2,700 of whom were actually engineers. The rest were managers, clerical and technical support people, and so on. We were now at our peak workload, churning out drawings for the 747. A lot of developmental testing was also in progress, identifying the need for running design changes, adding further to the load. My people were working *extremely* hard. I needed every single engineer.

I explained all this to Snyder, but he held fast and ordered me to show upper management a plan for dropping 1,000 engineers. At my request, he and I met to define the ground rules for these drastic cuts. How much further could the schedule slide, I asked? It couldn't, he replied. Then could we work more overtime? He grudgingly conceded that we could, but it was a meaningless concession; my people were already working about as much OT as was humanly possible.

"All right," I said as the meeting broke up, "I'll ask my engineering chiefs to assess how many heads they can drop according to these ground rules."

Snyder gave us four weeks to complete this painful exercise. We were only a week and a half into it when I received a sudden telephone call. Bill Allen was heading out of town for a few weeks and wanted to review our findings before he left. I was told to grab what information I could and report to the Management Control Center at Renton that afternoon to show our progress toward dropping those thousand engineers.

It was 10 AM and I was in Everett. I didn't think my fellows would have much of an analysis done by then. They were working like hell designing the airplane, and I'm sure this study wasn't their top priority. But I got hold of them, and they all trooped over to my office to show me what they had.

As I totaled up their preliminary inputs, I realized not one of them had proposed dropping any head count—they all needed more. I pressed them hard for concessions but they stuck by their guns, explaining how late their drawings were and how much remained to be done. I left Everett convinced that if we were going to make the 747 happen, we couldn't drop people. Hell, we needed more engineers, not fewer!

A long-smoldering pathology in my reporting structure was now hitting home with a vengeance. I'd suspected for some time that George Snyder wasn't communicating everything I told him to his boss, 747 program chief Mal Stamper. George's idea of managing was not to rock the boat or upset those above him. He felt that, given time, the situation would improve.

My relationship with Mal Stamper was equally troubled. In fact, the whole problem was that I *didn't* have a relationship with him. Despite his being in overall charge of the 747 program and our new

Everett Division—including my big part of it, the design of the 747—
he didn't seem to care about what I and my people were doing. As a
result, Stamper met with me in person only rarely in the course of the
747 program.

Stamper was a management wunderkind at General Motors before
coming to Boeing, a supporter of the arts, and very involved in the local community. On the work front at Boeing, he remained unflappable
in the midst of crises. In those areas where he took an interest, things
happened. I look to the construction of the 747 plant at Everett as the
best example, although the lion's share of glory for that achievement
rightly belongs to Bayne Lamb, the 747 program's director of facilities.

Mal Stamper had me reporting to George Snyder instead of directly to him, which would have been better for the program. As for
Stamper's idea of having me drop those thousand engineers, I think
he genuinely believed it was the right thing to do, and Snyder—for
reasons known only to himself—didn't see fit to tell him what a lousy
idea it was.

The stage was thus set for me to give Boeing's top people a nasty
surprise, and for Snyder and Stamper in particular to be publicly em-
barrassed. Being blindsided with bad news from below is something
no manager enjoys, so I needed to give them a heads-up as to what I'd
be presenting to Bill Allen and company.

By then it was 11 AM. I tried getting hold of both men but they
were tied up in a high-level meeting at Renton. I asked to have first
one and then the other of them pulled out to speak with me, but they
refused.

From Everett to Renton is about an hour's drive at the best of
times. I pulled out of my parking space a bit after noon, drove like a
crazed idiot, and arrived at Renton a little before 1 PM. Entering the
meeting room out of breath, I learned that Stamper and Snyder were
still at lunch. I set out to find them, determined to warn them ahead
of time about what I had to say.

They weren't in the executive dining room, so I strode the hall-
ways in search of them and bumped into Snyder. "Hey, George," I said

hastily, "I'd better show you the numbers I'm going to present, because you're not going to like what you're going to hear—"

"It's almost one o'clock," Snyder snapped, cutting me off. "There's no time. Just get in there and make your presentation."

I walked into the war room hoping to catch Stamper, but he was talking with someone else. Twenty or thirty high-level people had arrived and settled in, including Hal Haynes, the company's vice president of finance. Stamper and Snyder sat together off to the side as if hoping to attract as little attention as possible.

In strode Chairman Bill Allen with brisk efficiency. As he took his seat, he announced he would have to leave soon to catch an airplane. Settling beside him was T Wilson, who would soon succeed Allen as Boeing's chairman. Tex Boullioun, the head of commercial airplanes, joined them at center front. "I know this is preliminary," Bill said, dispensing with formalities, "but I'm anxious to hear what you have to say, Joe. Will you please summarize for us the 747 situation?"

Standing before this intimidating crowd, I put my first viewfoil on the overhead projector. Viewfoils are those transparencies we used in the days before video projection. This one showed us running about two months behind on the release of some 747 manufacturing drawings. I described the reasons why and the issues challenging my design team.

My status update finished, I hesitated. The remaining viewfoils got to the heart of why we were having that meeting: those 1,000 engineers I was supposed to drop.

I took a breath. Too many times I'd seen Boeing people fail at the helm of an important project or program. They generally were not fired from the company but their careers never recovered. In fact, they sometimes went downhill pretty dramatically. *I'm in my forties and have a lot of good years ahead of me as a Boeing designer,* I thought. *It's my profession. My life. My heart and soul are tied up in the 747. If I lose it . . .*

Bill Allen's expectant eyes drilled into me, pressing me to continue.

My next viewfoil itemized the ground rules that Snyder and I had agreed to for the head count reduction study my engineering leaders were performing. When I finished talking about that sheet, I put my final viewfoil up on the screen.

Visible to the room was the feedback I'd gathered that morning from the chief engineers for structures, systems, propulsion, air-conditioning, payloads, and the other engineering disciplines that were together creating the 747. All eyes focused on this sheet, which showed my head count going up, not down.

"What this tells me," I concluded, struggling to keep my voice calm, "is that I cannot give up any engineers. In fact, I need eight hundred more."

The room fell silent. T Wilson was the first to speak. "Hell, Sutter," he declared, "you know you're not going to get any more engineers."

"I know that, T," I replied. "I just wanted you to know why we're working so damn much overtime."

Bill Allen reserved comment but was clearly not pleased. "I have a plane to catch," he said, and stood up. "I'll leave it with you," he said to T Wilson as he left.

For a fleeting instant, I thought Allen had removed himself so that Wilson could fire me. But nobody spoke a word. T got to his feet, asked Tex to accompany him, and they too walked out. Everybody began leaving. Nobody looked in my direction or wanted a thing to do with me. It was as if I had the plague. As I gathered up my view-foils, the only person to speak was Mal Stamper, and that was only to convey his extreme displeasure with me.

I felt intensely alone, with no allies at Boeing, no supporters, no-body to speak up on my behalf. It was just me. And I had a family, a mortgage, college expenses, a broken-down old car, and not a hell of a lot of money in the bank.

Why had T asked Tex to accompany him? I found myself imagining their conversation in the hall. In my mind, T's words were something like this: "Maybe it's time somebody else took over for Sutter—he's too young and he wasn't the right guy for the job!"

But I knew there was no point dwelling on things beyond my control. With a hell of a lot of work waiting for me in Everett, I headed back to my car. *This may be my last day on my 747 program*, I thought bleakly during that long, miserable drive north.

———————

It felt good to be back with my team but the most loyal support, as always, came from Nancy. That evening I told her all about it. "Well, Joe," she asked, "are you doing what you think is right, and are you doing it to the best of your ability?"

"Yes," I replied.

"It seems to me you're probably doing as good a job as anybody can," she concluded. "Just hang in there and try to forget it for the time being. Get your mind off it by reading a book or something before bed."

I took her advice and resumed work at Everett. I had reconciled myself to the way things were even if I wasn't happy about them. Maybe what I was doing wasn't good enough—if that was what Boeing thought and they had somebody else who could do better, so be it.

Over the coming weeks, though, I didn't hear a word from anyone. That bothered me although I really didn't expect a call. That would have been out of character for T Wilson, whose style was always to let people stew. Tex Boullioun and I got along famously, but Tex was a salesman at heart and didn't insert himself into engineering matters. Stamper never communicated with me at the best of times, and I didn't expect him to now.

No news was definitely good news, I came to realize as the days passed. So what if you needed to read minds to know where you stood in this company? I still had my job as 747 director of engineering; that was all that mattered.

Only much later did I learn that T Wilson had told people he thought I was doing a good job. Apparently not everybody in that room saw me as a maverick who wouldn't follow orders.

Boeing's leadership was then focused on the bigger picture, and it was truly grim. Buffeted by external events, Boeing was now so financially overextended that its mushrooming debt load outstripped its entire stated net worth.

In less than a year, the SST program had gone from invincible to a shambles. Seemingly irresolvable technical hurdles and the airplane's computed poor operating costs had brought that high-flying program down to earth with a crash. The U.S. government was funding just 75% of Boeing's expenditures on this program, whose total cost ultimately ballooned to $500 million. By the time it ended in April 1971, Boeing would have spent $200 million of its own money on the 2707.

The 727-200 and 737 were also consuming Boeing resources. They had just entered service and were supposed to be generating cash now that deliveries were under way, but the 737 in particular required costly engineering revisions.

Boeing also faced major outlays on the space front, where it was building the massive *Saturn V* Moon booster for Project Apollo. And following the tragic deaths of astronauts Gus Grissom, Roger Chaffee, and Ed White in the launchpad fire of January 1967, a desperate NASA turned quietly to Boeing for help. Like someone trying to juggle too many balls, the U.S. space agency had lost control of managing America's race to the Moon. Bill Allen agreed to step in even though the timing could not have been worse. He appreciated Apollo's huge significance to the nation and the world, so he bit the bullet and sent NASA several thousand of our finest engineering managers.

Most of these Boeing rescuers came from the military side of Boeing, but a good many were pulled off the SST. Those Boeing professionals got the Apollo program straightened out. Without their efforts, President John F. Kennedy's vision of human beings walking on the Moon before the end of the 1960s would not have been realized.

Called the Boeing Technical Integration and Evaluation (TIE) program, this unsung Boeing contribution was kept quiet for decades to spare NASA embarrassment. Enough time has now passed, though, that it can be talked about. I suspect the temporary loss all at once of so many good Boeing people contributed to the trouble the SST program ran into.

The upshot of all this was that everybody was beginning to look to the 747 as Boeing's financial savior. In the commercial airplane business, you don't get very much money when airlines order airplanes. They put down a deposit and follow up with periodic progress payments, but it's when you actually deliver the airplane that you rake in the cash.

If Boeing could survive until the 747 came on line, our cash flow would turn positive and things would start to get better. With this strong shift in thinking, the company suddenly found itself trusting *me* with its fortunes. It was a very, very big responsibility!

We were in a real bind. We had to finish up and deliver the 747 to get out of our hole, yet financial institutions were increasingly unwilling to lend us the funds needed to reach that still-distant finish line.

Real leadership means having the courage to do what you know is right. That's what I did when I refused to drop those 1,000 engineers from my program. I could have obeyed what was arguably a direct order, but doing so would only have ensured my departure down the line, because the 747 program would have failed. Instead, I had stuck to my guns and kept my staffing at existing levels, which was workable.

In short, things were dire but my program was alive. I decided that the best course for everyone on my team was to concentrate on completing their assigned duties. We would trust Boeing's finance people to secure the funds we needed to get the 747 in the air.

8

THE WING AND WEIGHT CRISES

We had pretty much finished our 747 aerodynamics testing when a crisis erupted over the 747's wing. From an aerodynamic and performance standpoint, we had a wing that worked, but our structures people began getting lots of troubling data from wind-tunnel testing.

Analysis showed that the outboard wing was carrying too much load. The pressure distribution wasn't in the right place for this load to be properly supported by the internal structure. Because of the accelerated pace of development, this realization came quite late in the design process. Drawings had been released and the first wing parts were actually in production at our fabrication facility in Auburn, Washington. Stringers and wing skins had already been built and were about to be shipped up to Everett.

This was more than a problem; it had the potential to be a showstopper! As happened more than once during the 747's development, I found myself sitting squarely in the hot seat. But what to do about it? Al Webber headed up the structures section of my team, and one of his people had a suggestion. Jim Hoy proposed that we twist the entire wing from the root out to the tip to reorient it by three degrees. Doing so, he told us, would shift the wing's center of lift to the proper place on those outer wing panels for their internal structure to carry the flight loads.

Here we were with the first parts already being built, and people were talking of throwing them all away and starting from scratch. Twisting a wing three degrees doesn't sound like that big a deal until you realize it means redesigning the juncture where the wing and fuselage meet. Called the center section, this densely packed area is structurally the most important part of any airplane, meaning that twisting the 747's wing would be horrendously complex and expensive.

This full-blown crisis captured the immediate attention of Boeing's top management. Among the experts our leadership called on for an opinion was Jack Steiner, a very forceful and opinionated guy whose ego demanded that things be done his way. Steiner, of course, had led the 727 and 737 programs, and more than a few people on my team felt he was itching to get his hands on the 747 as well. Steiner stated his firm belief that our wing was unsalvageable. An entirely new wing would have to be developed for the 747, he said. Boeing's leadership gave him the go-ahead to gather a staff of engineers and lay out this new wing.

This was not an unusual thing for Boeing's leaders to do. Top management frequently convenes second engineering teams to assess situations and take over if need be. Steiner's presence in my camp was what the company refers to as an *engineering audit*.

Did it bother me to have Steiner insert himself in my program? Of course; I wouldn't be human if it hadn't. While I admired Jack for his accomplishments, he could be abrasive to work with and I'd chafed under him on the 727 and 737 programs. Now that I had a program of my own, the last thing I wanted was to have him show up claiming he would "pull my chestnuts out of the fire."

Even worse from my perspective, Steiner's proposed solution—an entirely new wing for the airplane—would deal a fatal blow to my team's schedule and budget. In my opinion, going his route would have scuttled the 747 and put Boeing out of business.

Steiner moved into one of our buildings with 50 aeronautical and structural engineers in what he melodramatically referred to as a "black parachute commando operation." Before any of us knew this was happening, he took over an auditorium and had its seats replaced with drafting tables. There his "troops" set to work designing a new 747 wing from scratch.

I was not initially aware of any of this. In fact, I was largely oblivious to the politics outside my immediate environment. I knew only that I had a job to do and that it involved meeting a schedule, holding to a budget, and achieving the 747 airplane's promised performance. A new wing simply wasn't an option; we would have to fix what was wrong with the current wing.

With this goal in mind, I gathered together Everette Webb, Al Webber and his structures people, including Jim Hoy, and other key engineers on my staff. I don't know whether it was Webb or I who finally said, "Well, you know, we've got to end this wing with a three-degree difference in orientation at the tip to shift the loads to the right place, but do we have to twist the whole wing to do that?"

Hopes rose at the idea of leaving the inboard wing intact and starting the twist only outboard of the outer engine nacelles. If it worked, it would be one tenth as difficult and costly as twisting the entire wing. At my instigation, Jim Hoy performed a rudimentary analysis to evaluate the concept and found that twisting the outer wings would actually yield 80% to 90% of the required benefit of twisting the entire wing.

On the basis of this quick-and-dirty assessment, I decided right on the spot that this was how we would proceed. My people redesigned the 747's wing for an outboard twist, which completely solved the loads problem. This expedient solution worked so well that it got the attention of the press, which labeled it the Sutter twist, a name it still has today.

Everette Webb felt it should actually be called the Webb twist, and maybe he's right. In team environments, ideas often occur to more than one individual at the same instant. The important thing is that we came up with a fix that did not compromise the aerodynamic qualities of our excellent wing.

In retrospect, I think I handled this crisis pretty well. I knew my job was in jeopardy, but I concentrated on working the engineering problem and didn't concern myself for a moment with politics. As it turns out, a hell of a lot of maneuvering was going on to cut me out of the picture and get that other wing on the 747. I learned the full extent of this story only in the early 1990s when reading Clive Irving's superb book *Wide-Body: The Triumph of the 747.*

If Jack Steiner had come up with a better engineering solution, I'd have been out the door before I knew what hit me. Instead, his determination that our wing was unsalvageable proved flat wrong. We defined and implemented a fix that got the 747 program back on track, and Steiner and his "black parachutists" packed up and retreated from the field of battle.

———

Like all airplanes in development, the 747 gained weight during its design. Compounding this problem, we'd taken a weight hit at the outset of the program by going to a very wide single-deck configuration instead of the expected double-decker. This alternative fuselage cross section had a larger diameter and made for a somewhat heavier airplane.

When I formed my study group and began work in the summer of 1965, we tentatively set 550,000 pounds as our big airplane's gross weight. By April 1966 and the signing of the contract with Pan Am that launched the 747 program, the airplane's projected gross weight was 655,000 pounds. A year later, it had risen to 680,000 pounds and was still climbing.

This weight growth threatened the entire program. A heavier airplane meant Pan Am and other customers wouldn't be able to carry as much revenue-generating payload—that is, not unless Pratt &

Whitney could come up with a corresponding increase in engine thrust, and Pratt already had its hands more than full just trying to meet the initial thrust targets.

Pratt was actually in dire trouble developing the 747's engine. High-bypass turbofan technology was so new and balky that the company hadn't even successfully run one yet, let alone met its targets, and suddenly we were looking to them for *uprated* engines! The 707-300's Pratt & Whitney JT3Ds, which generated under 16,000 pounds of thrust each, were then the most powerful jet engines in commercial service, yet now it looked like the ever-heavier 747 would need engines that each delivered more than 40,000 pounds of thrust!

Juan Trippe was personally monitoring the progress of the 747. Concerned about its weight growth, he spoke directly with Bill Allen. It was agreed that Trippe, his assistant Sanford Kauffman, John Borger, and other Pan Am officials would come out to Seattle so that I could brief them on this issue.

I got up and shared our latest data. Pulling no punches, I told Trippe to his face that this weight growth wasn't just a Boeing problem. In front of Bill Allen and the others, I pointed out that more than half the excess weight was the direct result of ongoing changes specified by Pan Am, which had added to the equipment and amenities they wanted aboard the airplane. The upgrades they had specified for the 747's seating, passenger lounges, lavatories, galleys, cargo systems, and so on made sense, but every bit of it added weight. "It's just as much your problem as ours," I concluded.

My Boeing colleagues, particularly our salespeople, were stunned that I'd dared say this to Boeing's most important customer. But I just didn't know how else to tackle it. Facts were facts, and I needed everybody to understand why our airplane was heavier if we were to reach consensus on what to do about it. First and foremost, we needed to agree on design weights and engine thrust.

Juan Trippe obviously didn't like what he'd heard but he reserved comment. Nobody else was happy with me either as that meeting ended, but I had no feedback from my management suggesting I should do anything differently. On the basis of that key meeting, we redefined the 747's takeoff weight from 680,000 to 710,000 pounds, which was clearly the right thing to do. If we hadn't taken that painful step in agreement with Pan Am, the airplane would have stayed at 680,000 pounds at delivery and would not have met its mission goals.

It seems to me essential that a project leader not fixate on one design parameter to the exclusion or detriment of others. Airplane design is the ultimate exercise in compromise. If you increase the fuel load, for example, you need a stronger, roomier structure to house it, so airplane weight and drag go up. You also need more powerful engines to lift it all, which means higher fuel consumption. The design team's job is therefore to define the optimal balance between these elements that yields the best results. The exception is safety, which is never subject to compromise.

Then as now, my guiding belief is that you're not living up to the faith placed in you if don't play things the way you see them. When you're in a position of responsibility, you need to do what's right. In the aerospace arena, if you don't have the courage to face up to difficult situations—and that includes making sure that unwelcome truths are heard and acted on—then you have no business being a chief engineer.

Weight was now the issue that woke me up at night in a cold sweat. The numbers were coming in very, very high. Worse still, we didn't know precisely where we stood. Our evolving design was so different in scale from anything the industry had built before that we couldn't estimate its weight with any certainty.

In an effort to slim the 747 down, I gave my project engineers a weight budget and asked them to pursue lower target weights than they had been coming in with. The single condition I imposed was that their suggested weight cuts could not be allowed to reduce the safety and airworthiness of the 747 one iota.

I thought we were doing pretty well when weight again became a focus of concern on the part of upper management. This time it wasn't just Boeing Commercial Airplanes that was worried; it was T Wilson, president of all Boeing. T worried that we might be so focused on getting the 747 out the door that we were dropping the ball on its weight. He assembled a team of top engineers and told them to perform a weight audit on the 747. This audit team was stacked with high-powered types including Maynard Pennell, Bill Cook, and Ken Holtby. Managing them was Charles Brewster, a hard-nosed old-timer. A confidant of Wilson's, Brewster had the president's ear and didn't hesitate to use the power this gave him.

Resisting the temptation to feel threatened ("Hey, these guys are undercutting my autonomy"), I chose instead to see this management-imposed review as an opportunity ("My team can certainly use the scrutiny of more engineers, so let's welcome them"). I ordered my people to support this audit to the best of their ability even as they continued their own efforts to slim down the 747. "Whatever the auditors need," I told them, "give it to them without protest. No matter how busy you are, drop everything and get them the data they want. And when they come back with suggestions for saving weight, we'll evaluate their ideas to see whether we think they make sense." The final decision, of course, was mine as director of engineering.

The inputs we received from the audit team were pretty much the same ideas my team was coming up with. We accepted these suggestions with thanks. There was only one audit team proposal that I disagreed with and refused out of hand. We had given the 747 a triple-slotted flap to keep approach speeds low. I felt strongly that even though the articulated flap array we designed was heavy, it was definitely the way to go for overall safety. The audit gang disagreed, saying we should get rid of the third slot of this triple-slotted flap. When I countered that a double-slotted flap would not meet our performance guarantees for approach, landing, and stall speeds, they replied that those promises should be renegotiated with our customers.

Our most important commitments were to launch customer Pan

Am. I volunteered to go back to Pan Am and ask whether they would settle for a higher approach speed, but Boeing management turned me down. The audit people felt I was biased and would not do an energetic job of selling this proposed change, which was true, so Maynard Pennell instead attended to it during an SST-related trip to Pan Am in New York. Maynard was well respected. I'm sure he presented this proposed design change as well as anybody could. John Borger heard him out and said, "If you want to take the third segment off, be my guest. But you still have to meet the approach-speed guarantee stipulated in our contract with you."

Pan Am was utterly unwilling to renegotiate the 747's promised low-speed performance. Going to a double-slotted flap would have dictated an eight-knot rise in approach speed, and they weren't about to accept that.

Eight knots is 9.2 miles per hour, or 15 kilometers per hour. That's not a very big difference, so why did it matter to Borger and me both? Because braking distance increases with speed and it's not a linear increase. Borger knew it would be meaningful in real-world operations and he stuck to his guns, holding us to our promise. I am grateful to him, because that triple-slotted flap is a key reason the 747 has consistently been so very safe in service.

We got the 747's weight well enough under control that the weight-reduction effort was terminated. Nothing but good came out of our being audited, which I chose to see as an opportunity rather than a vote of no confidence. My feeling was that we were all part of the same team and working toward the same goals, so I consciously viewed this situation without ego, fear, or a chip on my shoulder.

My welcoming of the audit actually led to some productive double-teaming, because some of those engineers pitched in and helped with the design work. Their participation and perceptions helped get the word out to our senior management that the key reason we had a weight problem in the first place was that we simply didn't have enough engineers working on the 747 program.

9

THE 747 ROLLS OUT

September 30, 1968, arrived cold and densely overcast. Today Boeing was introducing its big new airplane to the world. I sat in the brightly lit hangar listening to Mal Stamper's echoing speech about the development of the 747.

I had not been asked to give a talk, so I sat back and watched the hoopla. I must admit it felt a bit odd to be excluded, though. After all, Stamper and the others wouldn't have had an airplane to take bows in front of if it wasn't for its design team. But politics often holds greater sway than logic.

That first 747 sported FAA registration number N7470, but we insiders called it by its Boeing serial number, RA001. Hangar lights twinkled in its gleaming white paint and rakish red trim. On the jet's nose shone the colorful logos of the 26 airlines that so far had committed to purchasing 747s, among them Pan Am, JAL, BOAC, TWA, United, Lufthansa, Northwest, Braniff, KLM, Delta, El Al, American, Eastern, and SAS. Flight attendants from those 26 operators lined up for photos in front of RA001. Today their 1960s outfits look comically dated but the 747 itself doesn't. Dictated by aerodynamics, its lines have a pleasing rightness of form.

747 Rollout

After these festivities, an aircraft tug pulled the 747 out of the hangar by its nose gear. Just as that impossibly high nose emerged into the open, the sun finally broke through, lending dramatic impact to the scene. The crowd gasped audibly and broke into spontaneous applause. I knew how they felt; the 747 looked *huge* even to me, and I knew its dimensions down to the inch. That first airplane was 231 feet long and 196 feet wide and had a tail as tall as a six-story building.

The global news media covered that event with much greater interest than rollouts receive today, and they absolutely loved it. More important, a whole lot of bankers felt vastly relieved to see in the papers and on TV that Boeing had a real airplane to show for all that money we'd borrowed from them. In fact, this was the entire point of the rollout, which otherwise was decidedly premature. Oh, our jumbo jet might have looked ready to leap into the sky, but in reality it was only 78% finished.

After the rollout, RA001 went back in the paint hangar and we redoubled our efforts to get it ready for flight. That took until the following February, and even then it wasn't done. So compressed was our schedule, in fact, that we would actually complete the engineering cleanup *during* the 747's highly compressed flight testing and certification program.

———————

We were charting a lot of unknown territory with the 747, which was the world's first widebody (twin-aisle) airplane. It was also the first jetliner powered by high-bypass-ratio fanjets. With such severe time pressures, it seemed to me that the people on my team were coming up with new ideas and innovations almost daily.

Nowhere was this truer than in the 747's passenger accommodations. Nobody had ever attempted to define and configure the interior of a twin-aisle jetliner before, let alone one with a cabin 20 feet across. It was so large, in fact, that some Boeing and airline people thought airline passengers might find the 747 *too* big and object to traveling in an "aerial cavern."

Milt Heinemann was responsible for the design of the 747's interior as well as its cargo holds and loading systems. In addition to Milt and his team, we had the invaluable services of Walter Dorwin Teague Associates, a pioneering industrial design firm that shared our facilities and worked closely with us on the 747. Part of the U.S. industrial design movement that arose in the 1930s, Teague has long helped Boeing by focusing the imagination of its talented industrial artists to further enhance our airplane interiors.

Teague helped us define the jet age in the 1950s. The interior we together defined for the 707 was in many ways as great a leap forward as the airplane itself. It introduced a lot of features that subsequently became the industry standard. One example is the *passenger service unit* (PSU), that all-in-one overhead panel that clusters each seat's fresh air outlet, reading lamp, and attendant call button within easy reach. Plastic pull-down window shades also debuted on the 707, as did integral fold-down seatback trays, floor tracks to allow airlines to change the seat spacing, and a wide double seat that set the international standard for first-class comfort.

The 727 and 737 shared the same cross section as the 707 and followed its lead. But now we had this huge new challenge. With two parallel aisles, the 747 was fundamentally different. We were starting with a blank slate.

Frank Del Giudice headed up Teague's Puget Sound team. Mild-mannered, he was a good manager and a terrific industrial designer with an unmatched reputation. I'd known and worked with him for the better part of 20 years. It was easy to forget Frank worked for a different employer.

Structures, aerodynamics, propulsion systems, cockpit design, and many other areas competed for my attention, so I let Milt and Frank run with the interior design. I had no doubt they would once again come up with something as revolutionary as the airplane itself.

Using a process called human-centered design, the interiors team set about identifying and giving passengers what they wanted. For starters, survey data showed travelers strongly prefer window seats, yet by definition the 747 would offer proportionately fewer of these. What could be done to offset this seeming disadvantage? They decided to move the galleys, lavatories, closets, and other fixtures away from the sidewalls where they'd always been and instead mount them between and bracketed by the aisles to create center islands. This novel thinking solved two problems at once. More than just freeing up space for more window seats, it divided the 747's interior into five pleasingly proportioned "rooms," eliminating any sense of being in a cavernous tube. These islands provided forward walls every so often that could be used for the display of artwork and projection of in-flight movies.

Because the 747 is so big, its sidewalls are fairly straight, without the pronounced curvature of smaller jets. This characteristic enhances passengers' perceptions of being in a room, putting them at ease.

The windows in these sidewalls would be the same size as the 707's, but Frank made them seem bigger by setting them in something he called "architectural reveals." Surrounding the windows with these wash-lit reveals created a persuasive sense of being in a bright, open, and airy environment instead of a confined space. The psychological liking we humans seem to have for windows had been cleverly met. Above those windows Milt put the industry's first closable overhead stowage compartments. All previous airliners had featured an open shelf that was referred to as the hat rack. A significant and timely innovation, closable bins made it possible for passengers to bring increasing amounts of carry-on luggage on board with them. Occasional airplane encounters with in-flight turbulence also showed the wisdom of closable bins.

Boeing built a 747 interior mock-up at a cost of $1 million. A reporter who toured it dubbed it "the Waldorf Astoria with wings," while *Architecture Plus* magazine proclaimed it "the most interesting building of the decade." Milt, Frank, and their people used this mock-up to evaluate and refine their ideas, while Boeing sales and marketing people used it to show potential customers what the 747's interior would look like. All this activity occurred before the airplane ever flew, so the mock-up more than paid for itself in publicity and airline orders.

The design of the 747 was overweight and we were already taking remedial steps. However, I hadn't yet looked to the passenger cabin for weight cuts. I wanted Milt and Frank to define their interior first, and I had been meeting with them often enough to know they were moving in the right direction.

Once their design for the 747's interior was pretty well locked in, they invited me to review the mock-up. It was every bit as appealing and innovative as I had hoped. I knew its physical environment, systems, and amenities would redefine the experience of air travel.

I told Milt and Frank that everybody on our team was working very hard on weight reduction and that they too needed to wring excess pounds out of the airplane. Their reaction showed me they didn't think they could shave too many ounces off what they'd created.

Some of the magic I saw inside that mock-up was achieved through different types of direct and indirect cabin lighting. When they demonstrated this integrated system to me, I asked the total weight of their lighting scheme. The figure they quoted struck me as excessive.

"You've got four lighting systems in here," I said, looking around. "Let's turn them off one at a time and see what happens."

Each in turn, the four lighting systems were switched off while the remaining three were left on. We viewed the results, and then I told them which of the four systems I thought should go. It was the lights in the cove between the ceiling and sidewalls. Because this system ran the length of the airplane, its removal would save a lot of weight.

Frank Del Giudice made an impassioned plea for me to leave things as they were. This cabin lighting obviously meant a great deal to him. I stuck by my decision but made him a promise. "As this program progresses, Frank," I said, "we'll have more powerful engines that allow for higher takeoff weights. When that happens, we'll reinstate this fourth system, but for now it's out."

Frank, an artist at heart, got so emotional that a tear ran helplessly down his cheek. I felt bad about it, but I know he understood the reasons for my decision. As far as I know, that was the only time I ever made one of my employees cry. I went home that evening feeling that it's a tough job having to bring such dedicated people to that point. We all had strong feelings on the program even if we didn't show it. Above all, everybody wanted to make that airplane a success, to make it as good as it could possibly be. That's why we worked 10 or 12 hours a day, six to seven days a week, pouring our hearts and souls into it.

The story has a happy ending because soon after the 747 entered service we got those higher-thrust engines. To break the news that we could now reinstate the cove lighting, I took Milt and Frank to the mock-up. The first three lighting systems were on, and I'd arranged with the support crew to turn on the fourth while we were inside. The airplane brightened visibly, and so did Frank, who immediately understood. The news brought a great big smile to his face. "Let's all go have a beer and celebrate," he proposed. Not one of us had the time, he included, but the thought was pretty nice.

Mal Stamper felt his job as 747 program chief was to motivate the people below him to get the airplane done on time. He also firmly believed that the 747 design process could be accelerated through enhanced morale. Acting on these views, he launched a motivational campaign called The Incredibles. The star of this Boeing campaign was the mythical American lumberjack Paul Bunyan.

At Stamper's orders, Boeing artists worked up cartoon images of Bunyan, a giant, walking around chopping down problems with a big axe. Our Everett facilities were soon festooned with posters and banners of Bunyan. Huge footprints appeared on the factory floor to symbolize the giant steps we were taking with the 747.

Frankly, Stamper's campaign didn't sit well with my hardworking team, which had an attitude I'd describe as "get real or get out of my way." We engineers are a pragmatic bunch. We plan well, explicitly formalize our job requirements, track our progress against integrated schedules, and generally have a very clear take on what we can and cannot accomplish in a given time frame with given resources.

Our morale was already high because we were getting the job done in the face of adversity. Then along came Stamper's campaign, the intent of which—knowingly or not—seemed to be to push us to issue half-finished drawings just to meet unrealistic deadlines. It didn't take long for Paul Bunyan to become a source of irritation. My troops began griping about this inept campaign, which suggested to them that our senior management didn't understand or value what they were doing. The specific problem with it, I realized, was that it reflected two insulting assumptions, one offensive and the other patronizing. The offensive part was the idea that we were underperforming and needed to be motivated to achieve full productivity. The patronizing part, which added insult to injury, was Stamper's apparent belief that cartoons were the way to communicate with engineers.

We ended up ignoring Paul Bunyan. The clueless lummox was out of his element in Everett, a Washington State timber town suddenly at the forefront of commercial aviation. It didn't matter how big Bunyan's axe was; he couldn't cut it in our world.

Stamper's motivational campaign did make one lasting contribution to the 747 program, however. It bestowed upon my 747 team the well-deserved nickname "The Incredibles."

In those days, we designed airplanes by producing drawings, fabricating the components (or at least full-size stand-ins for them), and fitting all of this into a *class 3 mock-up*. This full-scale mock-up looked like the real airplane, although you'd sometimes see wood here or there instead of metal or plastic.

Our 747 program class 3 mock-up was an invaluable tool. Into it we installed air-conditioning ducts, mounting brackets, wire runs, and every single other component that would be in the actual airplane. This allowed us to quickly identify interference points where two parts were trying to occupy the same space. Seeing everything in place also gave us ideas for a host of design refinements.

Today, airplanes are digitally designed in three dimensions, which eliminates the need for a costly physical mock-up. The first airplane to be developed in this manner was the Boeing 777, which was launched in the fall of 1990 and entered service in mid-1995. Computer-aided design software automatically identifies interferences. It also lets Boeing designers "fly through" and view any part of the airplane's structure.

We did it the old-fashioned way on the 747. And with many of our drawings running two months late, it was obvious that our class 3 mock-up wasn't going to be completed in time to meet the program's stated deadline.

Managing the class 3 mock-up was ordinarily the task of the airplane's design team, which meant we should have been running it. However, Mal Stamper apparently felt that my engineers and I were not being aggressive enough on the schedule front, so he assigned Bob Bateman, a capable engineer not on my program, to run the 747 mock-up.

This produced a peculiar situation. My engineers knew that if they were too hard-nosed and refused to put something in the mock-up, they would be penalized and perhaps replaced. So they in effect produced drawings where you could install something—anything—in that mock-up to buy time while they finished the real drawings. Each time a section of the airplane was finished, Bateman put on an admiral's uniform and went up on the balcony to ring a big bell. Sometimes he'd have us all go out and have a big celebration in the afternoon to mark the occasion as another big section of the airplane was "finalized." Meanwhile, my engineers quietly kept working until those "finished" sections of the class 3 mock-up could actually be completed through modification. I don't know if Bateman and his team ever caught on to this schedule ploy.

It was clear to me that the 747 wasn't going to be ready to fly within the time frame Mal Stamper and other senior Boeing leaders wanted. Rollout had been scheduled for October 1968, and we had enough of the airplane done so that the 747 actually did roll out that month even though it was far from actually being finished. Fortunately, despite Pratt & Whitney's extreme difficulties, we came up with four presentable engines to hang on it so that it looked complete from the outside.

Stamper dearly wanted the 747 to fly on December 17, 1968. That would be the sixty-fifth anniversary of the Wright brothers' great achievement at Kitty Hawk, North Carolina. But although we were working 10 hours a day, 7 days a week, I could see that there was just no way we could possibly accommodate that desire.

I had been preparing Boeing's senior management, Stamper included, for the possibility of a schedule slide. By the same token, though, I knew that if I stated positively we'd miss it, I would only present Stamper and others with the opportunity to say, "If Sutter can't pull it off, we'll get somebody who can." My feeling all along had been: Why provoke a needless confrontation? The airplane would fly when it was ready and that was that. Meantime, declaring up front that it could not possibly fly on the Wright brothers' anniversary would do nothing but stir up needless attention and trouble.

If I felt bad about missing that deadline, it was only because we would soon be turning the 747 over to Boeing Flight Test, which was then led by Dix Loesch, director of flight operations for Boeing Commercial Airplanes. A good friend, Dix had joined the company at the same time I had.

Dix was open, friendly, and modest. Just talking to him, you'd never know he was an extremely well read intellectual with a degree in aeronautical engineering from MIT. You also wouldn't know that he had flown throughout World War II as a naval fighter pilot. Dix wouldn't talk about that, but it was well known that he had a number of aerial victories to his credit. He entered the history books when he downed a Japanese Emily flying boat, scoring the first victory for Grumman's famous Hellcat fighter. It had been a long war for Dix, who had been shot down and severely wounded but recovered and went right back for more.

Dix Loesch was a gifted test pilot and he ran BCA Flight Operations effectively. He agreed with me that attempting to fly the Boeing 747 before it was ready would cause nothing but headaches and frustration. Unlike me, though, Dix felt strongly that Boeing's leadership must be made aware that the first flight could not possibly take place on December 17. When Dix got a campaign going to this effect, he found he had unintentionally crossed swords with Mal Stamper. Stamper refused to believe his mandated schedule was unworkable, and he took significant exception to Dix's saying so. Dix ultimately left Flight Test, and I can't help but suspect that part of the reason for his departure was that he fought Stamper too hard over this issue.

When December 17, 1968, rolled around, RA001 was in the paint hangar with parts strewn all around the floor awaiting installation. That day, we ran safety checks on her landing gear, flight controls, and other systems. Stamper was bitterly disappointed. I don't think he ever forgave me for missing his chosen first-flight date, but it was unavoidable.

Believing the 747 would fly on the sixty-fifth anniversary of the invention of the airplane, Stamper had ordered a large number of models built of the Wright 1903 Flyer. These models had a wingspan of about 10 inches and were extremely intricate and pretty. Stamper planned to present them as 747 first-flight mementos to Boeing's senior leaders and directors, as well as to airline executives and other VIPs.

I didn't know any of this, of course. I also didn't appreciate how badly Mal Stamper wanted us to meet his decree that the airplane fly on December 17. That is, not until the following May when I received a call from Stamper's office saying he wanted to see me right away. One-on-one meetings with Stamper were definitely not the norm. My limited communication with him was always through the filter of George Snyder, the Everett Division's engineering VP. It was late in the day and I was getting ready to go home when this summons came. Why did Stamper want to see me? I wondered. I rushed over to his office and found him seated behind his desk.

The moment Mal Stamper saw me, he reached into a drawer and pulled out one of those delicate Wright Flyer models. "You know, Sutter," he said, "I was planning to give these out when we flew on the anniversary of the Wright brothers." He frowned. "But you guys didn't make it on time." He set that model down hard. It crumpled with broken wing struts and other damage, but he didn't seem to notice. He was really worked up. In a long emotional outpouring, he told me what a huge disappointment it had been to him to miss that anniversary. While he stopped short of pinning the blame directly on me, the inference was clear.

I heard Stamper out and calmly explained what our situation had been. I finished by apologizing for any personal distress that this situation might have caused him. That didn't end the session, though; it took another half an hour for him to get it all out of his system.

"Can I have the model, Mal?" I asked when we were finally done.

"Go ahead if you want it," he replied, still miffed.

I slid the damaged Flyer and its pieces onto a pad of paper and walked them carefully back to my office. The next day I asked one of my people for a favor. "Next time you're down in the wind tunnel," I said, "see if the Model Shop people can fix this for me, will you?"

They repaired it perfectly, and I took it home. That revealing souvenir has a place of honor in my study. Every time I look at it, it brings back the stresses that so many of us underwent to get the 747 designed, built, and into service. All the inevitable highs and lows of a major airplane program were magnified on the 747 program.

————————

Stereotypes notwithstanding, we engineers can be a pretty colorful bunch. However, we don't hold a candle to the manufacturing crowd, who are collectively referred to as *operations*. At Boeing, *operations* means *manufacturing*.

In the latter 1960s, seeming chaos reigned at Everett as Boeing geared up to produce the 747. Our new factory—the world's largest building by volume—was literally being erected around our operations people as they laid down the 747's assembly lines and figured out how to build an airplane that we hadn't even finished designing.

The 747 program's first vice president of operations was T. C. "Chick" Pitts, a volatile manufacturing guy from our Wichita division. Pitts combined an erratic and highly combative management style with a famously short temper. He disliked design engineers and dismissed us all as meddlesome busybodies who ordered changes simply to waste the company's money and make life more difficult for his "ops people."

Chick Pitts's background was military production, which made him a poor fit with the commercial 747 program. In military manufacturing, you roll out large numbers of identical airplanes, periodically interrupting this flow for a "block change" in which collected design improvements can be introduced all at once. The 747 program was much more demanding. Its accelerated time frame meant that the design and manufacturing phases overlapped a bit. We didn't have the luxury of time to finalize, fully debug, and lock in our design before the ops people started cutting metal and rolling out airplanes. And the airplanes themselves differed because they were being built for different customers.

Everybody understood this situation. Ongoing design changes were inevitable as the 747 airplane was finalized and fixes were made. Whatever side of the fence you worked on—engineering or operations—you just had to roll with the punches and do your best to make everything work. Morale was high in the operations community, where Boeing's manufacturing experts were generally champing at the bit to build our big new airplane. Its size made it a challenge they couldn't resist.

Willing as the rank and file was to do what it took to get our newest jetliner built, though, that wasn't the case with Chick Pitts. No matter how critical a design change might be, it didn't cut any ice with him. I'd hear an initial howl followed by expletives, then adamant opposition that blocked time-critical progress. Needless to say, Chick and I had some very interesting dealings as I strove to get the 747 built. This impasse threatened the success of the program.

An exchange I won't forget occurred after the rollout. We discovered a fatigue problem in the inlets we had designed for the 747's big fanjets. Our structures people put a sonic horn on those inlets and determined that high frequencies coming off the engines would cause the metal to crack.

My engineers identified a fix and put out a change order to correct the problem. With the airplane still scheduled back then to fly on December 17, 1968, though, it was decided to fly with the initial inlets, which were good for about 60 hours aloft before they would start cracking. After that we'd replace them with the new inlets.

Of course, the airplane didn't fly on December 17. By the time it did in February, those new inlets had been designed and Rohr, our supplier, had built and shipped the first set of four to Everett.

George Nible and Wally Buckley, two hugely talented Boeing managers, arrived on the scene late in November 1968 to straighten out the 747 "production mess," as it became known. Although Pitts initially retained the title of vice president of operations for the 747 program, Nible and Buckley took over the day-to-day operations in Everett. Thanks to them, Boeing would be ready to roll 747s out the factory door when the time came.

There's a no-nonsense air to George Nible. Probably the most brilliant ops person it has ever been my privilege to know, George singlehandedly restructured the 747 manufacturing processes to remove bottlenecks and get everything plugged together correctly. He didn't do it by applying business school training, because he never went past high school. Instead he did it through sheer hard work and old-fashioned horse sense of the highest caliber.

As a young man, George had worked briefly as a Boeing assembly-line worker. When the United States entered World War II, he decided to volunteer for the navy even though his war-worker status assured him of an exemption to the draft. So badly did Boeing need factory workers at that time that George's frustrated supervisor told him, "If you quit now, I'll make sure that Boeing never hires you again!" George fought the war and returned to find a different Boeing job. That supervisor later ended up working for him and they became friends. Over the years, George's miraculous ability to get things built, no matter how complex the challenge, saw him rise to ever higher levels. His energy and quick intelligence are legendary. He and I are friends to this day, and he still thinks and talks faster than any 20-year-old I know.

While George was straightening out Chick Pitts's mess, Wally Buckley was getting a handle on the administrative side of our manufacturing woes. He and his staff worked through a veritable mountain of paperwork to ensure that our operations billing and contract administration were up to snuff.

Wally called me one day about those replacement engine inlets that Rohr had sent us. "We've got a hell of a workload, Joe," he told me, "but we could probably put them on the airplane right now since they're here."

"It's your call, Buck, but it makes sense to me," I replied. "That'll spare us having to swap them out down the line, which would cost us time in the air."

Wally agreed and ordered his ops people to change those inlets. Word of this got back to Chick Pitts. Chick somehow got it into his head that I had ordered the work, so he snatched up the telephone. Chick's office was in the headquarters building at Everett and mine was in our new engineering offices there. So loud did Chick shout that he could probably have saved himself the call; I could have heard him even without the phone! "How dare you tell operations what to do!" Pitts bellowed. "Those orders have to go through me and my people!"

I tried to set him straight as to what had happened but Chick was too worked up to listen. Those old inlets were perfectly fine, he insisted. The new ones were nothing but a waste of money, and putting them on the airplane was disrupting his people's work.

This high-decibel browbeating was as heated a discussion as I've ever had. I consider myself a patient person who listens well, although I have been known to show a bit of temper on the job now and then. As the harangue continued, I found myself getting warm under the collar.

"What in hell am I supposed to do with these four old inlets?" Pitts concluded in an aggrieved howl.

The answer was that Boeing would modify them to conform to the new design and reuse them on another 747. But I wasn't about to tell Chick that because by then, I was fed up. "Well, Chick," I said, recalling what I knew about him, "you're a gardener, aren't you?"

The question caught him off balance. "Yeah."

"Do you have a patio?"

"Yes!" he barked. "What the hell does that have to do with anything?"

"Take those inlets, put 'em at the corners of your patio, and fill 'em with dirt. You'll have the world's biggest and most expensive flower-pots."

The wires sizzled as he slammed down the phone. Soon afterward, George Nible took over formally as vice president of operations, a job he was already doing on a de facto basis. I drew a huge sigh of relief. It was now more likely that the 747 would successfully enter airline service.

———

Taxi tests of the 747 began around the start of 1969. Before boarding the real airplane, though, Jack Waddell "taxied" a silly-looking 747 simulator composed of a dummy cockpit mounted on a frame high above a pickup truck. This crude device convinced him that pilots would have no trouble handling the actual airplane on the ground, despite the size of the 747 and the fact that its flight deck was three stories high.

In one of the first actual ground tests, Waddell tried to turn RA001 out of a tight parking stall and found the airplane simply wouldn't do it. He gave it more and more power, but the only result was a lot of ruined tires. Shutting down, he proclaimed the 747's ground handling unacceptable and ordered an immediate halt to testing until the problem was fixed.

The 747 has four main landing gears, two forward and two aft. Each of these struts ends in a four-wheel bogey. What was happening was that the 747's aft wheel bogeys were scraping sideways across the concrete as they tried to follow the axis of the turn defined by the forward wheels. This scrubbed the aft bogey tires, leaving them with bald spots that required their replacement.

The cure was to make the 747's aft main landing gear steerable so that its wheels could follow the forward set of wheels through a taxiing turn. My team and I had actually anticipated this problem during the design phase. We had specified a steerable gear, only to have a Boeing accounting audit team declare it unnecessary and delete it to trim costs.

Knowing that this steering system would be required, I had quietly ordered that it be designed and built anyway. As a result, the needed parts were sitting on a shelf ready for immediate installation. I'm sure it surprised a lot of people to see how fast we came up with a solution to this "unanticipated problem" during ground testing.

10

INTO THE AIR

February 9, 1969, was a cold winter morning. We had missed the Wright brothers' first-flight date but unintentionally hit another anniversary. As Boeing technicians readied the 747 to fly at Everett's Paine Field, we realized it was six years to the day after the 727 took flight at Renton, Boeing's center of single-aisle jetliner manufacturing.

Patches of snow dotted Paine Field. The clouds bunched thickly, but we elected to proceed because of a radio report from a 707 on a test flight over the Olympic Peninsula. Its crew described clearing weather pushing in from the west. On that hopeful note, Bill Allen and other key executives arrived.

Nancy was there with me. I described at the start of this book how she came to have the best view of all for the 747's first takeoff. With that event now imminent, I felt keyed up. There was no doubt in my mind that the 747 would fly; the only question was how well.

A quiet thrill of elation buoyed me as I chatted with our three-man flight-test crew. Project pilot Jack Waddell would take our baby aloft with the help of Brien Wygle to his right and Jess Wallick behind them in the flight deck as flight engineer. We called this fine team of aviators the "Three Ws."

Wygle was Waddell's boss as chief of Boeing Flight Test, where he reported to Dix Loesch, the director of flight operations. A superb flier, Wygle—a deft administrator who later became a Boeing VP—flew with the Royal Canadian Air Force in the China–Burma–India theater of operations during World War II. During the postwar years, he flew jet fighters and graduated from the elite USAF Test Pilot School, which he attended on rotation from the RCAF.

Jess Wallick was a Kansas farm boy who had followed his older brother, Boeing test pilot Lew Wallick, into the peculiar occupation of wringing out experimental airplanes for a living. Lew had been at the controls of the 727 when it first flew, with Dix Loesch his right-seater. For the 737's debut, Brien Wygle had been pilot in command, with Lew Wallick serving as copilot.

Jess zipped up his leather jacket and followed the others up the boarding stairs. Boeing technicians hastily completed last-minute adjustments. The door was closed, the steps taken away, and the engines came to life one after another.

I saw Boeing's new jet as 75,000 drawings, 4.5 million parts, 136 miles of electrical wiring, 5 landing gear legs, 4 hydraulic systems, and 10 million labor hours. In a few moments now, on an airfield 30 miles north of where I grew up dreaming of designing airplanes, we'd see whether all those pieces added up to a real flying machine.

A flaring roar pulled my attention to a gold-painted F-86 as it scrambled into the air. Another Boeing test pilot was at the controls of this surplus military fighter jet, now a Boeing-owned chase plane. It would take up station alongside our big jet, pacing it to keep an eye on things. If needed, its pilot was right there to inspect the airframe, answer any questions, and otherwise contribute to the safety of the flight. There was always an element of risk, I knew. You could mitigate this risk, but you couldn't totally eliminate it.

Buses drove onto the airfield to deposit journalists and photographers at strategic locations from which to cover the day's events. I dropped Nancy off at the calculated point where the 747's wheels would leave the runway. Returning to the flightline, I watched RA001 taxi like an oversize goose to the end of the runway. She turned to face us.

Waddell had set the brakes and the crew was now performing final checks, I knew. Long minutes ticked away and then the 747's huge engines spooled up. The world's first jumbo jet accelerated down the runway. Cheers and applause broke out as the nose lifted and it surged skyward.

A lump constricted my throat. Unable to say anything, I watched the plane bank into a shallow turn and return for a prearranged pass over the field for the benefit of Boeing workers and the global press corps.

Congratulatory pats on the back impeded me as I made my way to a Boeing vehicle. All I wanted was to share this moment with Nancy. Those tears of joyous relief I saw on her face when I picked her up spoke for both of us. We savored that too brief moment of intimacy, and then it was back to work for me.

I joined Everette Webb in the radio room, our flight-test telemetry center, just in time to hear Brien Wygle interrupt his technical chatter to exclaim, "The airplane's flying beautifully!" He and Jack Waddell continued to explore the big ship's low-speed characteristics until a minor structural failure occurred in one of the flaps, prompting them to cut short the first flight. They turned toward the field. I think I crossed my fingers at that point.

A lot of so-called aviation experts had been saying the 747 was too big for airline pilots to get it safely back onto the ground. How could pilots judge the landing, these critics asked, when the cockpit was three stories off the ground? This was definitely on my mind as RA001 turned from base leg to final approach. Before my eyes, it descended to the runway with the stately majesty of an ocean liner. It flared gently and touched down very, very smoothly.

That moment was my biggest thrill of the day. All my worries

747 Landing
(AUTHOR'S PERSONAL COLLECTION)

evaporated and I knew we had a good airplane. I took a grateful breath, happy to the core of my being.

———————

In an hour and a quarter aloft, Waddell, Wygle, and Wallick had learned that the 747 flew well, was stable, and had light controls with well-balanced forces. Although it was a gusty day, the big ship took it in stride and they never felt any turbulence. They also determined that our efforts to design out Dutch roll—that objectionable oscillation to which swept wings are prone—had apparently been successful.

"This is a flying arrow," Jack declared with a grin, "a pilot's airplane!"

We were euphoric. Boeing had a real airplane, and it looked to be a winner. An awful lot of celebrating took place that night. And with Boeing's survival now firmly tied to the 747's success, it wasn't just we engineers celebrating. It was our leadership plus a good many bankers.

In the days that followed, the airplane took to the air repeatedly. With an aggressive schedule to meet, we hoped to fly at least once a day. Those initial tests focused on cycling the landing gear, exploring landings more fully, and so on. From there we proceeded to low-speed tests to generate engineering data and let the pilots become more familiar with the airplane. No potential hazards or objectionable characteristics were identified.

We began taking the 747 to higher speeds. The plan was to gradually work our way up to the airplane's cruise speed of Mach 0.85 (85% the speed of sound) and then beyond to its maximum speed to ensure that its flight characteristics remained satisfactory to the extreme edge of the envelope. In addition to going faster, we started putting more weight into the ship to see how it handled all the way up to its maximum certified takeoff weight.

These efforts hadn't progressed very far when the program came to a screeching halt. We had run into low damping, and that, in turn, meant the potential for *flutter*, a word no aeronautical engineer ever wants to hear. Flutter is a potentially dangerous condition in which the natural vibration of one part of an airplane's structure couples with that of another to create a mutually reinforcing harmonic resonance. It is by far the most serious of the stability and control problems you can encounter in high-speed flight.

The structural components that make up an airplane are supposed to have different natural frequencies, or rates of vibration, so that each component damps out the other's vibrations. This is what we mean when we say an airplane is well damped. If two components instead are very close in frequency, they feed off each other in a mutually reinforcing harmonic vibration that can escalate rapidly to the point of tearing the airplane apart in flight. This is flutter, the seven-letter "F word."

Flutter had claimed a lot of early jet fighters. Fortunately, the 747 was a large machine with high inertias, so things weren't likely to get out of hand quite as fast. In plain English, this simply means that big airplanes are more ponderous, so bad things don't happen so quickly.

Most of the 747 structure's frequencies are low enough that we could pretty well determine when we were getting into areas of low damping. With proper controls, we knew we could work that margin to find out why the airplane was losing the damping it needed. In other words, given the right data, we could zero in on which components were harmonically reinforcing each other in a potentially destructive way.

We mounted accelerometers and motion sensors on critical parts of RA001's structure and then flew the airplane. At increasing speeds, the flight crew "pulsed" the controls (introduced a sudden jolt), or we'd use shakers to introduce vibrations into various parts of the airplane as it flew along. Doing this cautiously at different CGs and fuel loadings generated the data we needed.

Analysis of this information soon unmasked the culprit: The wings and outboard engine nacelles were vibrating together. Further testing confirmed that these were indeed the critical elements causing the problem. Our testing also showed that what little natural damping there was to counter this harmonic coupling quickly degraded when we put the weight of fuel in the outboard wing tanks. The overall situation was very worrisome because we were getting low damping long before we reached the 747's maximum design speeds, and FAA certification requires airplanes to have proper damping beyond their maximum design speeds.

All of our planned performance, engine, and systems tests with the first airplane went by the wayside. The schedule slipped and all that we did for a month was test to investigate and cure this flutter condition. We needed to restore full damping. The long-term solution was to redesign the outboard engine struts to change their natural frequency of vibration. In the meantime, the same results could be achieved by adding weights at the right places to the existing component.

Here is where Everette Webb, the head of my tech staff, came into his own. Structural dynamics were his engineering specialty and he thrived on the challenge. He was brilliant and knew his stuff. So impressive were his technical papers in the field, in fact, that professors had come all the way from Tokyo just to meet him. Webb later ran the Everett plant and ended up vice president of engineering for Boeing Commercial Airplanes.

In the early spring of 1969, Everette Webb and I sat down together to decide what to do about this low damping. This being his area, I stood back and let him call the shots. He pretty much took over the flight testing, and it amazed me how totally focused he was. Watching him tease clues out of reams of data was like watching Sherlock Holmes peer through his magnifying glass at something that was utterly meaningless to everyone else.

One day I sat in the radio room with Webb and his people as real-time telemetry came in from the test airplane in flight. A secretary showed up. T Wilson was on the phone, she said, and he wanted to know how our flutter tests were going. This latest crisis was obviously a source of considerable concern to Boeing's leadership, so the call wasn't surprising. Not appearing to hear, Everette continued watching his engineers plot the real-time data.

"Mr. Wilson wants to speak with you," the woman repeated more loudly.

"I'll call him back," Webb snapped, not shifting his focus.

At the end of the day as we headed to our cars, I remembered that call. "Hey, Webb," I reminded him, "you'd better call Wilson right away."

"Oh yeah, when I get to my office," he said distractedly.

There probably wasn't another person at Boeing so totally focused on the job at hand that he or she would put off the president of Boeing, a man soon to be our chairman. That was Everette Webb.

Going through all that together left Webb and me the best of friends. We didn't always see eye to eye but we could always reach agreement on what the program needed. The 747 airplane was always the better for those discussions.

Webb and his people cured the low damping without the delay of having to make structural changes to the wings or engine nacelles. They did this by putting small mass weights on those outboard nacelles to change their frequency of vibration. This interim fix wasn't the most elegant solution, but it cleared the 747 for flutter and let us get on with our flight testing. We later redesigned the parts and dispensed with the weights.

A month or two into the flying, I stopped by Boeing Field on my way up to Everett to watch the first 747 engine test at full rated power. We were taking an incremental approach here as elsewhere, which was fine because our lightly loaded prototype didn't need more than partial power to take off and fly its low-speed tests.

I watched as Jack Waddell started up the engines and ran them up to full power. Suddenly the number 2 engine stopped cold. It didn't spool down; it stopped instantaneously, and the resulting torque pushed the whole nacelle up toward the wing. This was a major and potentially very dangerous failure.

We removed that fanjet and tore it down in our shop. It turned out the fan shaft had snapped and jammed into the engine's stator blades, violently arresting the entire engine's rotation. I got right in touch with Pratt & Whitney and was dismayed to discover they weren't at all surprised. "Yeah, we know all about it," I was told. "We've redesigned the shaft and have made a whole bunch of replacements for you."

Within a few days, a DC-6 freighter landed and offloaded these shafts. I got our people busy tearing down the engines we had and installing those replacement fan shafts, which was a huge job.

I was enraged, but it wasn't about the added work. It was the lack of openness on the part of Pratt & Whitney. Keeping their problems from us could have killed someone on the ramp or even brought down our airplane in flight. We didn't do business that way at Boeing.

The relationship with Pratt, our close program partner, had begun to sour.

With the 747 in the air, hopes rose at Boeing that it might attend the 1969 Paris Air Show. Held each June in odd-numbered years, this international aviation display is the world's most prestigious air show. Boeing sales, marketing, and finance people in particular were pushing hard for us to show off the 747, especially since Douglas and Lockheed were now developing widebodies of their own, these being the DC-10 and L-1011, respectively.

A decision was reached at high levels: If we could do Paris safely, we'd go for it. We redoubled our efforts, but all through March and April I was pretty much thinking we were never going to make it. We left it to Jack Waddell as chief pilot to make the final determination as to whether the 747 could and should attend the show.

By far the biggest challenge was getting four adequate engines. Almost every JT9D we got from Pratt & Whitney in those early days lacked the reliability and surge margins needed to allow our test fleet to depart the immediate vicinity of our flight-test area. By then, more 747s had rolled out and our test fleet had grown to five airplanes, four of which would be delivered to customers after their flight-test duties. For Paris, we took the number 4 airplane and fitted it with the best engines we could find. After some flight testing, things looked good enough for a test flight from Seattle to New York and back without landing. If the airplane and its fanjets operated properly throughout this test, Jack decided, he'd release that ship for Paris.

I met Waddell as he landed after this New York trip. "Well, it worked okay," he said guardedly. Without another word being exchanged, we knew we were on. We also knew it was one hell of a commitment to make, particularly as we were going to fly nonstop from Seattle to Paris.

We took off from Seattle-Tacoma International Airport because it had a longer runway than Paine Field in Everett or Boeing Field in Seattle. There were just a few people on the flight and I was one of them. I'd been on a few 747 tests before, but this was different and a real treat. It gave me a good idea of how this big airplane would perform in an airline environment. The flight also provided us with long-range fuel consumption data that was gratifyingly close to our predictions.

Of course, all of us were a bit concerned about engine problems. If we lost one engine or even two, we could fly on, so there were no safety concerns. But not getting to Paris with four working engines would be a real embarrassment. Our crew nursed the power levers, avoiding any sudden throttle changes. Fortunately, those big Pratt & Whitneys performed flawlessly.

Among the new technologies the 747 would introduce to commercial service was inertial navigation, a system that told us where we were without any reference to external signals such as radionavigational aids. Comprising a platform of enormously sensitive accelerometers and gyroscopes, this system computed our position relative to the world solely by sensing the airplane's motion.

Relying on inertial nav, we hit our destination almost right on the nose. Le Bourget Aerodrome, the field where Lindbergh made his historic landing in 1927, was fogged in when we arrived. Our crew made an instrument approach with the intent of descending to minimums and, if we were in the clear by then, doing a flyby before circling around to land.

This arrival at Paris remains one of the great highlights of the early 747 program. An announcement had the huge crowd on the ground expectantly straining for any hint of our arrival. Because of the lifting fog, they heard us before they saw us and could tell it was something new. With those high-bypass fanjets, our airplane was quieter than other jets and had a very different tone.

Just short of the runway, we broke into the clear and flew at minimum altitude in a stately pass before the crowds, our vertical fin cutting the fog bank, or so I was told afterward. Our pilots then performed a visual go-around and made a very good landing. Nature's unveiling was thus more dramatic than anything Boeing's publicity people could have dreamed up.

As we taxied in to the display area, I saw we were being parked beside the Anglo-French Concorde SST. Fast as it was, the tiny Concorde seemed dwarfed to insignificance by the huge 747. As I exited, all I could think of was big brother looking down on little brother.

Dignitaries, Boeing executives, and well-wishers greeted us as we descended the steps. I spotted Maynard Pennell, our vice president of engineering and a friend and mentor. He shook my hand and congratulated us on the flawless flight. "You know, Joe," he said, "this is a day when I'm just happy to be an American and working for Boeing. Today we're showing what the United States can do."

The 747 stole the 1969 Paris Air Show. Crowds couldn't get enough of it, and we came home knowing our airplane was nothing less than a sensation with the public.

Just one month later, of course, the world had a far more dramatic demonstration of U.S. engineering prowess when Neil Armstrong and Buzz Aldrin walked on the Moon while Mike Collins orbited overhead.

Paris was quickly forgotten as our very high-pressure 747 flight-test program continued at Boeing Field. First and foremost, we had major propulsion issues to resolve. Surging and violent flameouts threatened to derail the entire 747 program.

Our engine, the JT9D, was Pratt & Whitney's first cut at a high-bypass-ratio turbofan engine. It was proportionately as huge a challenge for Pratt & Whitney as the airplane was for us, and because of weight growth during the 747's development, we were asking them for more thrust than originally requested. In fact, the JT9D would now have to develop more than 40,000 pounds of static thrust. By comparison, the intercontinental 707-320's low-bypass JT3Ds—the most powerful engines then in service—were rated at about 15,000 pounds of thrust each.

Everything worked well when the JT9D ran at a constant power setting during flight. But when the pilot moved the thrust levers to increase or decrease power, engine surges could and frequently did occur. These weren't simple flameouts, which are benign events. Instead, internal engine temperatures spiked so high that multimillion-dollar fanjets were toasted in the blink of an eye. Some of those initial JT9Ds seemed more stable than others. None was entirely free of the problem.

We were baffled by this phenomenon. Fortunately, I had some extremely bright engine guys on my team. They knew the JT9D fanjet just about as well as Pratt did.

The JT9D was built around two concentric spools rotating at different rates. Our investigations revealed that the low-speed and high-speed components (compressors and turbines) of this experimental engine weren't spooling up or winding down at exactly the same rate. This could trigger a sudden disruption, or *stagnation*, of the airflow through the engine. Sometimes there was too much fuel when the air bunched up, and other times too little. If there was too much fuel in the jumbled airflow, flames shot out an airplane's length in front and back of the engine. You felt a hard kick in the pants and heard a *bang*. This was a pretty good explosion that shook the whole airplane. Surges with too little fuel were less dramatic but no less damaging; either way, the engine suffered excessive temperatures and damaged turbine blades.

Now imagine four of these supremely ticklish engines on our experimental jet, and you can appreciate the horrendous situation we found ourselves in during the first half of our flight-test program. This was why it had been so hard to find four "good" engines for the 747's appearance at Paris.

Did Pratt & Whitney not understand the balance between the low-speed and high-speed portions of its engine, I wondered. Or was something unknown happening that adversely affected the computed airflow through the engine's core? The more we looked at it, the more it seemed to be the latter.

The frustrating thing was that this was a Pratt problem but they weren't doing much to address it. It looked to me like they'd just as soon have us—or even the airlines, after the 747 entered service—solve the problem.

Pratt was then run by a stubborn New Englander named Barney Schmickrath, and he was reluctant to step up to the challenge because it would cost his company money. This all came to a head in a meeting attended by T Wilson, Tex Boullioun, Mal Stamper, Jack

Waddell, and me across the table from Schmickrath and his crew from Hartford, Connecticut.

Waddell described his concerns as a professional test pilot about these damn engine surges. After he finished, Schmickrath made the mistake of saying, "What are you complaining about? You've got four engines. We've got reliability issues in single-engine fighters, and you don't hear those pilots bellyaching."

Waddell took that pretty personally. He looked like he was about to lunge across the table and give Schmickrath a broken jaw. Instead, he took that Pratt delegation up in the first 747 and demonstrated this problem, intentionally surging a couple of engines. It scared the hell out of Schmickrath and his crew. They went home and worked on the problem a lot harder.

Now that we were all on the same page, it wasn't long before we got a collective handle on the real culprit. The JT9D's casing was similar to that of other Pratt jet engines. That wasn't working here, because the JT9D featured this large-diameter fan at its front. Torque and gyroscopic loads coming off this massive fan unit were twisting the engine and distorting its casing, allowing the portion housing the turbines to go out of round. Pratt termed this problem *ovalization*. Because of ovalization, the tips of the turbine blades were rubbing against the inside of the engine casing in some places and gaps were opening up in others. Both occurrences cut way down on engine efficiency and jumbled up the airflow through the engine's core.

That was as far as Pratt & Whitney could get. Lacking the tools to understand in detail what was happening, they couldn't engineer a fix. Fortunately, we at Boeing had developed a much better structural analysis program than Pratt possessed. Using this in-house capability, we analyzed the loads on that engine frame and showed Pratt how to redesign the JT9D's casing and mounting system.

In the meantime, my people designed a temporary yoke assembly that would externally stiffen the existing engine installation. This yoke eliminated the violent flameouts and allowed our flight testing to continue. There was still the lesser problem of "insufficient surge margin" that saw less violent engine surges. While Pratt was not able to cure this problem right away, changes to the engine surge valves and throttle control monitoring alleviated it sufficiently for the 747 to enter service.

For the first time ever, a fundamentally new type of commercial airplane was being shaken out at the same time as a fundamentally new type of engine. I can't think of another time this has happened; in most cases, the engine is a year or two ahead of the airplane. The fates of Boeing and Pratt were firmly intertwined, because the failure of either company's ambitious development would have spelled disaster for the other.

I have heard comments over the years suggesting that I was too firm at times during the development of the 747. The term *hard-nosed* has even come up once or twice. If so, I was firm because I was trying to get the job done. One occasion in particular might have helped earn me this reputation. It involved a company called AiResearch and the auxiliary power unit (APU) it was developing for the 747.

The APU is a small gas turbine—in effect, a little jet engine—that supplies electrical power and compressed air for the 747 while it's on the ground. Housed in the tail cone, it can also provide backup power in flight if need be. Because of its size, the 747 needed an all-new APU, and its development by AiResearch was way behind. Unfortunately, that company showed little inclination to tackle and fix the problems in time for the overall program.

A row developed because we felt AiResearch wasn't improving its APU nearly fast enough. When matters came to a head, they showed up in Seattle with a contingent of about 10, including their chairman, the retired four-star general who led AiResearch's parent company. They made an engineering presentation in which they claimed that it was Boeing's fault their APU didn't work better.

It was clear to us that they simply weren't committing enough money or lab time to straightening out their troubles, and I told them so. The chairman immediately began dressing me down for what he saw as a lack of patience. He probably wasn't personally close enough to the matter to know where the truth lay, but that didn't stop him from trying to steamroll us. I said that if his people had done their job as agreed to under the contract, we wouldn't be having this meeting in the first place. It was definitely not a friendly exchange, and the mood was more than strained as both sides agreed to a course of action.

As this meeting broke up, one of the AiResearch executives caught me in the hallway. "You shouldn't have talked that way to our chairman, Joe," he said. "Don't you know he was a four-star general?"

I looked him right in the eye and replied, "And I was a lieutenant in the navy. What the hell does that have to do with anything? Let's get the job done."

Time was too short to put up with snow jobs or excuses. If I was guilty of anything, it wasn't of having a hard nose; it was of judging others by the quality of their work and their ability to meet integrated schedules, not by their titles or rank. This egalitarian approach is the dominant culture in Boeing engineering, and it's one reason we accomplished so much. Not all of our suppliers were as meritocratic as Boeing, and clashes of corporate culture—like this one with AiResearch—were inevitable.

After that meeting, AiResearch got a handle on its problems and delivered an excellent APU in time for the 747's service debut.

———

Some early jet transports had crashed on takeoff when the pilot *over-rotated*, which means he pulled the nose up too high, inadvertently placing the wing into a high-drag condition. When combined with insufficient thrust, such as during hot-weather operations (which rob performance by making the air less dense) or if an engine failed, those excessively nose-high takeoffs could be deadly. This was particularly true of the de Havilland Comet, which lacked leading-edge devices to keep the wing generating lift at high angles of attack.

To address this safety concern, the FAA defined a certification requirement under which manufacturers must demonstrate a premature takeoff attempt in which the pilot pulls the nose up so high that the aft end of the jet literally scrapes the runway! Called *minimum unstick*, or V_{mu}, this very dramatic departure must, by regulation, be performed at maximum takeoff weight with one engine pulled back to idle to simulate an engine failure at takeoff.

For our V_{mu} tests, we flew the 747 east across the Cascade Mountains to Moses Lake Airport in a sparsely populated region of Washington State. A former military airfield, Moses Lake offers long runways and few neighbors, which makes it a good place to conduct flying of this nature. I went along as an observer, and so did Boeing President T Wilson.

In preparation for this test, we fitted an oak plank to the underside of the 747's aft fuselage. That board's purpose was to prevent the airplane structure from being damaged when its tail dragged on the concrete. As last-minute preparations were being made, I asked project pilot Jack Waddell if I could join him in the cockpit, explaining that I wanted to observe the test from the inside. He agreed.

T Wilson strode over. "Sutter," he announced, "you're not going on that flight."

I was startled. Was T concerned about my safety? The 747 should be able to pass this test. If anything went wrong, professional test pilots and a long runway would together mitigate the risk. Hairy as it was, therefore, it shouldn't actually be dangerous.

"There's just one extra seat in the cockpit and I'm taking it," he continued, grinning as he pulled rank on me.

My disappointment was tempered by seeing this awe-inspiring test from the ground. Here's this huge jet careening down the runway toward you at maximum takeoff weight. I watched as Waddell pulled power off an engine and immediately overrotated the 747 until that oak strip dragged on the runway, shooting back a trail of fire. Despite this extreme nose-high attitude, the 747 broke ground and flew successfully away on the thrust of its three remaining engines.

I breathed easier knowing that another key certification requirement had been passed. As we watched three or four more of those

V_{mu} Certification Test

hairy V_{mu} takeoffs, it occurred to me that when the word got out that this test had been done with Boeing's president on board, it would speak to the company's confidence in the airworthiness of the 747.

—————

The next certification hurdle took us to Edwards Air Force Base in California's Mojave Desert, where we conducted our rejected takeoff (RTO) performance tests. Edwards was where Chuck Yeager broke the sound barrier in 1947. A lot of history has been made there. We chose Edwards for added safety. Its runways were part of a dry lake bed of vast proportions. If we needed an overrun (additional stopping area beyond the runway), there was as much as we could possibly use.

For RTO testing, the airplane is loaded to its maximum takeoff weight and accelerates to a calculated velocity known as V_1 speed. At this point, the pilot aborts the takeoff and brings the airplane to the shortest possible stop using wheel brakes alone. (For added safety, the rigorous FAA certification requirements do not allow the use of reverse thrust even though pilots use thrust reversers in real-world RTOs.)

Under FAA regulations, V_1 is the computed speed beyond which the flight crew will not attempt to stop the jet on the ground because too little runway remains for safety. V_1 isn't the takeoff speed; that's a slightly higher value known as V_R (rotation speed). What V_1 defines is the fastest the pilot can go on the runway and still elect to abort the takeoff. Beyond V_1 it's safer to proceed with the takeoff even if an engine has just failed.

In our RTO test at Edwards, Jack Waddell would chop the 747's throttles at V_1 and slam on the brakes to see whether the 747 would stop within the certified field length. This dumps a tremendous amount of energy into the brakes, which on the early 747s were made of steel. Today the industry relies on composite brake discs, which perform better and last longer than steel.

The RTO test definitely had safety concerns for those of us watching from the ground at Edwards. For one thing, the brakes on those 16 main wheels would have to stop more than 700,000 pounds of airplane in a relatively short distance, something that had never before been attempted. Those brakes would get so hot they'd catch fire, ruining the tires. The heat would have exploded them except that aircraft wheel rims are designed with built-in fuse plugs. These melt in high heat, safely releasing the tire's pressure to avoid a hazardous explosion.

Making this test even more exacting, FAA requirements further stipulate that the jet must sit for five minutes before any firefighting equipment can begin extinguishing the flames. This requirement simulates the time it might take to get equipment out to a real jetliner following an actual RTO.

The test began. I watched the 747 barrel down the runway. At what looked like flying speed, Jack Waddell chopped the throttles and initiated maximum braking. Cringing at the squeal of tortured brakes, I focused on the careening jumbo jet's wheel hubs. They began to glow a dull red. This rapidly became bright orange and continued to intensify as the jet stopped short with an abruptness that said tremendous forces were at play. Flames broke out in its wheel bogeys.

I sweated out the interminable five minutes until FAA regulations said hoses could be brought to bear. The time finally passed and the airport firefighting crew quickly knocked down the fires. Framed in the cockpit windows above was a very calm-looking Jack Waddell.

Test pilots are a funny breed. At Boeing, you find the spectrum of personalities among their ranks, but they all have a few things in common: They are understated, stick to the facts, and don't burden you with their inner thoughts and feelings. If Waddell's crew had any concerns about the underbelly of their jet being exposed to open flames, they didn't show it. They also didn't seem concerned that a wheel might fly apart because a fuse plug didn't work. It was all business as usual for them.

———————

Preparing for FAA certification also meant performing hundreds of stalls as we fully probed the 747's flight characteristics out to the edges of its flight envelope. For safety's sake, stalls are performed at altitude. In the basic power-off stall, the airplane is taken to below its landing speeds and the pilot continues pulling back on the control yoke. When the jet runs out of flying speed, the airflow separates over its wings and it quits flying. The nose drops as the stall breaks. Then the pilot releases backpressure on the control wheel, allowing the jet to regain flying speed.

It all sounds gentle and easy, but in fact stall tests have a high "pucker factor" in very large airplanes, particularly the ones known as accelerated stalls. During the 747's flight-test program, we performed many accelerated stalls in power-on turns to evaluate the jet's tendency to drop a wing and perhaps flip over. We were pleased to find out that the 747 displays very little tendency to fall off to either side during aerodynamic stalls.

We also performed stalls with different engines throttled back to investigate the effects of asymmetrical thrust (that is, more power on one side of the jet than the other), and with every combination of landing gear and leading- and trailing-edge device extensions. All of this was done over and over again at different CGs, since an airplane handles differently depending on whether its CG is forward or aft.

If it sounds like it could make you pretty miserable, it can. The secret about stalls is that they don't bother the guy doing them (or gal, since Boeing also has enormously talented female test pilots) because the person at the controls knows exactly what's coming. However, everybody else on the airplane turns green pretty fast.

Also rigorously tested in flight were the 747's hydraulics, air-conditioning, and other systems under normal conditions and with simulated failures and combinations of failures. This exhaustive test effort—the most comprehensive certification program performed up to that time—kept our five 747 test airplanes flying seven days a week.

We used Ship 1 (RA001) to clear the 747 for flutter and probe its basic aerodynamics, including stalls. Ship 2 did engines and systems testing. Ship 3 flew structural tests. Ship 4 (which attended the Paris Air Show) and Ship 5 did service testing. Two more 747 air-frames were sacrificed to "static testing" that saw them intentionally destroyed to verify the airplane's strength.

We completed the 747 developmental and certification flight test-ing in just 10 months. This set another record, since we took our big bird through to government certification faster than any commercial jet transport before or since.

———

Two weeks before the FAA was scheduled to certify the 747, the third ship in our test fleet crashed while landing at Renton Airport. Seated in the flight deck at the time, I had a close-up view of the event.

That accident happened on a drizzly Saturday morning in Decem-ber 1969. My day had started out at our Flight Test Center on Boeing Field. I found myself with time on my hands when instrumentation problems delayed the test I was planning to run. It would be several hours before the plane could take off.

"Hey, Joe," suggested one of my people, "why don't you fly over to Renton on the number 3 ship? As long as you've got nothing better to do, you might as well observe that short-field landing for yourself. It should be quite a sight seeing something so big land there."

Our number 3 airplane had finished up its testing duties and was being flown to Renton to have its test equipment removed and an airline interior installed prior to delivery to an airline customer. That would ordinarily have been done at Everett but that plant was too busy, so the work had been relocated to Renton, where Boeing builds its single-aisle jets.

Renton Municipal Airport and Boeing's Renton plant are located at the southern tip of Lake Washington, some five miles southeast of Boeing Field. Whereas Boeing Field's runway is 10,000 feet long and Paine Field's is 9,000, Renton's is only a bit more than 5,000 feet long. It's geared to small airplanes, not jetliners.

Back then, Boeing probably had about 50 air-transport-rated pilots on the payroll—more than many of the world's airlines. Some were production test pilots who would wring out our jets as they rolled off the production lines. Others were training pilots who instructed the flight crews of our customer airlines. The third group was Boeing's engineering test pilots. These were the people I worked with. In the old days, they might have been called experimental test pilots, but that had come to smack of Clark Gable in a leather helmet and white scarf. Besides, most of the members in this group actually had engineering degrees and knew airplanes inside out.

Jim Gannett, one of these elite fliers, had been slated to fly the 747 on its brief hop over to Renton. He was traveling for the company, though, and had been delayed getting back. Fellow engineering test pilot Ralph Cokely got the assignment instead.

I went to Dix Loesch's office and found Cokely looking quite worried. He repeatedly expressed concerns about the 747's ability to use Renton's short runway. To put his mind at ease, I called one of my engineers and asked him to bring performance charts describing the 747's stopping performance. That engineer arrived and gave an impromptu briefing that showed what the rest of us already knew: Our very lightly loaded 747 test ship would have no problem setting down at Renton.

Cokely asked for additional reassurances and didn't appear to believe them. I followed him and his crew aboard the airplane and buckled into a jump seat in the flight deck. We taxied out and took off, and Cokely banked us in a wide circuit to approach Renton from the north over Lake Washington.

Watching him from behind as we flew down final approach, I could see he was really sweating it. His knuckles were white on the controls. He was determined to use every available inch of pavement ahead. As we descended toward the water, I saw that we were too low. *By God, we're not going to make it!* I thought.

Our right landing gear caught the lip of the concrete seawall and ripped off, dumping us to the side. Cokely jumped on the brakes and called up full reverse thrust. The engines surged from affected airflow as their nacelles scraped the ground.

We came to an abrupt halt with three quarters of Renton's runway remaining ahead of us. There was a rope ladder on the flight deck for emergency exits. Using it, we climbed out through the side window and were standing glumly inspecting the damage when the field's rescue vehicles raced up, lights flashing.

Wally Buckley joined us. Wanting a front-row seat for the landing of a 747 at Renton, he'd parked his car by the end of the runway and had been there watching. Our right wing had missed hitting his vehicle by inches. His was probably the luckiest escape of the day.

I was a bit concerned that this crash might jeopardize the 747's certification, but the accident was so clearly a case of pilot error that the FAA hardly took note of it. Their brief investigation turned up plenty of testimony documenting Cokely's worried review of those performance curves and his subsequent fixation on landing short.

The robustness and crashworthiness of our jumbo jet impressed the hell out of the FAA. Boeing designs its landing gears with shear pins so that, in the event of a collision, they will tear safely away without puncturing the fuel tanks or otherwise endangering the airplane and its occupants. This is what had happened at Renton, and there was little damage to the airplane.

Factory workers towed the 747 to the plant's refurbishment area. It took surprisingly little time to repair this ship to like-new condition and roll it out for customer delivery. As for Ralph Cokely, a good pilot who'd had a terrible day, he probably didn't feel he could live down that landing at Boeing. So he jumped ship to Lockheed, where he flew the L-1011 TriStar widebody through its certification testing.

———

On December 30, 1969, the FAA awarded Approved Type Certificate A20WE to the Boeing 747. This government certification cleared the way for us to start delivering 747s, which would soon begin flying in the colors of the world's great airlines.

As for our five-ship test fleet, the second through fifth airplanes were reworked and delivered to airline customers. RA001, the first 747, stayed a Boeing-owned and -operated test ship until donated by Boeing to Seattle's Museum of Flight. Located at the southwest corner of Boeing Field, the Museum of Flight is one of the best air museums in North America. It displays RA001 and other large jets, including a Concorde, diagonally across East Marginal Way from its main building. The museum's Web site calls the 747 "perhaps the most significant engineering achievement ever undertaken by private industry without significant governmental support." From my perspective, that's entirely true.

In the early 1990s, Boeing leased RA001 back from the museum and flew it during the 777 test program. People in the Puget Sound region got to see this historic prototype in the air again, this time with a 777 engine in place of one of its regular inboard engines. The 777—the world's biggest twinjet—is nearly as large as the 747, and its engines are much larger in diameter.

———

So all-consuming was the 747 program that those of us involved sometimes saw little of our homes and families. In my case, home was in West Seattle where Nancy and I built our dream house and raised three wonderful children.

I still live in this West Seattle house tucked into a verdant bluff high above Puget Sound. It has a spectacular view with greenery framing the blue waters below and the snow-covered Olympics off in the distance. The Vashon Island ferry—dazzlingly white and looking like a model—arrives and departs silently all day long.

It's a modest home, not large or luxurious, but it felt great to own our own place, particularly as Boeing didn't pay much back in the Bill Allen days. Nancy filled it with love, humor, and her artistry. When work kept me away, as it so often did, she uncomplainingly shouldered the load. It became her job to manage the household and attend to the parenting. She did a heck of a good job, although it wasn't easy on any of us.

Our children could not be more different. Gabrielle, the eldest, came along about the time I started at Boeing. From the time she was tiny, Gai loved painting and art projects. As she got older, she spent a good portion of her time outdoors swimming and playing with friends.

Jonathan came next and immediately seemed to want a wrench in his hand. He built himself a go-cart at an early age. In high school he bought a worn-out old Plymouth whose aft body had been replaced by a truck bed. He took that vehicle's engine out, tore it apart to see how it worked, rebuilt it, and it actually ran! He showed real initiative on other fronts as well, like the time he harvested oysters and made enough money to buy himself a new set of skis. He was pretty proud of that.

Adrienne came last and was a particularly happy little girl. She had a great friend named Kari, who lived nearby in West Seattle. The two girls got interested in hamsters and raised a lot of them. Periodically another of their hamsters would die. They'd bury the animal with due ceremony and have themselves a good cry.

I tried not to shortchange the kids or myself during their rich childhoods. When they were younger, I made time to tell them countless bedtime stories. They could never get enough of those, and I was sorry when they inevitably outgrew them. Of course, we have great memories of our times at the cabin at Hood Canal, where the beach, swimming, wildlife, and a leaky little sailboat were magical parts of their childhood.

Fortunately, the 747 program came along when our children were largely grown and gone. Gabrielle had graduated from college, worked briefly at Boeing, and then moved to Hawaii, where she still lives. Jonathan was in college, so he too was gone much of the time. That left only Adrienne, then in her late teens, at home during the 747 years.

Adrienne tells me she doesn't recall that period as being unusual. There wasn't any high drama at the dinner table, just ordinary conversation. While she knew I was working on airplanes at Boeing, she had no idea at the time that I was designing what would for decades be the biggest airliner in the world.

There was something on the home front back then that gave me a welcome sense of balance: Nancy's work. On those many occasions when problems on the 747 seemed overwhelming, her situation showed me that my big job wasn't everything.

All of us need a productive role to play in this world, a sense that we're making a difference and a contribution. This was every bit as true of Nancy as it was of me. A nutritionist by training, she was a caring human being, and with our children mostly gone, she felt she should be out doing something worthwhile.

Nancy found an outlet for her restless energies in a government program called Head Start. It addressed the needs of children of preschool age in the daytime when their mothers and fathers were working. Nancy became a nutritionist for Head Start in High Point, an area of Seattle where many lower-income people lived in public housing.

Nancy was supposed to arrive at work at 9 AM, prepare lunch for these children, and then head home by 1:00 or 1:30. Sometimes, though, she'd get home as late as I did because she took so much on herself. She couldn't stand to see these little kids not getting proper nutrition, so she went the extra mile in getting good food and preparing very healthy and satisfying lunches for them. She really accomplished miracles on a limited budget, and the program was enormously grateful to her for all the excellent work she did.

All through the busiest and most demanding days of designing the

Nancy Sutter
(AUTHOR'S PERSONAL COLLECTION)

747, I'd come home with big problems and share them with Nancy. She'd listen carefully and offer support and suggestions. Then it was my turn to listen while she described her problems at work. Sometimes hers were bigger than mine, because I could at least tell people what to do. In contrast, Nancy wasn't in a position of authority, so she could only try to coax and persuade others who lacked the capabilities, desire, or gumption to get the job done.

It was very discouraging for her at times, but caring for those disadvantaged kids was also a real source of joy and inspiration for her. Sometimes it broke her heart because no matter how she tried to take care of them at school, she knew that when they went home they didn't get what they needed. Gentle questioning revealed that many of them got nothing more to eat at home than a slice of bread, dry cereal out of a box, a cold hot dog out of the refrigerator, or nothing at all.

I think she ultimately just couldn't stand the sorrow of it, so she gave it up after three years. She also had a hard time with the bureaucracy.

After being there for a couple of years, for example, she actually would come in below her budget. When her bosses saw that, they told her, "You've got a surplus, so go out and buy a new refrigerator and stove." Well, they'd bought brand-new appliances two years before, so more appliances were the last thing they needed. As someone who grew up in the Depression years, Nancy couldn't believe her ears. She couldn't understand wasting money like that when there were so many crucial human needs that could and should have been met. This bad side of bureaucracy was disillusioning, but she stuck with it for another year. There were times when I was gone for days or even weeks on Boeing travel, and she was eager to have work of her own.

11

TRANSFORMING THE WORLD

I was at a meeting in Pan Am's boardroom in New York decades ago. Coffee and sandwiches were brought in and we were taking a lunch break. Charles Lindbergh, one of the attendees, came over to where Jack Waddell and I were standing by one wall eating our sandwiches. "You know," he announced quietly, "this is one of the great ones."

He meant the 747, which was then new in service, and he pointed out that it was the first airplane ever to make air travel broadly available. He added that he considered its emergence one of the most significant milestones in the entire history of flight.

This observation from none other than "Slim" Lindbergh, a hero of mine since I was six, was what first opened my eyes to how important the 747 would be. For me personally, his words remain a treasured gift. They more than make up for every bit of stress I endured during those incredibly demanding years.

———

Financial woes were catching up with Boeing, which desperately needed to start delivering 747s. That would bring in huge revenues, pushing the company's cash flow back in the right direction. But just when things should have been better, the pain got worse: Pratt & Whitney did not meet its contracted delivery schedule for JT9D engines. The Connecticut manufacturer had its hands too full trying to get the engine to perform reliably at rated power. While I understood the issues they were contending with, their schedule default came at a very, very bad time.

We found ourselves rolling 747s out of the factory with 5,000-pound concrete blocks dangling from their wings where their engines should be. Without those weights, the airplanes would have sat back on their tails. The ramp at Everett soon filled up with all these beautiful 747s, brand-new and resplendent in their bright airline paint schemes, ready to go except that they were missing their engines.

JT9Ds finally began to arrive, letting us finish up those 747s. It was a very satisfying feeling to watch them fly off to new homes around the globe. The airlines' own crews were at the controls, often accompanied by Boeing pilots seeing to the last of the airline pilots' training.

————

The 747 debuted in service on January 21, 1970, when Pan Am's *Clipper Constitution*—a brand-new 747-100—flew from New York's John F. Kennedy International Airport to London's Heathrow Airport with 324 passengers on board. That inaugural flight generated a tidal wave of popular interest and media attention.

A major economic recession was in full swing at the time, though, and our new jet was clearly a gamble. The conventional wisdom was that it was much too big, and more than a few aviation experts castigated Boeing for being so audacious. They predicted that, like Icarus in the ancient myth, we would suffer the consequences for flying too high.

In those days, Pan Am was the undisputed powerhouse of international air travel. TWA and Northwest struggled to compete, the former across the Atlantic and the latter the Pacific. Pan Am had a worldwide network, so it also competed against foreign carriers such as Lufthansa, Air France, and Japan Airlines, all of which were overshadowed and playing catch-up after the setbacks of World War II.

When Pan Am bought the 747, a lot of international carriers felt compelled to buy 747s of their own just to compete. They saw that our jumbo was going to attract a lot of business and couldn't afford to be left behind. Sure enough, passengers flocked to the 747, which immediately set higher standards and expectations for intercontinental travel.

One of the great pleasures of my life was watching passengers board the 747 when it was new in service. They would halt abruptly just inside the doorway and gape in amazement. *This isn't an airplane*, their astonished expressions said, *it's a large room!* That feeling of wonder continued throughout the flight.

The public was so taken with the 747 that, despite the recession, our sales picked up as more and more airlines jumped on the bandwagon. They discovered that stepping up to the 747 brought more than just prestige; it brought market share and competitiveness. Despite its size, they found it a very easy airplane to maintain and fly.

If Boeing's new jumbo gave airlines more capacity than they needed immediately, they knew that it was just a matter of time before the fast-rising demand for international air travel saw their jets filled. And when airlines filled their 747s, they made *lots* of money. The reason was the 747's per-seat operating costs, which were an astonishing 30% lower than those of any previous jet. In an industry where a difference of 1% or 2% can mean millions of dollars per year, we at Boeing had rolled out an unprecedented moneymaker.

Douglas and Lockheed were hot on our heels with widebody jets of their own, of course. The Douglas DC-10 and Lockheed L-1011 TriStar both had three engines and entered service in the early 1970s. Unfortunately for their builders, though, they offered transcontinental range when the world's airlines wanted widebodies with intercontinental range like the 747. Lockheed designed its TriStar with too small a wing, a mistake that drove that company entirely out of the airliner business. As for Douglas, it was able to increase the DC-10's range quite a bit but never matched that of the 747. The McDonnell Douglas MD-11, a major derivative of the DC-10, also didn't fly far enough because McDonnell Douglas simply wasn't willing to invest sufficiently to give the airplane the new wing it needed.

A new European consortium called Airbus brought a fourth wide-body to market during the 1970s. Placed into service in 1974, the Airbus A300B was a twin-aisle twinjet with very limited range capability. As originally delivered, it was intended for service between Europe's capitals and perhaps to North Africa and the Middle East. It sold poorly, though, and Airbus quickly learned that the world didn't want a twin-aisle jet that couldn't even fly nonstop from Chicago to the West Coast.

The DC-10, MD-11, L-1011, and A300B today all fly as freighters, although none of them is as well suited to the role as the 747. It alone of that first generation of widebodies was designed from the outset for intercontinental range as well as main-deck freighter use.

Needless to say, our foresight has paid off for Boeing over the decades. The world knew we had something really good from the very start.

––––––––––––

The 747 caught the eye of more than just our airline customers. Before it even entered service, it attracted the attention of celebrities, the media, Hollywood, and just about everyone else. Everybody wanted to get a look at our big airplane, it seemed.

One Saturday a few weeks before the first 747's first flight, I was at work when a call came in from Tex Boullioun. It turned out he was up flying with famous golfer Arnold Palmer and was speaking to me from a helicopter. Palmer was an aviation buff who traveled in a Lear-jet that he owned and piloted himself. He had made a special trip to the Seattle area just to see our new airplane. We gave him a tour of RA001 and it absolutely floored him. I watched him contemplate this huge flying machine with unguarded amazement. I guessed he was wondering what it would be like to fly. We were actually all wondering that at the time.

That was the first of many pilgrimages made by VIPs who wanted to see aviation's next great jetliner for themselves. It took me away from my busy schedule, but it generated valuable publicity outside the company and was an enjoyable break from my usual duties.

The tours continued after the airplane was in service. Bob Six was then the president of Continental Airlines, which had ordered the 747 but not yet taken delivery. He was married to Audrey Meadows, an actress who had starred in an early television series called *The Honeymooners* before she moved on to movie roles. They were both in Hawaii when we flew through in Qantas's first 747, which we were delivering to that airline in Australia. We had just one day's layover in Honolulu. Nancy was with me on one of the rare occasions when I was able to combine business with pleasure.

As was true for most Boeing people, I had few days off, and they were precious. To maximize our time together, Nancy and I went to the pool right after checking into our hotel. I had on my swimsuit and was about to jump into the pool when a Boeing salesman hurried over. "Boullioun wants you out at the airport right away because Bob Six wants to tour the Qantas airplane," he told me.

With a quick apology to Nancy, I changed and hurried to the airport. Tex and the salesman were there, and so were a couple of proud Qantas representatives who didn't want anybody to scuff their brand-new 747. But it turned out that Six was interested in only one part of the airplane, this being the upper-deck area behind the cockpit. Back then, airlines were using that area for lounges and restaurants. Only later did they turn it into additional seating space, generally business class. The upper deck of Qantas's first 747 was laid out in a very attractive nautical motif that Quantas called the Captain Cook Lounge. Those early 747-100s had only a few windows in that upper area. We were just coming around to the idea that airlines could make more money by putting paying passengers upstairs too, so we had designed rows of windows for the upper deck to give airlines this option.

I told Bob Six that he could have his choice of just a few windows, as on that Qantas jet, or a full row down both sides of the upper deck. Bob felt the extra windows would be best, whereas Audrey felt just as strongly that Continental should go without the extra windows because it created a more intimate lounge atmosphere.

Bob and Audrey began arguing about it. Tex and this Boeing salesman, who had together been leading the tour, now found themselves strictly on the sidelines as the window discussion became more heated. Then Audrey walked up to me and began asking more questions. I gave straightforward replies but found that conversing eye to eye with a very animated and attractive movie star made it difficult to concentrate completely on engineering matters. She had a real presence and could be very persuasive.

The tour came to an end. As we all exited that Qantas jet at Honolulu International Airport, Bob came alongside me. "Go ahead and build our jets with those extra windows, Joe," he told me with a quiet smile. "Don't worry about Audrey—there's going to be a little pillow talk tonight, and she'll come around."

———

Once the 747 was in service, we engineers found we still had a lot on our plates. The reason was that the airlines immediately wanted more range out of the 747. We met this customer requirement by modifying the design to permit an increase in gross weight from 710,000 to 775,000 pounds. We'd intentionally designed growth capability into the airplane by giving it a more robust structure and bigger wings and tail surfaces than it needed, to allow for such things as higher gross weights and a possible fuselage stretch.

With its technical problems now largely resolved, Pratt & Whitney was able to support this early gross-weight increase with uprated JT9Ds. Each of these new engines developed more than 50,000 pounds of thrust.

The result of all these improvements was the 747-200B, which we certified at the end of 1970 and placed into production beside the

747-100. We put a huge amount of effort into this new model, which consumed 1.7 million engineering labor hours. The first 747-200B went to KLM in January 1971, and before that year was out, this model was also flying in the colors of Air India, Alitalia, Condor, El Al, JAL, Lufthansa, Northwest, Sabena, SAS, South African Airways, Swissair, and Qantas.

General Electric and Rolls-Royce soon brought to market 50,000-pound-thrust engines of their own. GE's CF6 was an entirely new fanjet developed for the McDonnell Douglas DC-10. As for the Rolls-Royce RB211, it was developed for the Lockheed L-1011 TriStar. To give our customers more choices, we certified both these engine types for use on the 747.

Rolls-Royce had originally tried to get the RB211 onto the 747 in 1967 or 1968, but the engine was then at a very early stage of development. At that time, it presented us with too many unknowns. Not willing to take on those risks, we said no but encouraged Rolls to approach us again once the engine was more mature.

That didn't sit well with the British Overseas Airways Corporation. BOAC, which would later merge with British European Airways to form British Airways, wanted its 747s to be powered by British engines, as was their tradition. To keep this key customer happy, a lot of Boeing people pressured me strongly to change my mind and approve the early RB211 for use on the 747.

At the time, Rolls-Royce's chief propulsion engineer was Adrian Lombard, a British jet-engine pioneer. As head of the RB211 design team, Lombard believed strongly in his team's technically ambitious high-bypass-ratio fanjet, which was built around three concentric shafts instead of the usual two. He also believed wholeheartedly in its weight-saving fan blades, which were made of a lightweight composite material called Hyfil. Hyfil was a matrix of fiberglass and glue sheathed in steel. It was still largely untested, so nobody truly knew how well it would stand up to real-world events such as hail or "bird strikes," as collisions with geese and other large birds are called. I was very leery of these "oatmeal blades" and wasn't about to allow them on the 747 no matter how much it upset people at BOAC or within Boeing.

Compounding my suspicions about Hyfil, Rolls-Royce continued to refuse to provide my propulsion people with the technical data we had been requesting. The British firm appeared to be counting on its sterling reputation to assuage our reservations. Known for the quality of its products, Rolls-Royce—a true industry pioneer—had introduced the world's first commercial fanjet engine, the R-R Conway, to service aboard the 707 back in 1960.

I first met Adrian Lombard during the Conway's development. At the time, he and his design team in England didn't know how to design nacelles for pod-mounted engines, so they requested Boeing's technical data on the subject. That body of hard-won knowledge was just about to be handed over to Rolls when I pointed out that it had cost us a lot of time, money, and effort to develop it. We should at least be reimbursed, I said.

Boeing agreed and sold that proprietary information to Rolls-Royce instead of just giving it away. That got Lombard and me off to a bad start. He didn't take kindly to my speaking up, particularly since I was just a junior engineer at the time. Now a decade later, I was again being a thorn in his side as he tried to get us to certify the RB211 on the 747.

Hoping to get around me, Lombard went to Ed Wells, Boeing's senior statesman and vice president of product development. This end run resulted in a lot of top Boeing people viewing me as an obstructionist. My reputation as a hardnose rose to new heights, although I didn't think I deserved it; I was just doing what was in the best interests of the 747 program and Boeing. Fortunately, chief engineers at Boeing traditionally have final say in such matters, so I was able to keep the RB211 off the 747 until they addressed our concerns.

At Wells's request, I flew to New York during this period and met with Lombard at the old Ritz Tower Hotel. I walked into his suite at the appointed time and found a buffet breakfast so lavish it would have fed 20 people, even though there were just the two of us.

We exchanged pleasantries and helped ourselves to the breakfast. I was hoping Lombard would finally provide the technical data we'd been requesting about Hyfil, but instead he launched into an impassioned diatribe about the strength of those fan blades. To make his point, he jumped up, ran into the bedroom, and returned an instant later with an actual Hyfil blade.

It was long and curved like a scimitar. Brandishing it like a weapon, Lombard raised it over his head and swung it down as hard as he could with a menacing swish. To my astonishment, I saw that the blade had sliced right through the room's coffee table. That demonstration certainly attested to Hyfil's utility as a knife, but it still didn't mean the blade would hold up to years of airline use. I also very much doubted the hotel would appreciate Lombard's treatment of their furniture.

It turned out my reservations were well founded. Despite Rolls-Royce's claims about those composite RB211 fan blades, they failed a critical test. Rolls-Royce was forced to abandon Hyfil in favor of all-metal blades. All of this came at a challenging time for Rolls-Royce Aero Engines, which survived a brush with bankruptcy only by dint of a government bailout. It regained its financial health and went on to develop higher thrust versions of its RB211. We certified them for use on both the 747 and 767 widebodies.

By holding fast, I pushed Rolls-Royce in the right direction and ended up bringing them a lot of business they would otherwise not have had. At the time, though, I was definitely cast in the role of the bad guy—not just at Rolls-Royce but also by people within Boeing. But if we had adopted that original RB211, there's no doubt in my mind that Boeing and Rolls would have taken a financial bath and our reputations would have been badly tarnished.

I'm pleased to say that in recent decades I've enjoyed a very cordial relationship with Rolls-Royce. People at this great British firm acknowledge and express appreciation for the role I played in helping them put a lot of excellent engines on Boeing jetliners.

Traveling in Europe for Boeing in the spring of 1973, I briefly attended that year's Paris Air Show. This was the year of dueling SSTs, with the Anglo-French Concorde and Russia's Tu-144 taking turns performing for the assembled crowds.

The day I visited, it was raining and no flying was slated. This pause worked to my advantage because I found myself invited—along with Lynn Olason, Jack Waddell, and a third Boeing colleague—to tour the Tu-144.

The plane looked to me a lot like the Concorde, which I had also toured. Our hosts were the SST's Soviet flight crew plus a couple of Russian aeronautical engineers and industry executives. After showing us the passenger cabin, they ushered us into the cockpit. We all squeezed in there, and our hosts produced caviar and vodka. Amid much laughter and good camaraderie, we drank a toast with them and had quite an enjoyable conversation. I've had a lot of contact with the Russians over the decades and have always found them to be very fine people.

Flying home the next day, I was seated in first class aboard a United 747 when the flight attendant invited me to visit the flight deck. The pilot wanted to chat with me about the 747, she explained. This was back in the days before the FAA required cockpit doors to be locked in flight against hijackings.

The three-man flight crew welcomed me and pointed to a jump seat. I sat down and we had a relaxed discussion during which they told me how much they loved the 747. The captain frowned, remembering something as I stood to leave. "Have you heard the news, Joe?" he asked.

"No, what?" I asked.

"The Tu-144 crashed while performing for the crowds at Paris. Everybody aboard was killed."

The news hit me very hard. From him I learned that the Soviet crew had apparently lost control of their SST while attempting to avoid a camera plane. I'd just visited with those guys and we'd had a wonderful time. They were so full of life and laughter. It was a hell of a shock to learn they were dead.

The Tu-144 was built primarily for prestige and wasn't a very good airplane. Its engines were too thirsty, its operating economics were dreadful, and it reportedly vibrated so badly in flight that Aeroflot initially used it to carry mail and cargo, not people. It's hard to imagine freight needing to go anywhere that fast.

There were two crashes after passenger services finally began. Those accidents put an early end to the Tu-144's troubled career. Only 17 were built, 3 fewer than the total number of Concordes.

The bloom was certainly off the rose for SSTs. By the time the Tu-144 crashed at Paris, it was pretty clear that SSTs weren't the next big thing in aviation. That honor pretty much belonged to the 747, which was proving to be more versatile and successful than anyone had imagined.

Just how versatile is the 747's design? Consider an early derivative we built for a use totally different from the long-haul operations we designed the airplane for: the 747SR, a short-range shuttle we built expressly for Japan. To this day, the 747SR—and its successor, the 747-400 Domestic—remain the only jetliner models ever developed by any manufacturer to address the needs of just a single nation.

Of course, Japan isn't just any nation. Back in the 1970s, it was experiencing phenomenal economic growth that saw huge increases from one year to the next in air travel demand. The 727s we had sold to Japan starting in 1964 were suddenly way too small to meet this galloping demand. Something much bigger was needed for the Tokyo–Sapporo, Tokyo–Fukuoka, and other interisland Japanese routes, which are among the busiest in the world.

I was then leading the entire 747 program as general manager of the Everett Division. Row Brown reported to me as head of 747 product development. He and I had been meeting with Boeing's commercial salespeople, who were eager to help their Japanese customers find solutions to their growth challenges. Row and I also met directly with representatives from JAL and All Nippon Airways (ANA) when they visited Everett, and heard firsthand how urgently they needed more lift.

Row came up with the remarkable idea of considering the 747 for shuttle use in Japan. This concept was nothing less than shocking, because the 747 was strictly a long-haul airplane. It flew once a day or maybe twice at the most. We had not designed it for the stresses of frequent pressurization cycles or the poundings of all the landings it would make in very short haul shuttle use.

A shuttle would also be very different on the inside. Instead of three service classes (first, business, and economy) with comfort levels and galley provisioning geared to long flights, we were talking a walk-on, walk-off airplane with almost nothing but seats.

Row looked at how many people we could put into a 747 shuttle, and the number was somewhere between 525 and 575. But even after that had been established, there were many doubters at Boeing. Was it possible to make a long-range airplane like the 747 suitable to dozens of short hops each and every day, year after year, for 20 or even 30 years?

When we examined the 747 design with an eye toward this unanticipated use, we discovered that many minor changes would be required but nothing too major. The landing gear and some internal structures needed beefing up; that was about all. Turning the 747 into a robust shuttle wouldn't have a big impact on operating costs or airframe weight.

JAL introduced the 747SR to service in October 1973, and ANA, the country's largest domestic operator, later inaugurated 747SR operations of its own. Those Boeing shuttles each had 525 passenger seats and often flew entirely full. Needless to say, the people at both airlines were hugely pleased that we went the extra mile to give them something most people thought wasn't in the cards.

In 1993, JAL and ANA began replacing their hardworking SRs with 747-400 Domestics, a 568-seat version of the much improved 747-400 of 1989. These ongoing shuttle services have been a very,

very good operation for both airlines and for the country itself. Without them, Japan's economic growth would have been stifled and people there wouldn't have enjoyed as much freedom of travel about their country.

———

Because the 747 was also designed for use as a main-deck freighter, there was considerable interest from the very start in that role. The 747-200 Freighter was the first cargo 747 to roll off Boeing's assembly lines. Lufthansa introduced it to service in April 1973. Seaboard World Airlines, JAL, Air France, Northwest, Cargolux, and many other airlines were soon operating it as well.

Back in the early 1970s, of course, a lot of cargo was being carried by converted propeller airliners finishing out their days as tramp freighters. Compared with them, the 747 provided an astonishing increase in capability and productivity. Light-years ahead of the competition, it has since become the backbone of intercontinental air freight.

Another variant also developed early on was the 747-200 Combi. It's a hybrid 747 that's half passenger plane and half freighter. It came into being at the specific request of Sabena, Belgium's national airline, which was a highly successful 707 operator. One of Europe's prestige air carriers back then, Sabena was the first airline based on the European continent to introduce jets across the Atlantic—not Lufthansa, not Air France, but Sabena.

At the start of the 1970s, this airline took delivery of two 747s. They carried the Belgian flag to New York but their passenger loads were way too thin. While Sabena had no trouble filling the lower holds of its 747s with revenue cargo, the airline simply didn't have enough passenger demand on its Brussels–New York route, or any other route that Sabena flew for that matter.

If Sabena couldn't break even with their new 747s, why had they bought such a big airplane in the first place? The reason was that Congo had won its independence from Belgium a decade earlier. As a colony, the African nation had provided Belgium with heavy trade and travel to support its national airline, but that had evaporated after Congo left Belgium's political and economic sphere. Sabena apparently placed its 747 orders before it caught up psychologically with the realities of these reduced circumstances.

At that time, a Boeing man named Hans Ott handled Sabena in our European sales division. Hans asked me to accompany him to Brussels in the early 1970s to see if we could help Sabena find the formula for success with its 747s. As stated, they did have good cargo loads, particularly across the North Atlantic.

During our meetings in Brussels, the Sabena people suggested that we look at dividing the passenger cabins of their 747s so that the forward section catered to passengers and the aft to cargo. This involved more than just a partition, of course. A cargo door would have to be installed aft of the wing, and the rear flooring would need to be strengthened to support heavy freight pallets.

When Hans and I came home, Boeing's management gave us the go-ahead to look into this intriguing concept. We developed an engineering program under which Sabena's two 747s were brought back to the Everett factory for these modifications to be made. Meantime, our marketing people dubbed this hybrid 747 the Combi, which stands for "combination airplane."

Lynn Olason and Row Brown did the design work. Having helped at least initiate this 747 variant, I went out to the Everett factory to watch the work being performed. I saw this beautiful white-and-blue Sabena 747 sitting in jigs to preserve its fuselage alignment while the airplane's structure was compromised. It shocked me to see factory personnel grab Skil saws and cut a gaping hole in its side. It seemed a real shame when I thought of how much effort went into designing that structure and building it, but in fairly short order a stiffened door frame had been installed, followed by the big cargo door itself.

The rest of the modifications were completed and we redelivered these two jets—once again looking resplendently new—to Sabena. The airline put its Combis into service over the Atlantic and immediately began making money hand over fist. This soon attracted the attention of Sabena's neighbors, particularly KLM in Holland.

————

The biennial Paris Air Show came along about this time. Lynn Olason and I attended with many members of Boeing management and our salespeople. Lynn has always had a lot of initiative. He proposed that, building on the Sabena modifications, we make the Combi a regular Boeing product offering. To this end, he had a model built of the Combi that was shipped to Paris ahead of us.

Boeing always has a chalet with a great view of the runway at Le Bourget. That's where we entertain airline clients and other high-level visitors. When Lynn and I checked in, they were still unpacking the Combi model and getting it ready for visiting customers. Clancy Wilde, Boeing's vice president of commercial sales, entered with his people in tow. They saw the Combi model and promptly got all worked up about it.

KLM was very close to signing for the 747, they told us, but the Dutch airline had heard about the Combi and was starting to express interest in it. With KLM ready to sign on the dotted line for all-passenger 747s, Clancy didn't want the Combi model in plain sight when it could send everybody back to square one in the complex sales negotiations. He told Lynn to get rid of it before the KLM people arrived. An airshow chalet is not a place with a whole lot of extra room, so this model ended up inside a bathroom, and not a very big one at that. Lynn was told not to sit in on the meeting with KLM because contractual rather than engineering matters would be discussed.

The KLM officials arrived in due course and discussions started between them and Clancy and his people. Just as those talks were reaching what seemed a successful conclusion, one KLM person remembered the Combi and asked to hear more about it.

Not at all happy, Clancy summoned Lynn to make an impromptu presentation using available charts. The KLM people kept wanting more information until finally Lynn couldn't bear it anymore. "Well," he announced, "I could answer these questions a lot easier if I just showed you the model."

"What model?" they all asked.

"The one in the bathroom," he replied.

With that, three or four rather large gentlemen from KLM plus Clancy and Lynn all squeezed into that bathroom for a highly technical discussion about our combination passenger plane–freighter. By the time this peculiar session ended, KLM was ready to sign up for the Combi.

Boeing would of course make just as much profit selling 747 Combis as regular 747s. The Combi became a very popular model, because it allowed airlines that couldn't use the total passenger capacity of a 747 to fly a combined passenger and main-deck freight operation. Many, many airlines around the world bought it, including some smaller nations that wanted the prestige of a 747 but didn't have the high-density passenger routes needed to fill it. The 747 became the primary long-range airplane for many of the world's airlines, including British Airways, Air France, Lufthansa, Japan Airlines, Singapore Airlines, Cathay Pacific Airways, Qantas, Air New Zealand, United, Northwest, and of course Pan Am.

———

Pan Am's New York–Tokyo route generated a lot of business traffic and was an important source of revenue. However, these cities were too distant to fly nonstop. The airline badly wanted an airplane capable of flying that mission and looked to Boeing and other manufacturers for help. This was in the early 1970s when Pan Am had about 33 747s in its fleet.

The 747 then had the longest range of any airliner, but New York–Tokyo was well beyond its capabilities. The Douglas DC-10 and Lockheed L-1011, both of which entered service in the early 1970s, had less range than the 747, although Douglas talked up developing an improved version of the DC-10.

Out of consideration was the L-1011. Lockheed knew that it could never get that kind of range out of its airplane, so it declined Pan Am's overtures. Airbus Industrie—a European consortium with French, German, British, and Spanish participation—was then fielding its first airplane, the A300B. However, it had the least range of all, so it was not a contender.

We at Boeing believed it was up to us to provide Pan Am with its New York–Tokyo airplane. This was one hell of a challenge, though, particularly since flying this route westbound also meant fighting the prevailing winds.

The good news was that we had designed the 747 with plenty of growth capability. Once the engine manufacturers developed higher-thrust engines capable of lifting the high takeoff weights of greater fuel loads, the 747 would be able to fly this mission. However, Pan Am wasn't content to wait. Fortunately for them, Row Brown had another idea.

Row proposed that we shrink the 747 by taking a full 47 feet out of its fuselage length, a very dramatic decrease in size! Although the resulting jet would look like a flying football, and its per-seat operating costs would not be great, his preliminary studies showed that it could do the job for Pan Am.

These studies were labeled 747SB. The initials stood for "short body," but some wag at Boeing claimed the designation stood for "Sutter's balloon." The joke caught on and made the rounds. There were quite a few chuckles inside the plant over the extreme lengths—in reverse—to which my people were willing to go to adapt our jet to meet customer needs.

It so happened that John Borger and Bill Hibbs, a subordinate of Borger's at Pan American World Airways, came to Boeing to be briefed on preliminary studies for what would be the 767. I had not been following that work very closely and was pointedly told I didn't need to attend those meetings. It didn't bother me to be excluded, because I understood what the 767 people were thinking. Pan American was here about the 767. They knew Borger and I were friends and didn't want him distracted by our 747SB studies; that wasn't what he was in town for.

Borger and Hibbs spent the day being thoroughly briefed on the 767, after which Danny Palmer and some other Boeing people invited them to dinner. Borger accepted but there was something he wanted to do first. "You know," Borger said, "I would really like to talk to Sutter and his people and see if they've made any progress on meeting this New York–Tokyo requirement of ours."

The salespeople tried to dissuade him but he insisted on coming over to my area with Bill Hibbs. In typical Borger fashion, he barged into my office without pleasantries and launched into a diatribe against Boeing for not being responsive to Pan American's requirements. Douglas was willing to try to meet the Tokyo–New York need with an improved DC-10, he concluded, so perhaps Pan Am should take its business there.

"Well, John," I replied, "we probably don't have anything you'd be interested in but here's what we've done."

When I showed Borger and Hibbs our drawings and data on the 747SB, their eyes lit up and they insisted on seeing more. I agreed to work it up and meet them downtown at the dinner being hosted for them by the 767 team.

I got Row Brown's people to put together a little report. Since I hadn't yet shown it to our management for their blessing, I wrote on the cover, "Preliminary and subject to change without notice." When I got to the restaurant and presented this promised document to Borger, he frowned at the handwritten disclaimer. "That's how we buy *all* our airplanes from you," he groused. "I suppose it's as good a commitment as we'll ever get out of Boeing."

Quite a bit of time was devoted that evening to discussing the 747SB before Borger and Hibbs departed for the airport to take the red-eye back to New York. As we all split up, it was obvious that more than a few of my Boeing colleagues were highly annoyed with me for derailing the evening's focus on the 767 with what they called "Sutter's balloonacy."

The next morning at work, I'd hardly sat down when I got a call from Clancy Wilde, who in turn had received one from Mal Stamper. It seemed Borger and Hibbs spent the entire night flight going over this data and checking the 747SB's characteristics against their New York–Tokyo mission requirement. They'd hurried from the airport straight to their offices in the Pan Am building. New York being three hours ahead of Seattle, they had already found and briefed their president.

Pan Am's vice president at that time was Laurence Kuter, a retired four-star U.S. Air Force general. A West Pointer, Kuter had learned to fly at the end of the 1920s and had advanced quickly through the ranks during World War II. Instead of calling Tex Boullioun, the head of our commercial division, Kuter, being new to the game, called Mal Stamper, who was now president of the Boeing corporation. "Are you serious about this airplane you showed my people yesterday?" Kuter demanded.

Stamper knew nothing about it and had never heard of the 747SB. That was not unusual, considering that it was just a preliminary design concept and not an offerable product. Taken aback at being caught off guard, he called Clancy Wilde and demanded to know what the hell was going on. Clancy explained that what Pan Am had been shown was a preliminary design study for a much-modified 747 with greater range.

The upshot was that Clancy, Danny Palmer, and a few other key Boeing people trooped over for a meeting with Stamper. They didn't include me. I suspect it was because they were annoyed with me. Whatever the reason, they closeted themselves without engineering participation in an all-day session to define what action Boeing should take with respect to the 747SB.

This was a bad situation. Stamper did not know much about the technical side of the commercial airplane business. Without me in that meeting, the 747SB might not be properly represented in terms of its capabilities, characteristics, and reason for being.

I was more than a little curious as to what had transpired in Stamper's meeting. When people returned late that afternoon, I sought Danny out and asked him what the outcome had been.

"Well," Palmer said, "we talked about the program and came to a big decision."

My heart skipped a beat. Had they killed the 747SB? Were they going ahead with it? "Yes?" I asked.

"We can't call an airplane 'Sutter's balloon,'" Danny replied. "It doesn't sound right!"

As he filled me in on the meeting, I realized incredulously that they had spent the entire day discussing nothing more than what to call the airplane! For whatever reason, Stamper did not like our working designation and focused on coming up with an alternative. Because this shortened 747 would address a unique requirement—sufficient range to fly from New York to Tokyo despite the limited engine thrusts then available—they settled on 747SP, the new initials standing for "special performance."

Sometimes it's good when a committee gets caught up in inconsequential details.

————————

In the days that followed, lots of different Boeing organizations took a good hard look at the 747SP. Our sales and marketing community liked the airplane well enough to climb on board, and the decision was reached to pursue it as a product offering. Fortunately, nobody at high levels shot the SP down, even though it looked like Walt Disney had stormed Seattle and taken over our design halls.

The 747SP looked to me like a 747 had taxied into a wall and collapsed in on itself like a telescope. Despite its truncated appearance, it was the only airplane on anybody's drawing board that could fly very long intercontinental routes. Our marketing people concluded that other airlines besides Pan Am would also need that kind of range capability. Their analysis predicted a market for the SP and identified five airlines as likely launch customers.

On the basis of this assessment, Boeing's board decreed that the program would go ahead if we got enough orders from enough different airlines. Aside from Pan Am, none of the airlines we expected bought the airplane, but sufficient orders materialized and the program went forward.

747SP

This special 747's design differed in significant ways from that of the standard 747. Being smaller and lighter, it didn't need as much flap area and could make do with single-slotted instead of triple-slotted flaps. In contrast, its tail surfaces needed to be larger to make up for the reduced "moment arm" (degree of leverage) that resulted from not being mounted so far aft.

These factors, and the airplane's changed aerodynamics as a whole, could make for a very different airplane from the pilot's perspective. I felt strongly that we couldn't let that happen. The reason was safety. In real-world operations, the same flight crew might be called on to fly a standard 747 one day and the short-body SP the next. If there were meaningful differences in how these airplanes handled, it could get the pilots into trouble. For this reason, I decreed that the flying characteristics and operating procedures had to be identical from the perspective of the pilot.

Our talented engineers met this rigorous design constraint. They also kept the basic maintenance requirements the same despite the necessary repositioning of some systems to accommodate having more than a fifth of the airplane's length removed. As a result, the SP became just another 747 from the airline's point of view.

We ended up delivering a total of 45 747SPs. People have been tempted to conclude that it wasn't a good program because we built so few of them. This misses an important point, because the SP actually benefited the entire 747 program: It introduced many countries and airlines to the 747 and showed them that it is an easy airplane to operate.

Mainland China's intercontinental airlines were just gearing up at that time. They badly wanted to be competitive and had very long routes to serve. However, they were hesitant about committing to big airplanes they couldn't yet fill. The 747SP was the perfect "starter airplane" for them.

The 747SP was also a good fit for Iran, another country experiencing significant growth in air travel demand. Having had success with the 707, Iran needed more capacity and range but was very concerned about the excessive size of the 747. The country did not have a big freight market at that time, so a Combi wouldn't have worked for it.

Over time, as demand for air travel matured in these markets, their airlines moved up to full-size 747s and in some cases purchased large fleets. This experience offers a valuable lesson to financial and marketing types who tend to think short term and look too hard at the bottom line. In manufacturing, you'll do better in the long run if you look beyond an individual model's sales to see what it does for your overall product line.

––––––––––

John Borger worried throughout the 747SP's development that it would come in overweight and not meet its New York–Tokyo range and payload commitments. To reassure him, I proposed a simple wager. If his fears proved correct, I would pay him a dime for every pound the airplane came in above its specified target weight. But if Boeing did better than promised, he would pay me a dime for every pound. As it turned out, the 747SP came in a full 6,500 pounds below its committed weight. Pan Am was ecstatic, since that savings translated directly into additional payload capability and thus revenue opportunity.

Borger surprised me by paying up in memorable fashion. During a Seattle dinner at a Polynesian restaurant, a cloth sack was brought in on a blue Pan Am cushion. This hefty bag was ceremoniously presented to me. Opening it, I discovered a treasure trove of dimes! I learned later that Pan Am people had scoured Manhattan for enough dimes for Borger to spring his surprise.

I kept that bag at home and it delighted our grandkids. At the end of their visits to Nancy's and my West Seattle home, we'd let them reach in and take home as many dimes as their little fists could hold. It took more than two years for that bag to empty out.

———————

Further engine and other improvements allowed us to increase the 747-200's range to the point where it matched that of the shortened 747SP. For many years, the 747-200B was the long-haul jetliner of choice for airlines worldwide. It flew about 5,600 nautical miles. Boeing delivered 389 between 1971 and 1990, including two 747-200Bs to the air force to replace the presidential flight's Kennedy-era 707s.

Starting in 1983, Boeing began delivering 747-300s, a model characterized by an extended dome for additional upper-deck seating. Because we didn't add gross-weight capability, though, this model paid for its additional capacity with reduced range and thus wasn't popular with airlines. The last of 126 747-300s rolled out in 1990.

By then, the most successful 747 model was already in service. This was the 747-400, the first "major derivative" of the 747.

12

NEW ASSIGNMENTS

The 747 program went through incredible traumas on more than just the engineering front. Many of the program's other directors left. Both 747 Materiel and 747 Finance changed leaders several times, for example.

In April 1969, Mal Stamper had moved on to other duties at Boeing, and George Nible took his place as vice president and general manager of the 747 Division. At the very end of that year, Nible invited a bunch of us to the executive dining room for a festive lunch. We settled at a table in a small private lunch room off the main area.

During a lull in the conversation Nible looked around. "How many of you were here from the beginning of the program?" he inquired. It turned out that just two of us had seen the 747 all the way through. One was Bayne Lamb, the program's director of facilities who had done the impossible in erecting that huge factory in Everett. The other was me.

"Well, hell, we should record this somehow," Nible said, impressed.

"Why don't you name this room after Lamb and Sutter?" somebody suggested.

"That's a hell of a good idea!" Nible replied.

The next day there was a little sign on the door: "The Lamb-Sutter Room." The last time I checked several years ago, that room wasn't being used for the same purpose anymore but the sign was still there.

Life can be ironic. During all those problems and crises I contended with on the 747 program, I thought each time that my replacement was just around the corner. But Bayne and I saw the 747 all the way through. Everybody else who started in a leadership position under Stamper was gone, as was Stamper himself.

It is a great personal satisfaction that, as director of engineering, I saw the 747 through its definition, design, flight testing and certification, and entry into highly successful revenue service with the airlines. That four-and-a-half-year sprint was so arduous that I felt like a grizzled veteran and a survivor.

———————

For having successfully developed the 747 and introduced it to service, Boeing, Pratt & Whitney, and Pan American World Airways were named the recipients of the 1970 Collier Trophy. First presented in 1911, the Collier is aviation's highest award. I attended the presentation on May 20, 1971, and felt happiness and pride listening to Bill Allen's remarks. Najeeb Halaby, Pan Am's chairman after Juan Trippe's retirement, spoke next, followed by United Technologies Corporation Chairman William Gwinn (UTC is the parent company of Pratt & Whitney).

Unfortunately, Congress chose that very day to announce they were cutting funding for the Boeing 2707, effectively killing the U.S. SST program. Like the race to the Moon, the U.S. SST had been named a national priority by President Kennedy early in the previous decade. Half a billion taxpayer dollars had been spent in addition to a huge amount of Boeing's own money. Twenty-six airlines around the world had ordered some 120 Boeing 2707s, and two prototypes were currently under construction.

This cancellation was not entirely unexpected in light of the technical difficulties, cost overruns, and environmental concerns that beset the SST program. Still, it was a bitter pill for Bill Allen because it came when his company was just a shadow of its former self.

———

At the start of the 1970s, Boeing's financial woes came home to roost with a vengeance. Bankruptcy was imminent unless costs were drastically reduced. And the only way to accomplish that was through massive employment cuts.

T Wilson, Boeing's president, saw all this. He also realized that if Boeing went into receivership, changes would be imposed on what was left of the company as its debt was restructured. But aerospace is a complex business, and Wilson suspected those external fixes, however well intentioned, would do more harm than good. No, if Boeing was to survive, he had to do the cutting himself. Hard as it was for him to conceive of such draconian measures, he stepped up to the plate and saved the company.

Boeing's recent employment peak was 148,650 people in 1968. A moderation of work for the Apollo program and cuts in the Pentagon's Vietnam War spending had reduced this figure slightly, but the head count was still in that ballpark. Then Wilson and his team set to work. By the time they finished, our total employment stood at just 53,300. The effect on Seattle was little short of catastrophic. Businesses that supported Boeing or its employees also had to let employees go. Many went out of business.

Houses suddenly flooded the market and residential real-estate values collapsed, because people left town in droves seeking employment elsewhere in the United States. It got so bad that a highway billboard, with grim humor, said: "Will the last person to leave Seattle please turn out the lights?"

This was the situation when Congress canceled the SST in May 1971. But by then, the 747 was in service. With this big new cash cow selling well, Boeing was once again in the black and paying down its debts.

All that the reporters wanted to talk about at the Collier Trophy award ceremony was the cancellation of the SST. Ignoring the 747, they peppered Bill Allen with questions. "Some members of Congress say Boeing should continue the SST without public funding," one of them asked. "How do you feel about that?" Bill was always a gentleman but this was more than he could take. We left shortly after, and he was madder than I had ever seen him. Even a couple of scotches didn't improve his mood on the flight home.

The following year, he retired at the age of 72. T Wilson took over as Boeing's chairman. Bill's tenure was phenomenally productive, and he's widely hailed as one of the most successful leaders in the history of aerospace.

On September 30, 1970, George Nible—who had replaced Mal Stamper as vice president in charge of the 747 Division—promoted me to assistant general manager of Everett. I handed the 747 engineering reins over to Ed Pfafman and moved into the office next to Nible's.

Sad as it was to leave "The Incredibles," I knew the 747 was in good hands. I would miss my magnificent team. I wouldn't have to miss the 747 itself, though, because I never really let go. I watched over her continuing evolution through the rest of my career at Boeing, and I'm still doing it today!

On November 19, 1970, George Nible left Everett to run Boeing Customer Support, which was then becoming a much bigger organization. In terms of economic activity, that Boeing organization already ranked as one of the biggest corporations in the country because of the dealings we have with the world's airlines.

When George got tapped for that job, he called me up. "Joe," he said, "you're taking over Everett—I'm leaving you in charge." That was how I came to assume what for so long had been Mal Stamper's role. It was a natural and easy step up the career ladder. As head of the 747 program and Everett Division, I found that my new duties were still largely engineering oriented. They drew on management skills I'd developed over a quarter century at Boeing. I thoroughly enjoyed the work.

Our relationship with Pratt & Whitney was still sour in 1971. Deliveries of JT9D fanjets continued to run late, hampering our ability to deliver 747s to customers. Pratt's engines also weren't living up to their promised fuel efficiency, so our 747 operators weren't getting as much range out of their 747s as they expected. Worst of all, Pratt had not resolved its ongoing surge problems, which dragged on.

This last issue became such a concern to the FAA that it threatened to ground the 747. That didn't happen, but it brought matters to a head. Mal Stamper decided we needed to tackle these issues and put them behind us. The way to do that, he felt, was through frank discussion in neutral territory where we and they could get away, lock out all distractions, and really thrash things out.

Stamper selected Bermuda as the venue for this gathering, which became known as the Bermuda Love-In. The name was ironic, since there was little if any love lost between Boeing and Pratt & Whitney at that point. But both of us wanted a successful outcome, and that was half the battle.

Stamper led the Boeing contingent and I represented the company's engineering findings. I pushed hard to get to the bottom of these issues, which made the Pratt people very defensive. Arguments broke out about engine reliability, surge, and the fact that the engine was burning too much fuel.

With regard to fuel efficiency, Pratt claimed their engine was fine and the problems were with our airplane. They put their data up on the board and I put ours there. Together we examined all the underlying assumptions and methodologies used to generate those numbers until we were on common ground. At that point, we had a clear picture of where the JT9D engine stood.

It became obvious to all that the Boeing numbers were right. As a result, the Pratt people went home and put more money into straightening out their engine. It wasn't long before Pratt & Whitney began delivering the fuel-efficient, reliable fanjets we'd expected all along.

I give Mal Stamper full credit for taking the initiative here. It was thanks to him that these significant concerns got elevated up the line at Boeing and Pratt. Without this added visibility and the very productive meeting it gave rise to, our chronic engine problems might have dragged on for quite some time.

Back during the 747's development, BCA Sales called on me from time to time to go along on trips and help them conclude purchase agreements with the airlines of various nations. Boeing had a very fine sales department under Clancy Wilde. Quite a few of his people had come out of engineering. All of them knew Boeing's products and how to sell them. Most important of all, they knew their customers.

There is probably nothing harder in this world to sell than a commercial jetliner. Beyond the enormous complexity of the product itself, there's the issue of how it will be used and what the customer needs to keep it airworthy and profitable. Consequently, our salespeople traditionally maintain extremely close ties with our customers to be sure they fully understand their business requirements.

Clancy would enlist experts from elsewhere around Boeing Commercial Airplanes to help him make his case. People from BCA Engineering, Contracts, Marketing, and Finance would often be called on to go along on trips and help consummate a purchase agreement.

I was asked to participate in many such customer meetings over the years, even at the height of the 747's hectic development. It gave airlines confidence to hear the chief engineer speak about the capabilities

of a new airplane that hadn't flown yet. Moreover, I'd been dealing
with customers for two decades, and those relationships had blos-
somed into friendships.

When wives were invited on these working trips, Nancy sometimes went along with me, and she always did a great job representing
Boeing and the United States. Among our most unforgettable trips
was one to China in the late 1970s. I have traveled there a number of
times and have come to know Beijing, Guangzhou, Xi'an, Guelin,
Wuhan, Shanghai, and many other vibrant cities across that wonderful and truly amazing land.

I have had a number of particularly interesting experiences in China.
While there in 1980, I accompanied Boeing sales representative Matt
Chen and Wally Buckley, who at the time was general manager of the
Everett Division, for a special tour of the Y-10, a Chinese-built copy of
the 707. There at Shanghai International Airport was its Asian clone.
Almost every part of this amazing jet—from its aluminum skin to its
wiring to windshield glass—had been made in China in hopes of jump-
starting an indigenous commercial aircraft industry. The Chinese even
wanted to build engines for the Y-10 but found that too challenging, so
they used Pratt & Whitney JT3Ds purchased as spares for their fleet of
U.S.-built 707s.

Matt, Wally, and I walked around the airplane with upwards of 50
Chinese engineers and officials in close attendance. They watched my
inspection with supreme interest, clustering around me and looking
where I looked at the fuselage, wings, and landing gear. When I announced that the Y-10 looked like a good airplane, they were obviously relieved. I felt like a general conducting a military review.

We boarded the airplane and entered its flight deck, which was
laid out almost exactly like that of a real 707. I tried the controls and
found I had to use both hands to turn the wheel. The forces were
many, many times higher than they should have been. The same was
true with fore-and-aft movements of the control column. I explained
to them that there was way too much friction in the control system. I
told them they would have to fix it before the airplane's first flight,

which was imminent. For guidance, I recommended that they match the feel of the Boeing 707s in Chinese service.

They built only two Y-10s, which quietly disappeared after being flight-tested. China's plans for production of a small fleet of Y-10s for domestic use went by the wayside, perhaps because warming relations with the West made U.S. jets available at far lower cost than building their own.

At the start of the 1990s, I was in England working as a Boeing consultant. I knew the Farnborough International Airshow was in progress but wasn't planning on attending. Then Matt Chen tracked me down and asked me to be the Boeing host for the chairman of China Southwest Airlines in a special dinner at the Majestic Hotel.

During that dinner, the conversation somehow came around to the airline's hesitancy to serve Lhasa, Tibet, with twin-engine jetliners. At 12,040 feet (4,334 meters) above sea level, Lhasa is one of the world's highest and most challenging airports. I explained to the chairman that the Boeing 757—our rocket of a single-aisle twinjet—could fly that route easily and safely. I attended the demonstration, which was duly arranged, and it made the sale. China Southwest inaugurated regular 757 services there starting in 1992.

I had a very interesting Cold War encounter with Russians at the start of the 1970s. It was altogether different from that collegial dinner in Paris that the State Department had arranged in the late 1960s. This time a group of 20 or so Russians visited the Boeing plant in Everett to discuss the purchase of up to 25 747s.

None of us really believed they were here to buy airplanes. Back then, airlines behind the Iron Curtain flew only Soviet-built transports. The U.S. State Department likewise harbored doubts about their stated intentions but permitted the visit in the interests of détente.

I asked my people to treat this Soviet delegation like any other airline customer. Because the Soviet Union was known to be active in industrial espionage, though, I alerted security and told my people to be on guard. It was a safe assumption that a sizable percentage of the party would be KGB agents.

A Soviet Ministry of Aviation official led this visiting delegation. I believe his name was Marmsarov. He spoke excellent English and was, if I recall correctly, their minister for aircraft construction and operations. We rolled out the red carpet for him, giving his group a cordial welcome and treating them to the same engineering presentations we'd give any potential customer.

Ken Luplow, the Boeing sales executive who specialized in that part of the world, showed up in my office the next day. "Joe," he said, "the Russians are very upset. They think we're holding out on them. Mr. Marmsarov wants to meet with you tomorrow morning to settle this matter."

I didn't understand what the problem could be. While I hadn't personally accompanied the delegation, I knew what orders had been given and was sure my colleagues were doing their best for our unusual visitors.

Marmsarov and a couple of his people showed up the next morning with Ken. We sat down in my office and I served them coffee. After exchanging pleasantries, the Soviet official came to the point. "We came here expecting to talk to your experts, but you're having junior people talk to us," he asserted indignantly.

"That's incorrect," I replied. "The people briefing you are the individuals heading up key posts in the 747 program."

He named Jim Johnson as an example of somebody too young to have such a job. I assured him that Jim was the top aerodynamicist on the 747 program and that he knew the 747's performance inside out.

"He can't be," Marmsarov protested. "He's too young."

I began to realize that the dilemma was all a cultural misunderstanding. Marmsarov came from a highly centralized and controlled society where people were appointed according to seniority. In contrast, the United States was much more of a meritocracy.

Ken and I finally managed to convince Marmsarov that Jim was indeed the 747 program's lead aerodynamicist. He was mollified but still couldn't understand a youngster like that having the job.

The next day I had another meeting with the Russians. In the interim, they had learned about a very thick document called *Boeing 747 Design Objectives and Criteria*. They badly wanted a copy and were very upset we weren't giving it to them. I was a little chagrined that our people had even told the Russians of its existence. We called our 747 DO&C "the bible" because its pages held the collective engineering wisdom of our company. Everything that our engineers, past and present, had learned over the course of a lot of decades about building safe airplanes was reflected in its pages. Written at the start of the 747 program, this document listed the thousands of individual requirements—airline, Boeing, and FAA—that the 747 would have to meet. It went on to spell out in precise detail exactly how these design goals were to be met. It was thus a veritable compendium of Boeing design expertise and a how-to manual for creating a great jetliner.

Our 747 DO&C built on similar documents prepared for earlier Boeing airliners. In turn, this 747 bible would provide a foundation on which the engineers for Boeing's next jetliners would build. Everything that we had learned was in this one amazing book, which was the repository of our hard-won knowledge and evolving philosophy about safe airplane design.

I sensed excitement behind Marmsarov's tightly controlled features as he stared at me across my desk. He repeated his demand that we give him this book.

"The *747 Design Objectives and Criteria* is a proprietary document," I said, shaking my head. "It's not for release outside the company."

"We would like to purchase this document," he persisted.

"No." I said it as firmly as I knew how.

With this exchange, the true purpose of his visit was out in the open. The Russians hadn't come to buy jets from Boeing; they were here to learn how to build vastly better airliners than their own industry was capable of producing. That Boeing built the best jets was true then, and it's still true today.

"We will pay for it," Marmsarov said. "I will pay you one million dollars."

I was flabbergasted to be offered a million bucks just like that, but I didn't let it show. Marmsarov upped the ante: I could name my own price—whatever I thought the 747 DO&C was worth. "You can offer me one million dollars, ten million dollars, or a hundred million dollars," I told him with finality. "It's not for sale!"

This was quite upsetting to the man. Seeing that there was no use pursuing the matter any further, he abruptly left my office. *What consequences await him for returning empty-handed?* I wondered, having no way of knowing if my guess was right.

The moment Marmsarov was gone, I put Boeing security on alert. Then I summoned an assistant. "Go and collect every one of those documents, starting with mine, which is right here," I said. "Once they're all accounted for, I want them locked in a safe. It's not to be opened again until we know those Russians are on their way back to Moscow."

For security reasons, those 747 DO&C documents were given only to the lead engineers, so we knew where every copy was. All of them were numbered, so we knew they were all accounted for. I still have my copy of that hefty tome. Reading it brings to mind a lot of important decisions we made in the design of the 747. It also makes me very glad the Soviets didn't get their hands on it.

————————

Nible had been vice president and general manager of the 747 Program and Everett Division. When I succeeded him, I naïvely assumed that this would be my title as well. However, Boeing listed me as *acting general manager* and there was no mention of any vice presidency even though all the other division general managers were VPs. This was okay with me. I've never paid much attention to titles, and I had a great job that I enjoyed. If Boeing was grudging in dispensing vice presidencies, I thought it might be as much my fault as theirs. I'm not a political creature and I certainly hadn't fought for the title.

Joe Sutter and Brien Wygle flying RA001 to celebrate Joe's promotion to vice president, 1971

Consequently, I was caught off guard in April of 1971 when T Wilson called me up one day after I'd been on the job half a year or so. This was highly unusual; T and I had spent time together on any number of occasions, but I certainly couldn't say I was ever a confidant of his.

"Sutter, we're making you a vice president," Wilson said with his usual bluntness. "We should have done it when you took over the 747 Division, but we were testing you. Now we have to do it because we're sending Bob Bateman to Washington to run our DC office, and that calls for a vice president. We couldn't make Bob a VP without making you one, of course, so as of right now you're a Boeing VP."

The lack of any ceremony or appreciation was typical of T. I didn't hold it against Boeing. In fact, I had recently turned 50 and chose to see this lofty status as Boeing's birthday present to me. I was thrilled to see the word *acting* finally disappear from my title. To celebrate, Brien Wygle took me up on a test flight in RA001 and I flew her to my heart's content. Of course, Nancy and I celebrated that evening at home!

Years later, T and I were chatting and he confirmed what I had long suspected. "You were so young that we would have replaced you if we could have found somebody better to head up the 747 program," he said, presenting me with a backhanded compliment.

———————

In June 1976, a delegation of Iraqi VIPs arrived at Boeing to take delivery of that nation's first jumbo jet, a Boeing 747-200C. Iraqi Airlines was already a valued 707 and 737 customer, so we feted them lavishly during their stay. Our visitors particularly enjoyed a boat trip we arranged to Blake Island in Puget Sound. There they feasted at a salmon bake in the tradition of the Native Americans who first inhabited this part of North America.

In return, the Iraqis invited some of us along on their delivery flight back to Baghdad. In the interests of good customer relations, I and a number of other Boeing people accepted this kind invitation. We had no idea how memorable it would be.

On landing, we found ourselves part of an elaborate event celebrating the arrival of Iraq's brand-new 747. Sheep were slaughtered during those festivities by having their throats slit. As a welcome, it left something to be desired.

Baghdad itself was every bit as exotic as I had expected. I didn't have a chance to explore its ancient bazaars or walk the banks of the Tigris River, though, because our hosts had planned a full itinerary for us.

Our first adventure found us on a bus heading south to the Euphrates River. It was over 100 degrees Fahrenheit outside and hotter still inside that bus. Our hosts had provided sodas in a tub filled with ice that turned immediately to water. Unfortunately there was no bottled water. Our hosts' image of Americans was apparently that we drank nothing but soft drinks.

We arrived at what we were told was the archaeological site of the legendary hanging gardens of Babylon, one of the seven wonders of the ancient world. Two thousand years had taken their toll, though, and it was impossible for us to get any sense of what those gardens might actually have looked like.

The most unforgettable event of the visit was a fish fry obviously meant to reciprocate for the salmon bake we'd treated the Iraqi delegation to on Blake Island. For this event, our Iraqi hosts picked us up at our Baghdad hotel at five in the evening and drove us to a dock on the Tigris River.

Waiting there was a sizable group of men and women. We all boarded a barge pulled by a small tugboat. On the barge I saw chairs, bottled libations, and a large number of freshly caught freshwater fish in tubs. We settled expectantly into our seats as the tugboat pulled into the river.

We'd hardly started when the barge ran aground on a sandbar. About an hour later, we were finally pulled free and proceeded upriver for another hour until we reached an island. There we debarked and helped offload all the chairs and supplies.

Iraqis with machetes set about cutting brush that grew on the island. Others laid Persian carpets and positioned our chairs while cooking fires were stoked using the cut brush. Traditionally clad Iraqi women began doing what looked like belly dances to exotic Mesopotamian music played on instruments I couldn't identify.

It was now well into the evening and again there was no drinking water. There wasn't even any beer, which we would have welcomed. Instead, perhaps reflecting another stereotypical misconception about Americans, the potables consisted of nothing but a very large supply of scotch. Iraq being a Muslim nation, the presence of alcohol was clearly a significant gesture on their behalf. Just as obviously, we were expected to drink what we were served. I began sipping my scotch just for the sake of having something liquid.

It took a very long time to cook the fish, which were finally ready at around ten o'clock. By then the black sky was full of stars, the air was fresh, and we were all ravenously hungry. The fish smelled wonderful, but when our hosts started to serve it, they realized they had forgotten to bring bread. Without giving us any say in the matter, they promptly dispatched the tugboat for a slow roundtrip to Baghdad to bring the missing foodstuff, which delayed our dinner by several more hours.

It was at least midnight before we got a bite to eat. By then we were dead tired and the scotch on an empty stomach was having its inevitable effect. In the wee hours of the morning we helped load the barge for a return journey that seemed endless. The first blush of dawn showed in the east by the time we reached the dock.

––––––––––

Boeing began shuffling senior people around in the late 1970s to accommodate the company's continuing growth. In September 1978, I was very pleased to find myself the Boeing Commercial Airplanes company's new vice president of operations and product development. My office was in Renton, where Boeing builds its single-aisle jetliners.

I live in West Seattle, a neighborhood at the other end of a long causeway. While I would miss the people and programs in Boeing's Everett Plant, I knew I wouldn't miss that daily commute. It took me through my neighborhood, across the West Seattle Bridge (a causeway over Seattle's harbor facilities and the Duwamish River), north through downtown Seattle, and then another 30 miles farther north after that. Door to door, it took more than an hour at the best of times.

In contrast, the Renton Plant (named for the town it's in) is at the southern tip of Lake Washington. That's not too many miles southeast of Seattle. It cut my driving time to less than half an hour, giving me quite a bit more time in my day. The BCA headquarters was then at Renton. Today, it's in a campuslike setting south of Seattle at a former track for horse racing that Boeing purchased. My current office is in this new headquarters building.

My new duties saw me managing Boeing's existing jetliner product lines and helping create new product lines. The organization charts showed 45,000 people reporting to me, and I must admit it was quite a task managing them all. Fortunately, I didn't have to worry about finance, customer support, sales and marketing, and the many other areas that were outside my area of responsibility. This was still an engineering assignment.

Wally Buckley, who had done so much to fix our production problems in Everett, helped me manage this new empire. Having worked with him on the 747 program, I knew him to be a first-class operations guy. Wally was definitely of the old school. He had spent his entire career in manufacturing and production control. I don't think his formal education was all that broad, but he had a lot on the ball and a great deal of hard-won expertise. As we worked it out, I led engineering and product development while he managed the production operations of the various divisions.

Although this was before the universal use of computers, Boeing developed computer programs to manage the ordering of parts and production control. Even though Wally had probably never sat in front of a computer in his life, he knew that this was the way to go. He had an assistant, Ernie Fenn, who also was of the old school but who likewise appreciated the importance of computers.

One of the earliest production control programs used at Boeing was called Online Planning. Buckley and Fenn worked very hard to get it up and running. It was quite a struggle and there were a lot of naysayers. The old fellas in particular were reluctant to adopt it, but those two individuals bulldogged that system into use. It was the first real effort to computerize the Boeing production system.

Today, of course, Boeing's production, financial, engineering, and planning functions are completely computerized and talk to each other. The only thing you can't computerize is the human brain. You still have to think.

Wally's chief asset to me was his ability to understand that engineers work in a development cycle and that not everything they do is right the first time around. If we had an engineering problem or issues with airplanes out on the field, it took only one meeting to get it addressed. "We've got a problem out there, Buck, and we've got to fix it," I'd say. "The engineers will be issuing change orders and putting out drawings. We really need the cooperation of the operations people to get these fixes implemented."

Thankfully, he was never one to blame such situations on the engineers and drag his feet because of the extra workload we were throwing at him.

In September 1981, I received my final promotion as a regular Boeing employee. I'd been with the company more than 35 years and would hit the mandatory retirement age of 65 in another five years.

My new title was executive vice president for engineering and product development at BCA. As those are my two favorite areas, and since Boeing was then the biggest and most successful commercial airplane maker, I guess I had topped out in my chosen profession. It was a great concluding assignment.

As the 1970s wore on, Boeing perceived a growing need in the marketplace for intermediate-size jetliners. British Airways and Eastern were pushing for an efficient twin-engine, single-aisle jet bigger than the 737, and United Airlines wanted a medium-size twin-aisle jet for one-stop operations in North America. These emerging requirements saw me spending a lot of time working with Boeing teams to define and develop the 757 and 767. With the help of people like Ken Holtby, we worked on these two Boeing airplanes simultaneously so that they could share a common cockpit and type rating. This meant that crews trained to fly the single-aisle 757 could also fly the twin-aisle 767 or vice versa. This concept offered airlines the powerful benefits of lower training costs and greater flexibility.

The 757, which is now out of production, used the same cross section as the 707, 727, and 737. To that proven cross section we added a very good wing and good engines. The result was a high-performance airplane that for many years was the most cost-effective intermediate-range airplane in service.

As mentioned, the airline that exerted the most influence on the 767's design was United. Its president back then had come out of the hotel business and had very different thoughts about what was needed in an airliner. For instance, he wanted a widebody, but he wanted it to be extremely efficient. He didn't even want it to be able to fly coast to coast nonstop, because that would mean a heavier airframe and thus slightly less fuel efficiency. It was pretty hard to take the engines that we had, wrap an airplane around them, and not exceed his objectives.

Airbus was then developing an airplane called the A310. They put a small wing on that airplane because they were strongly influenced by European airlines that had very short routes to serve. Airbus was after the best efficiency for its short-haul A310 and didn't see the need for a larger wing that could carry more fuel.

Because the 767 would use the same engines as the 747 (although just two of them), we had engines already available that could generate a lot of thrust. We had discussions with many airlines around the world and found that some of them could probably use more range than United was specifying as launch customer.

At Boeing, we made a critical engineering decision: We would not inhibit the 767's range by giving this airplane too small a wing for the loads it could carry with the engines we had available. We believed that the 767 should be capable of flying all the way across North America nonstop. It should be capable of flying the North Atlantic—then by far the busiest intercontinental air market—and even handling Pacific routes with one and two stops. With this in mind, Boeing's engineering community put a fairly large wing on the 767 relative to the A310. We were immediately and very strongly criticized by carriers such as Lufthansa, who felt we had misjudged what the market wanted. But we did convince United of the benefits of this large wing. The 767 used very little more fuel than it would have with a small wing, and it had superior takeoff and landing performance. This made getting into and out of medium-size airfields no problem for the jet.

United bought the 767-200, which was the first member of the 767 family of twinjets. Meantime, Airbus brought its A310 to market. To make a long story short, if you look at the 767 program today and the A300–A310 program over at Airbus, far fewer A310s than 767s have been built because its restricted range did not make it suitable for very many of the world's airlines. And whereas the 767 went into service with United on short routes like Cleveland to the West Coast, the airline also immediately began using its 767s for transcontinental nonstops and on North Atlantic routes.

We sold very few 767-200s because that big wing plus the higher engine thrusts we had available allowed us almost immediately to bring out a stretched model: the 767-300. This model carried another 50 to 60 passengers and could easily fly the Atlantic. The 767-300 became a very, very popular airplane for U.S. and European operators.

Of course, long-haul airliners are the backbone of intercontinental travel. Like the 747 before it, the 767 introduced new technical capabilities never before available. Specifically, it combined low operating costs with long-range capability and a passenger capacity that was just half that of a fully loaded 747. Airlines used this formula to fundamentally transform air service patterns across the North Atlantic.

Before the 767, intercontinental travel relied on a skeletal route network that linked a small number of gateway hubs in each of the world's regions. Air service was via these gateways, so flying from one continent to another usually required several flights. Flying to Europe from the United States, for example, meant taking a domestic flight to New York, boarding a jumbo jet for the flight across the Atlantic, and then taking a third flight from the gateway airport you arrived at—generally London or Paris—to reach your final destination in Europe.

Today, in contrast, people increasingly fly direct, whether it's Atlanta to Milan, Cincinnati to Zurich, Orlando to Düsseldorf, or Philadelphia to Manchester. What happened? Airlines that used to funnel their domestic traffic to New York as a jump-off point for Europe found that they could fly these passengers to Europe themselves instead of giving the business away to Pan Am, TWA, or European airlines at John F. Kennedy International Airport.

Because the 767 carries just half as many passengers as a 747, it allowed airlines to fly directly between secondary population centers where total travel demand was insufficient for a 747-size airplane. This "bypass flying" fleshed out the skeletal route network with additional services, avoiding hubs to bring nonstop services to a much larger and still rising number of cities on both sides of the ocean. The result has been the *fragmentation* of the North Atlantic air market.

Before fragmentation, Pan Am and TWA were the powerhouses of American–European travel. Then United, American, Delta, Continental, and many other North American and European airlines launched transatlantic services of their own, and a lot of business went away for those two industry giants and their European 747 competitors. Of course, the 767 didn't kill Pan Am or TWA, and neither did that era's trend of deregulation. But both factors did allow other airlines to undercut Pan Am's and TWA's business by operating more flexibly and giving travelers more of the direct flights they prefer.

Almost single-handedly, the 767 demonstrated to the world the safety, reliability, efficiency, and utility of twin-engine jets in long-range service. On the basis of this success, Boeing went on in the 1990s to develop the 777, which has become one of the key long-haul airplanes in the world. Larger and longer-ranged than the 767, the 777 is doing over the Pacific what its predecessor did over the Atlantic. So successful has this formula been that 767 and 777 twinjets today account for fully two thirds of all flights across the North Atlantic.

In light of these transforming trends, I believe that matching the 767's wing to the available engines—thereby giving the 767 a lot more range than anyone was asking for—was one of the most important decisions I helped push through at Boeing.

In 1979, ANA in Japan signed on as an early customer for the 767, which Boeing was then developing. The airline took delivery of Japan's first 767 twinjet early in 1983, half a year after the type entered service.

The 767, being a widebody, is ordinarily a long-range jetliner, but

Boeing 767

ANA's traffic loads are so high that the company also wanted to use it in domestic Japanese services the way other countries use single-aisle jets like the 737. Although ANA liked the 767, it was having a tough time operating the airplane at Hiroshima and other small airports in its route system.

My duties at Renton placed me above the level where I would be expected to work on such a problem myself, but I have always loved Japan and have rich and rewarding memories of helping its airlines over the years. Such being the case, I took a personal interest in seeing whether Boeing could help ANA out by improving the 767's low-speed characteristics to achieve improved field performance. This was a somewhat unusual engineering effort because the 767 was already in service.

I worked with Dave Norton, an extremely fine engineer who was in charge of 767 aerodynamics. Dave and his team identified changes to the trailing-edge flaps that did the trick. They also modified the brake system. Together these changes gave this widebody the field performance of a single-aisle airplane.

Hiroshima was a critical airport for ANA. To convince the

company that the revised 767 could now serve it routinely and safely, I traveled to Tokyo and made a presentation myself in the boardroom at ANA headquarters.

When ANA placed the 767 into service, it was a huge success. The airline has taken delivery of 80 767s since then, and more were coming off the line for this Japanese carrier at the time this book was written. ANA is the largest operator of 767s outside the United States. It's the company's signature airplane the same way that the 747 is JAL's.

———————

I understand that I have a pretty good reputation in aviation, particularly in the Asia-Pacific region where the 747 has done so much for so many countries. If so, it's purely the result of helping customers around the world meet their unique operational challenges.

I hasten to add that I'm not a paragon of virtue. In the past, for example, there were occasions when I got a little hot under the collar at Boeing or when dealing with companies supplying parts for our jetliners. I have been known to raise my voice, but I did so calculatedly and for effect. It's not in my nature to fly off the handle.

I'm also remembered by former colleagues for a management style that employed humor. I might say, "If you don't finish this up by tomorrow, I'll have you transferred to Bangladesh!" or otherwise jokingly suggest a move far from Seattle. And if I passed the office of a hardworking Boeing salesperson burning the midnight oil, I might pop my head in the door and say, "Why aren't you out selling Boeing airplanes? There are no airlines in Seattle!"

It was all tongue in cheek and generally well received. It's the result of having grown up as one of five siblings, all of whom loved to tease each other.

What I'm most grateful for at Boeing over the decades has been the support and good morale of my troops. I let my people run with the ball and made sure to give credit where it was due. I also strove to communicate well. On the 747 program, I was the one making the decisions—I'm not a consensus guy—but I generally did so only after hearing everybody out with an open mind.

In 1985, I learned I would be one of a select group of Americans to receive the U.S. National Medal of Technology. President Ronald Reagan would present it to us in a ceremony at the White House. It was a distinct honor. Nancy accompanied me to Washington, DC.

Before the ceremony in the East Wing, White House staffers explained what we recipients were to do when the president called our names. They showed us footprint outlines on the carpet and instructed us to stand right there so that photographs could be taken of the medal award and handshake.

The secretary of commerce made a short speech, after which the president entered and mounted the platform. Sitting in the audience, I assumed the medals would be presented alphabetically and I would be among the last called. It caught me by surprise to hear my name called first. I stood, mounted the few steps, and strode across the platform.

Reagan leaned forward and spoke softly in my ear. He then shook my hand heartily and handed me my medal. The other honorees got medals and handshakes but no words. It tickled me how they crowded around after the ceremony bursting with curiosity. What had the president told me, they wanted to know?

I considered keeping it a secret or making something up, but honesty got the better of me. "He didn't know that we'd been told about the foot marks," I explained, "so he said, 'Now Joe, you just keep standing right here.'"

To this day, part of me regrets not keeping everybody wondering what the president of the United States told me privately.

13

THE *CHALLENGER* DISASTER

Returning from a short vacation in Hawaii at the start of 1986, I reflected with mixed feelings that I had just three more months to go at Boeing. In March I'd turn 65, the age at which the company expects its executives to turn the reins over to younger people.

January 28, 1986, was my first day back after that vacation. A little after 9 AM, my secretary entered the office. "The *Challenger* has exploded," she announced breathlessly. There was a Canadian business jet called the *Challenger*, so I thought she was talking about an airplane accident. "No," she said, "I mean the space shuttle *Challenger*!"

She switched on a television set and we watched the replay of the shuttle launch and subsequent explosion. "What a terrible tragedy," I recall saying. "This will really set the space program back."

It was the first time the United States had ever lost an astronaut in flight. With the spacecraft so thoroughly destroyed, I thought it might be an impossible mystery to solve. Commercial aviation accident investigation seemed easy by comparison.

At home that evening, I discussed the day's shocking event with

Nancy. "I've had a lot of problems on my plate," I told her, "but not like this. I'm glad I don't have to worry about it."

Shortly thereafter the telephone rang. It was the White House, and the caller explained that President Ronald Reagan was chartering a commission to investigate the accident. He would like me to be on this panel. Would I care to participate?

I didn't know what to say. "If the president wants me, I'll accept," I replied, "but I have to check with my company first."

"Boeing has already approved your participation," I was told.

This is how it came to pass that I helped investigate a very sad chapter in the U.S. manned spaceflight program. There were 14 of us on that presidential commission to investigate the *Challenger* explosion, which killed six astronauts and a New Hampshire school teacher serving as a payload specialist.

Our chairman was William Rogers, the former U.S. attorney general and secretary of state, and our vice chairman was Neil Armstrong, the first person to walk on the Moon. Since leaving the astronaut corps, Armstrong had been teaching aeronautical engineering in Ohio.

In addition to me, this commission's remaining appointees were David Acheson, an attorney with aerospace expertise; Eugene Covert, who headed the Department of Aeronautics and Astronautics at MIT; brilliant physicist and Nobel Prize winner Richard Feynman; Robert Hotz, a former editor-in-chief of *Aviation Week & Space Technology*; USAF Major General Donald Kutyna, a military expert on space; astronaut Sally Ride, who holds a Ph.D. in physics and had two shuttle missions in the *Challenger* under her belt; former TWA Vice President Robert Rummel; astrophysicist Arthur Walker; Hughes Aircraft Executive Vice President Albert Wheelon, a physicist by training; and retired USAF Brigadier General Charles "Chuck" Yeager, the World War II fighter ace who broke the sound barrier in 1947. Alton Keel, a public servant with a doctorate in engineering physics, was our administrator.

Our presidential mandate had two parts. The first was to review the circumstances surrounding the accident and establish its probable cause or causes. The second was to develop recommendations for corrective or other action on the basis of our findings and determinations. We were given 120 days plus lots of administrative and clerical support to get the job done.

Bill Rogers and Neil Armstrong began by forming subcommittees. I led the subcommittee tasked with reviewing space shuttle engineering and production. Sally Ride had the related area of flight operations.

The *Challenger* had flown successfully nine times before it exploded 73 seconds after liftoff from Kennedy Space Center. Delivered in the early 1980s, it was the third shuttle in a NASA fleet that began with the *Enterprise* (a nonspaceworthy prototype) and *Columbia* and continued on with *Discovery*, *Atlantis*, and *Endeavour*.

Being on that investigation was a real eye-opener. As we set to work, it quickly became apparent to the other commission members that I viewed things differently from the rank and file at NASA. Sally Ride and several others took exception to my approaches and many of the comments I made.

The point of contention was safety. In the world of commercial aviation, safety is paramount. Airplane and engine manufacturers, government regulators, and the world's airlines have always worked hard and continue to strive to make air travel as safe as humanly possible.

Boeing has always made it a policy to consider government certification requirements as *minimum* acceptable standards, not design goals. And to further elevate safety, Boeing makes each engineer responsible for the safety of his or her design and provides help and guidance if it is needed. To my thinking, this unstinting commitment to safety has always put Boeing above the competition. Everybody working for me on the 747 program made the airplane as airworthy as they possibly could. Nobody would have dreamed of making a decision that would compromise safety. If they had, they would have been violating our company's rules.

In short, I'd spent my entire professional life in a world that lives and breathes safety. That's why it came as such a shock to me to find the same wasn't true of NASA. It's also why my point of departure was so markedly different from that of many of the other commission members. It's not that they weren't equally focused on safety but simply that it was difficult for them to hear how bad things were from my perspective.

But I'm getting ahead of myself. I'd better tell it the way it unfolded.

When I arrived in Washington, DC for our initial meetings, I was still concerned that the orbital vehicle's near-total destruction might make it difficult if not impossible to determine what had gone wrong. Fortunately, this proved not to be the case. Imagery of the liftoff clearly pinpointed the accident's cause: hot, high-pressure combustion gases had leaked from the right-hand solid rocket booster (SRB) on the side that faced the *Challenger* and its large external fuel tank. Starting at liftoff, this leak had quickly grown to a large hole from which issued a flaming efflux. The dynamic pressure of the launch deflected this blowtorch downward, causing a mounting support to fail, which in turn allowed the SRB to penetrate the external fuel tank.

Confirming this reconstructed sequence of events, telemetry from the liftoff recorded falling internal pressures in the right-hand SRB and then the external fuel tank. Very shortly thereafter a massive explosion blew the vehicle apart, scattering wreckage in a wide swath from the Atlantic Ocean all the way to Texas and Louisiana.

We thus identified the immediate cause of the accident as a bad design that allowed a joint to fail where one body section of the SRB met another. The integrity of this joint depended on an O-ring, or circular gasket, to maintain a seal. This O-ring was never supposed to be subjected to combustion gases, yet it clearly was. We also learned that it was made of a material that became brittle and thus less effective as a seal at low temperatures.

At the time of the *Challenger*'s launch, the temperature at the

John F. Kennedy Space Center had been an unusually chilly 36 degrees Fahrenheit, which was 15 degrees colder than that at any previous shuttle launch. Moreover, the leak had occurred on the colder side of the SRB, where it faced the cryogenic external fuel tank.

It all added up. But this "immediate accident cause" was just the tip of the iceberg. Behind the scenes another failure had occurred that set the stage for avoidable disaster and let down a trusting crew. I think my background gave me a much clearer sense at the outset of what wasn't right. At the very least, I suspected that the affected organizations weren't plugged together properly and that important safety-related engineering processes weren't in place.

Morton Thiokol, the SRB's manufacturer, had refused to believe the implications of early tests that revealed an unsuspected design flaw. The company's official stance, a matter of record, was that "the condition is not desirable but is acceptable."

Likewise, NASA's management hadn't listened to its own engineers and technical experts when they identified that SRB "joint problem" as a safety concern that demanded attention. Even when the number and severity of SRB joint incidents grew during the early years of space shuttle operations, NASA management briefings and reports continued to downplay this issue.

Thus, engineers in both organizations had repeatedly warned about what in retrospect was clearly a potentially catastrophic design flaw. Despite that, their managements had taken no action other than to downgrade the problem to "an acceptable risk." NASA could and should have ordered that a fix be designed and then suspended flight operations until it was implemented. Instead they just kept flying.

Why did this happen? One reason was NASA's organizational structure, which comprised various regional centers with different responsibilities. In addition to the Kennedy Space Center at Merritt Island, Florida, and the Lyndon B. Johnson Space Center in Houston, Texas, there was the George C. Marshall Space Flight Center in Alabama, the Goddard Space Flight Center in Maryland, Langley

Research Center in Virginia, Dryden Flight Research Center at California's Edwards Air Force Base, and so on. All these organizations functioned rather autonomously under the loose leadership of NASA headquarters in Washington, DC. The decisions these regional centers made, including those involving safety, were generally just rubber-stamped in Washington. There was no unified and formalized safety reporting structure to give this vital concern the visibility it needed and ensure that potential problems were properly addressed.

Another factor was an excessive focus on schedule. Safety had been sacrificed to an aggressive launch schedule. For example, Huntsville, Alabama, was in charge of the solid rocket booster program. We found that some NASA people there had really browbeaten Thiokol to get them to continue supporting the firing of their SRBs even though repeated usage had been found to enlarge and distort the rocket tube diameters. We identified this ignored distortion as a contributor to the failure of the improperly designed seal.

In short, NASA lacked an organization-wide safety structure. Of course NASA had safety processes and procedures, but these were ad hoc and disjointed. There was no top-level safety leadership position to remind people that it must always come first. *This is no way to run an airline*, I remember thinking in dismay.

I was very vocal in my criticisms of the failings that denied NASA's engineers and technical experts the ear of management and set the stage for disaster. I stated my conviction that NASA's chief safety official should be the director himself or herself, and that a new and fully empowered executive position should be established devoted solely to safety and reporting straight to the director. During any shuttle launch, these two individuals should be fully apprised of all anomalies and concerns, and should be the ones who ultimately make the go/no-go decision. It pleases me to say that this proposed restructuring to implement a proper safety management system was one of the key recommendations put forward by our commission in its final report. I feel very proud of my participation.

My teammates never seemed to realize I live in Seattle. Many of them were on the East Coast, and they had a chronic habit of calling meetings for the next day. My requests for sufficient notice to allow for daytime travel went unheeded. The only way I could attend was to red-eye it, which I did a dozen times in four months. These night flights took me to meetings and fact-finding sessions in Washington, DC, Houston, Cape Canaveral, California, and Utah. They were all the more uncomfortable and tiring because the government did not see fit to provide anything more than economy-class tickets. Partly as a result, I ran on too little sleep throughout the investigation.

All in all, though, the public was certainly well served by the *Challenger* presidential commission. I and the other appointees signed that report without any reservations. I parted good friends with everyone, including the remarkable Dr. Sally Ride who graciously thanked me for my efforts on NASA's behalf.

We arrived at the White House on June 6, 1986, to deliver this document to President Reagan. It felt funny to be back at the executive mansion for the second time in two years. We were ushered into a waiting area near the Rose Garden, where the presentation was to take place. There we found coffee, refreshments, and one of the president's signature jars of jelly beans. All of us were invited to bring White House jelly beans home as souvenirs. I gave my supply to my kids and grandkids.

Reagan was not a man of great detail, but he did the right thing in the sad case of the *Challenger*. Instead of letting NASA investigate itself, he'd turned the job over to Rogers and Armstrong and let the two of them pick the right people for the presidential commission. And then after we submitted our findings, he gave NASA a direct order to fully implement every one of our recommendations. Too many past presidential commissions have made recommendations only to see them tabled and largely ignored. Because Reagan held NASA's feet to the fire, that didn't happen here. The space agency initiated thoroughgoing reforms and structural changes in the wake of the *Challenger* tragedy.

To Joseph Sutter
Thanks for a job well done

Ronald Reagan

Joe Sutter and Ronald Reagan
(AUTHOR'S PERSONAL COLLECTION)

The space shuttle remains the riskiest of all flying vehicles, particularly since it depends on those SRBs to achieve orbit. The SRBs consume more than a million pounds of rocket fuel in 128 seconds. Once they're ignited, they can't be throttled or shut down because they're actually a controlled explosion. It's absolutely amazing to me that the space program has accepted and lives with this risk.

The loss of the space shuttle *Columbia* in February 2003 reflects the inherent risks of manned spaceflight. It shows that we still have more to learn on this front.

14

CONSULTING IN RETIREMENT

The time had come for me to retire from Boeing. I was 65 in 1986 and had been with the company for four very busy decades. It amazed me how the years had flown by.

The president of Boeing Commercial Airplanes at that time was Dean Thornton. When I told him I had picked June 1, 1986, as my retirement date, he asked me to consider staying on as a consultant. "You know what you're interested in, Joe," Thornton told me. "Just go ahead and define your own duties. Do what you think is worthwhile and we'll talk from time to time to see what progress you're making."

I have continued to maintain an office at Boeing over the two decades since my retirement. I've done a lot of work as a consultant on the engineering and production fronts, but my main focus has been product development.

Probably the biggest effort I've been engaged in has been the future of the 747. We designed it with significant growth capability in mind, but so far it's never been stretched beyond the original fuselage length that it entered service with back in 1970. The potential is certainly there.

Working on the 747-400 was my last major activity as a regular Boeing employee. As soon as the airlines got their hands on this much-improved 747 derivative and found out what it could do, it became a best seller.

Improvements in technology set the stage for that updating of the original 747. On the propulsion front, manufacturers had learned to design fanjets that generated thrusts of 60,000 pounds or more and were fundamentally more fuel efficient. Pratt & Whitney's improved successor to the JT9D is the PW4000 series.

At Boeing, meantime, a design aid called computational fluid dynamics (CFD) had emerged. This entirely new field harnesses massive computing power to model the behavior of airflows as they pass around airplane structures or through jet engines. Combined with and verified by wind-tunnel data, CFD provides an amazing new tool for aerodynamic refinement.

Technology had advanced on other fronts as well. For example, composite materials and aluminum–lithium alloys were coming into use that would allow airframe weight reductions. This in turn would translate directly into greater payload or range capability.

By the mid-1980s, a significantly more fuel-efficient, wider-ranging 747 was definitely possible. Row Brown and his team had been doing their best all along to incorporate improvements on a piecemeal basis, and as a result the 747 already offered somewhat greater range and payload than any other airliner. But as usual, our airline customers were clamoring for more. In particular, customers wanted us to incorporate advanced features from our new 757 and 767, which entered service in the early 1980s with electronic flight instrument system (EFIS) cockpit display screens and a "two-crew cockpit" that was simpler and dispensed with the flight engineer.

To meet these customer desires, Boeing identified 14 specific technology improvements that in one jump would take the airplane to a much higher baseline in terms of performance and fuel efficiency. This was what the airlines wanted.

Boeing's finance people strongly resisted making *any* changes to the 747. So much money had gone into it and our other airplane programs that they all but ordered us engineers to cease and desist so that Boeing could earn stronger profits. Against this bottom-line mentality, it was impossible for us to sell the idea internally of a major 747 derivative.

By the early 1980s, our meetings with customers showed they were frustrated and discouraged that Boeing wasn't committing aggressively to further 747 improvements. One key international air carrier, Germany's Lufthansa, was particularly critical of the "half steps" Boeing had been taking with incremental improvements to the 747.

Reinhardt Abraham, Lufthansa's deputy chairman at that time, was one of the key architects of commercial aviation in Europe. He made a special trip to Seattle so that we could give him a full briefing on the spectrum of changes that we felt we could make to the airplane to improve its payload-range capabilities and operating economics.

Abraham had degrees in aeronautical engineering and industrial management. This technical background let him fully appreciate what we showed him. He was also acutely aware of the lack of enthusiasm on Boeing's part to pursue these changes, so he took it upon himself to give Boeing a lesson in customer responsiveness. His weapon of choice was *Aviation Week & Space Technology*, the aerospace industry's most widely read trade publication. In the May 28, 1984, issue he gave an interview about the changes Boeing was capable of making and what they would do for 747 operators. The benefits included greater range, greater payload, and a fuel savings of 20% per passenger seat! Abraham's article stated in part:

> Boeing is working on all of the proposed improvements but Lufthansa is concerned that they will make them available in a piecemeal fashion. Abraham said this would increase the development cost, which will be passed along to the airlines, and result in airlines operating a fleet of 747 aircraft that have little remaining commonality.

"We don't like the piecemeal approach," Abraham said. "We want one full package on the airplane. It would be a big incentive for new orders." He said he believes the entire package could be available for delivery by 1989–90 if Boeing begins work this year. . . . But the airline is concerned that the development work will be delayed because there is little incentive for Boeing, which has a monopoly in the long-haul widebody market, to make the required investment.

This article triggered a veritable clamor of demand from airlines. Taking note, Boeing's leadership launched the 747-400 program in October 1985.

———————

The 747-400 is distinguished from earlier 747 models by the winglets at the tips of its increased-span wings. The first prototype flew in April 1988, and Northwest Airlines took delivery of the first airplane in January 1989.

All of the 747 operators worldwide were immediately interested in this new model. Singapore, Northwest, JAL, Lufthansa, Cathay Pacific, United, KLM, Air France, Air China, and many other airlines jumped on board with orders that made the 747-400 the best-selling 747 model of all. At the time of this writing, 747-400s account for no fewer than 660 of the more than 1,400 total orders Boeing has received for the 747.

The 747-400 isn't a single airplane type but rather a family of models. Building on the success of the basic 747-400 passenger plane, for example, Boeing delivered the first 747-400 Combi to KLM in 1989 and the first 747-400 Domestic—a successor to Japan's 747SR interisland shuttles—to JAL in 1991.

In the fall of 1993, Boeing delivered the one thousandth 747 to Singapore Airlines. That November, Luxembourg's Cargolux placed the first 747-400 Freighter into commercial service. Today, airlines also have the 747-400ER (extended range) and 747-400ER Freighter to choose from, both of which entered service in 2002. The 747-400ER

A Cargolux 747-400 Freighter transports the long mast of a large sailing ship in 2005.
(PATRICK JEANNE/CARGOLUX AIRLINES INTERNATIONAL)

has a gross weight of 910,000 pounds (412,770 kilograms) and can fly 7,670 nautical miles (14,205 kilometers) nonstop.

Boeing has delivered more than 1,350 747 jumbo jets to the world's airlines over the decades. Some early 747s have logged 100,000 or more hours of flight time and are still going strong, showing what a robust airplane it is. Considering the size of the 747, and the fact that the world needs fewer big jetliners than little ones, this program has been an astounding success.

———

In the 1990s, key customers began asking for further improvements beyond the 747-400. Boeing started looking at another major updating of the 747.

Two key Boeing Commercial Airplanes experts spearheaded this study, one from the sales community and the other from the engineering ranks. As a consultant to the company, I was asked to participate as the third member of this product development team.

I found myself working with two good friends. The first was Larry Dickenson, who then directed the company's Asia-Pacific jetliner sales and is today a BCA Sales senior vice president. Able, energetic, and an authority on Asia-Pacific airline operations, Larry brought to the table unmatched expertise in customer requirements for a new 747.

Just as capable on the engineering side was John Roundhill, who was then BCA's vice president of product strategy and development. For many years, John, Larry, and I worked closely with airlines around the world—particularly in the Asia-Pacific region, which has the greatest need for very large jetliners—to define this new 747 for the twenty-first century.

Launched recently, the Boeing 747-8 will use the same engines as the ultra-efficient 787 Dreamliner, although twice as many of them. It will also incorporate other technological advancements, including a revised wing and a slightly longer fuselage. It is scheduled to enter service in 2009. How good will this third-generation 747 be? Compared with today's 747-400, which seats about 416 passengers in three service classes, the 747-8 will carry 450 passengers in three classes. It will carry 20% more revenue cargo in its lower holds than today's airplane. This coming 747 will fly farther—up to 8,000 nautical miles, or 14,815 kilometers—and will use 15% less fuel per passenger seat. In light of today's rising fuel costs, this will be enormously helpful to airlines.

Successful airplanes breed additional requirements. The airlines see what an airplane can do and they immediately start clamoring for more from the manufacturer. The 747-400 made good on these demands back in 1989, and I predict the 747-8 will do the same when airlines begin operating them. I also predict that there will be yet another major derivative down the line. If so, the final 747 won't roll out of the Everett factory for decades to come.

People often ask for my opinion of the new Airbus A380 super jumbo, which is flying and a year away from entering service as I write these words. With 550 seats, the A380 is a remarkable achievement and a tribute to pan-European collaboration.

I am fascinated that Airbus Industrie adopted the configuration that my design team abandoned in the 1960s: the double-decker. We looked at all the problems associated with double-deckers and decided to avoid them by opting instead for a wide single-deck design. When the A380 enters service in 2006, its characteristics will be known more fully than at the time of this writing. However, the world is already seeing Airbus contend with significant challenges in terms of airplane weight, operating economics, and passenger emergency evacuation.

After I retired from Boeing, I traveled to Asia many times as a company consultant to visit with friends and associates at airlines in Japan, Korea, Singapore, Hong Kong, mainland China, and elsewhere in the Pacific Rim. Aviation's a relatively small community, so personal relationships mean a lot, particularly in Asia.

My return travels generally took me through Tokyo's Narita International Airport. I would arrive there in the late afternoon and sit around for a couple of hours until my flight to Seattle was finally announced. That waiting area faces one of Narita's runways. Tiring of reading, I would begin watching the airport activity and notice 747s at almost every terminal gate I could see. They wore the colors of many airlines and clustered as thickly as single-aisle 737s do at U.S. airports.

At that time of day, a constant stream of jets was flying in from many of the world's regions. I saw familiar tail emblems as one 747 after another landed. Once in a great while there would be a trijet or a twin-engine widebody, but the 747 predominated by a huge margin.

From the mid-1980s through the next 15 years or so, 747-watching became a regular part of my travels and something I looked forward to on my way home. As this scene repeated itself before my eyes one day, I for some reason started counting those 747s. I saw a total of 55 in the two hours before my flight was called.

Walking down the jetway, I did some quick mental arithmetic. Assuming a 75% load factor for those 55 747s (that is, imagining that they were on average three-quarters full), I had just witnessed upwards of 20,000 people arriving in Japan within a span of two hours. All of them had been delivered by Boeing 747s.

The last time I did this, I had the strongest feeling that the guys who helped me design the 747 were standing right there with me. So many members of our team are gone now, of course, but I found myself wishing we could all have a reception at Narita. There would be no need for entertainment—just standing there seeing all those 747s touch down, one after another, would have been enough.

It would have shown them how we changed the world.

POSTSCRIPT

I started this account by observing that the world was a very wide place when I was born. Then along came Lindbergh. He blazed an intercontinental trail that changed the world and my life, beginning a profound shrinking of the globe. Decades later my team and I accelerated this trend by developing the Boeing 747, the long-range jetliner that more than any other has brought far-flung peoples and cultures together.

I am often referred to as the father of the 747. If people want to call me that, that's fine as long as they recognize that I wasn't alone. The 747 has three fathers, the other two being Juan Trippe of Pan American World Airways and Boeing's Bill Allen. Trippe pushed hard for a high-capacity airliner in the 1960s. Bill Allen shared his friend's vision and had the courage to launch the 747 despite a long list of very good reasons not to. If it weren't for them, history would have taken a different course.

As Clive Irving so ably demonstrates in his excellent book *Wide-Body: The Triumph of the 747*, and as I too have attempted to show, the huge gamble that was the 747 came at the worst of times for Boeing. I feel incredibly fortunate in having been selected to lead this effort. More than just the high point of my career, it was what I had dreamed of doing since I was a boy.

Developing the 747 was never a drudge. In fact, those were the happiest days of my professional life, although I probably didn't realize it at that time because we were working so darn hard. But there's no greater joy than tackling challenges with a superb crew of gifted problem-solvers.

Because I tended to be younger than my team, the majority of them are probably gone now, but their legacy lives on. I see it in the Boeing 787 Dreamliner and other audacious new programs. This younger generation of engineers will emerge with the same shared sense of closeness, loyalty, and satisfaction at achieving something of benefit to the world.

I have received a lot of recognition over the years for having led the 747's design. It's good to be recognized for one's contributions, but whenever I receive an award, I feel that I am accepting not for myself but rather on behalf of "The Incredibles," the amazing group I was so fortunate to lead. What we went through left us with a shared sense of closeness and the strong satisfaction of having presented something valuable to the world.

As for the 747 itself, I see it as a beautiful and inspiring piece of technological sculpture. Like the Wright 1903 Flyer, the DC-3, the 787 Dreamliner, or any other truly great airplane, it shows what we human beings can achieve when we collaborate.

In January 1970 when the 747 entered service, its competition was the Concorde and its U.S. counterpart, the Boeing 2707. Both those SSTs were going concerns with political and financial backing. Additional competition arose with Douglas, Lockheed, and Airbus all introducing twin-aisle subsonic jetliners of their own before the middle of the decade.

The Lockheed L-1011 TriStar is long out of production. So are the McDonnell Douglas DC-10 and its successor the MD-11. The Airbus A300–A310 series is very near the end of its production life. Concorde is gone from the skies and the U.S. SST was never built. All those other programs are pretty much history, yet the Boeing 747 is going strong.

Why? I keep coming back to Lindbergh's comment: "This is one of the great ones."

INDEX